The
Tapestry
of Christian
Theology

The Tapestry of Christian Theology

Modern Minds on the Biblical Narrative

Gregory C. Higgins

Paulist Press
New York/Mahwah, N.J.

Cover and book design by Lynn Else

Library of Congress Cataloging-in-Publication Data

Higgins, Gregory C., 1960-
    The tapestry of Christian theology : modern minds on the biblical narrative / Gregory C. Higgins.
        p. cm.
    Includes bibliographical references and index.
    ISBN 0-8091-4120-5 (alk. paper)
    1. Theology doctrinal—History—20th century—Textbooks. 2. Bible—Criticism, interpretation, etc.—History—20th century—Textbooks. I. Title.
    BT28.H54 2003
    230'.09'04—dc21

                                                                    2003012906

Published by Paulist Press
997 Macarthur Boulevard
Mahwah, New Jersey 07430

www.paulistpress.com

Printed and bound in the
United States of America

Contents

For the living and deceased Christian Brothers (F.S.C.)
of the New York Province

Preface

I would like to thank a number of people without whose help this book could not have been written. First, I need to thank Kevin Coyne, Eileen Higgins, Joseph Incandela, and James Massa, who read the manuscript and offered their very helpful comments. Second, I would like to thank the faculty and students at both Christian Brothers Academy and Georgian Court College for sharing their wisdom with me over the years. Special thanks to Peter Santanello and Br. Daniel Gardner, F.S.C., of Christian Brothers Academy. Third, thanks to Christopher Bellitto of Paulist Press for his editorial guidance. Finally, I have dedicated this work to a remarkable group of men with whom I have been associated for more than half my life. The Christian Brothers taught me when I was in high school. I have worked with them now for nearly twenty years, and they continue to teach me much about Christianity. For that, I am deeply grateful. Thanks to Br. Andrew O'Gara, F.S.C., for hiring me years ago. Special thanks to Br. Ralph Montedoro, F.S.C.

Acknowledgments

The author would like to thank the following publishers for granting permission to reprint previously published material:

Sexism and God-Talk by Rosemary Radford Ruether. Copyright © 1983, 1993 by Rosemary Radford Ruether. Reprinted by permission of Beacon Press, Boston.

A Theology of Liberation by Gustavo Gutiérrez. Copyright ©1973, 1988 by Orbis Books. Reprinted by permission of Orbis Books, Maryknoll, New York.

Moral Man and Immoral Society by Reinhold Niebuhr. Copyright © 1932 by Charles Scribner's Sons, New York. Renewal Copyright 1960 Reinhold Niebuhr. Preface © 1960 Reinhold Niebuhr. Reprinted with the permission of the Estate of Reinhold Niebuhr.

Reprinted with the permission by Simon and Schuster, Inc., from *Letters and Papers from Prison*, Revised, Enlarged Edition by Dietrich Bonhoeffer. Copyright © 1953, 1967, 1971 by SCM Press Ltd.

Theological Investigations, Volumes IV, V, and XIII by Karl Rahner. Copyright © Volume IV, 1966; Volume V, 1966; Volume XIII, 1983. Reprinted by permission of the Crossroad Publishing Company, New York.

The Crucified God by Jürgen Moltmann. Copyright © 1974 by SCM Ltd. Reprinted by permission of HarperCollins Publishers, New York.

On Being a Christian by Hans Küng. Copyright © 1976 by Doubleday, a division of Random House, Inc. Used by permission of Doubleday, a division of Random House, Inc.

Wolfhart Pannenberg, "Constructive and Critical Functions of Christian Eschatology." Selections reprinted with permission from the managing editor of the *Harvard Theological Review*. Original publication: Wolfhart Pannenberg, "Constructive and Critical Functions of Christian Eschatology," *Harvard Theological Review* 77:2 (1984), 119–39. Copyright © 1984 by the President and Fellows of Harvard College.

Introduction

The purpose of this study is to provide college students and general readers with an introduction to the study of theology by examining works by nine influential twentieth-century theologians in which they grappled with the problems and possibilities of Christian life in the modern world. This project, therefore, has three goals. First, an introductory text needs to demonstrate to the reader how theology is done. Second, a theological text needs to offer some means by which students can help better understand the Christian way of life. Third, a historical text needs to acquaint students with the leading thinkers and movements of a particular era (in this case, the twentieth century).

I have employed the concept of tapestry-making in various ways to help achieve these three goals. First, the process of weaving a tapestry serves as a useful analogy for how a theological position is crafted. Second, I will suggest that the structure of the tapestry with its intersecting horizontal and vertical strands may be a useful model for understanding the Christian life. Third, the nine thinkers presented are masters of their craft who tackled the dominant questions of twentieth-century theology.

Tapestry-Making and Doing Theology

The construction of a tapestry and the crafting of a theological position are similar processes. They both (1) begin with the selection of materials, (2) continue through the painstaking process of arranging and weaving those materials into one piece, and (3) end in a public display of the work.

In both tapestry-making and theology, the first step in the process is the careful selection of materials. For weavers of tapestry, wool has been the most common material, though silk, linen, cotton, and even gold and silver were also used.[1] Weavers also had to select

1

from the thousands of available colors of thread. Theologians draw upon scripture and tradition. This, too, calls for a careful selection of materials from the wide range of possible choices. The cries of the psalmist, the wisdom of the proverbs, the warnings of the prophets, and for Christians, the words of Jesus in the Gospels and the instruction found in Paul's letters are but a few of the Bible's riches. The Christian tradition is the 2,000-year repository of the insights of those who have delved into the central mysteries of the Christian faith. Theologians draw upon those insights as they continue to develop new positions in the ever-changing world of Christian thought.

The second step in the process is to assemble the various elements. Tapestries are based on designs called "cartoons." Weavers will at times strictly follow the outline of the design and, at other times, deviate from the template as they see fit. Tapestries are woven on looms that are placed in either the vertical or horizontal position.

> Tapestry is woven by passing weft threads (those that run horizontally across a textile) over and under warp threads (the vertical framework of threads) so that the latter are completely covered by the coloured weft. Tapestry differs from other types of weaving in that only rarely are the weft threads carried across the complete width of the fabric. Specific colours are carried across only as far as necessary in a given row to create a particular section of the design. The final design is only apparent after much slow and meticulous work by the weaver.[2]

The theologian operates in a similar fashion. In theology as well as tapestry-making, there is a healthy tension between tradition and innovation. The theologian does not merely copy the works of the great masters. Rather, a theologian resembles "the master of a household who brings out of his treasure what is new and what is old" (Matt 13:52). In addition to scripture and tradition (which obviously expands with each passing era), theologians draw upon their own personal insights as they fashion their own distinctive theological positions.

In the third and final step, a tapestry is displayed and critiqued. A tapestry is both practical and beautiful, and its value has historically been judged by both criteria. Tapestries served a number of purposes: when hung on the walls, they provided much needed insulation against the cold and served as decoration. Their images could be drawn from the Bible, Greek mythology, or national histories.[3] Despite this diversity, however, tapestries functioned as both practical household items and works of art. As such, they were judged both pragmatically (for example, Will it help keep the castle warm?) and aesthetically (for example, Is it pleasing to the eye?). These same two types of questions can be applied to theologies. There are pragmatic questions (Does this work help us better understand the Christian life?) and aesthetic questions (Does this work convey a compelling spiritual vision?) to be raised.

Tapestry-Making and the Christian Life

The second goal that we outlined in the opening paragraph of the Introduction was to provide students with some means of helping them better understand the Christian way of life. The structure of the tapestry provides such a means. The images in the tapestry emerge when both the horizontal and vertical strands are joined. If the horizontal line represents the Christian understanding of history as moving from creation to the end of time, and the vertical line represents the individual person living at a particular moment in time reaching out to God, then from the intersection of these two lines would emerge the Christian life.

If the image of the continual intersection of the biblical narrative with the events in an individual's life, with a gradual picture emerging, accurately reflects the process of how individuals live the Christian life, then we can describe the Christian life in the following manner: *The Christian life may be understood as the gradual interiorization of the biblical narrative so that it eventually becomes the overarching interpretive framework through which believers understand the events of their lives.* Readers will, of course, be the final arbiters as to the usefulness of such a description in understanding their own journeys of faith, but for now, let us pursue this idea a bit further.

The Biblical Narrative

From its seven-day creation story to the banishment of evil at the end of time, the biblical narrative provides the grand vision of God's relationship with the world. The Bible invites the reader on an epic journey with patriarchs, judges, kings, and prophets that culminates for Christians in the appearance of the Son of God. Along the way, we meet saints and sinners, witness the miraculous and the mundane, and encounter human frailty and heroic virtue. More important, however, we read the Bible in the hope that along the way we might come to know a bit better the central character of the work, the One shrouded in mystery, who is at the same time the One in whom we live and move and have our being.

The biblical odyssey begins with the two creation stories in the opening chapters of Genesis. Immediately following the creation accounts are the familiar stories involving Cain and Abel, Noah, and the tower of Babel. The bulk of Genesis details the glorious and ignominious moments in the lives of Abraham, Isaac, and Jacob. From the horrifying scene of Abraham's near-sacrifice of Isaac to the mystical vision of Jacob's ladder, the patriarchs never fail to inspire, anger, or confound the reader. The final cycle of stories in Genesis involves Joseph as we follow his trials and tribulations to his final reunion with his father and brothers in Egypt.

The situation in Egypt changes dramatically in the first chapter of Exodus. Here we learn that Joseph has been forgotten and the Egyptians have enslaved the Israelites, who cry out to the Lord for liberation. At this point we are introduced to one of the towering figures in the biblical narrative. Placed in a basket in the Nile River as an infant, adopted by Pharaoh's daughter, and called by God at the burning bush, Moses plays a role in some of the most memorable scenes in the Bible: the ten plagues, the parting of the sea, the Ten Commandments, and the golden calf. As we move to final chapters of the Torah, Moses feasts his eyes on the promised land, but dies before entering it.

Moses is succeeded by Joshua, who will lead the people into the land of Canaan. After sending spies into the city, Joshua leads the Israelites into the land of Canaan with a miraculous crossing of the Jordan River that is meant to recall the parting of the Red Sea.

Angelic forces gather to assist in the taking of Jericho, one of the most dramatic events in the entire Bible. God places the city under the "ban," which consists in nothing less than the total annihilation of all living creatures there (Josh 6:21). The book of Joshua recounts the subsequent conquest of the land of Canaan.

The conquest did not secure permanent possession of the promised land for the Israelites. After settling there, the twelve tribes slowly moved from a loose confederation to a unified nation under a single monarch, centered around a single religious sanctuary, the Temple in Jerusalem. Tribal loyalties, however, simmered underneath the surface, and in 922 B.C.E., after the death of Solomon, those tensions erupted. The result was a divided nation: a northern kingdom comprised of ten tribes, known collectively as Israel, and a southern kingdom comprised of two tribes, known collectively as Judah. Though politically and economically the stronger of the two kingdoms, Israel was no match for the armies of the Assyrian Empire. In a fatal political misjudgment, the last Israelite king refused to pay the annual tribute to Assyria. The Assyrian response was swift and sure: in 721 B.C.E. the Israelite capital city of Samaria fell, and its inhabitants were deported. The Babylonians would eventually succeed the Assyrians as the overlords of Palestine, and Judah would soon suffer a similar fate to that of Israel. Sensing a weakness in the Babylonian resolve following a difficult battle with the Egyptians, the king of Judah refused to pay the tribute to the Babylonians. The Babylonians responded by raiding the Temple and the royal treasuries and exiling many of the leading citizens of Jerusalem to Babylon in 597 B.C.E. Ten years later, after more political miscalculation, the unthinkable happened: the Babylonians burned the Temple to the ground and exiled many of the remaining inhabitants to Babylon. The Israelites would eventually return to the promised land, where they were ruled successively by Persians, Greeks, and then Romans.

At this point, the biblical narrative shifts into what Christians call the New Testament. Christ appears, preaches first in Galilee and then in Jerusalem, where he is arrested and crucified at Golgotha (*Calvary* in Latin) by Roman authorities on charges that he claimed to be "the King of the Jews." The gospel that Christians proclaim does not end at the cross. The horror of Christ's death was surpassed by the glory of his resurrection. So central, in fact, is the resurrection that

Paul insists that if Christ has not been raised from the dead, Christianity is a fraud (cf. 1 Cor 15:13–19). In Acts of the Apostles we learn of the empowerment of the apostles to carry on the ministry of Christ, who now reigns in heaven but who will return to judge the living and the dead.

This "biblical narrative" is the indispensable context for understanding Christian beliefs and practices. For example, the Apostles' Creed summarizes Christian belief by recounting the central events in that drama, from the creation of heaven and earth to life everlasting. The sacraments only make sense when situated in this larger narrative framework. Christian marriage requires the creation story, baptism requires the gospel, and anointing of the sick for those about to die requires the hope of everlasting life. Any theology or spirituality that rightly calls itself Christian in general, or Catholic in particular, must intersect with the biblical narrative. The biblical narrative contains countless events and persons, but I have chosen to focus our attention on nine particular moments in the biblical narrative: Creation, Exodus, Conquest, Exile, the Incarnation, Crucifixion, Resurrection, Pentecost, and the End of Time. While arguments certainly could be made to include other moments, I believe there is a general consensus that these nine are critical to any adequate understanding of the whole of the biblical narrative.

Christian Spirituality as the Interiorization of the Biblical Narrative

I am proposing that the Christian life can be understood as the gradual process by which we interiorize the biblical narrative to such a degree that it becomes the primary framework for understanding ourselves, our lives, and our world. More formally stated, the narrative world presented in the Bible becomes, in the words of George Lindbeck, the "interpretive framework" by which we make sense of our lives. Commenting on the canonical writings of religious communities, Lindbeck writes, "For those who are steeped in them, no world is more real than the ones they create. A scriptural world is thus able to absorb the universe. It supplies the interpretive framework within which believers seek to live their lives and understand reality."[4]

Lindbeck's provocative comment that the scriptural world absorbs the universe suggests that the biblical world is the overarching, though not exclusive, framework in which we understand the events of our lives. As we interiorize the biblical narrative, we see the natural world as a creation of God, we describe our own pain and alienation as "exilic," and see our sufferings in light of the cross.

This process of the interiorization of the biblical narrative requires that we recover the medieval practice of seeking the "spiritual sense" of scripture. Sandra M. Schneiders explains the four senses of scripture sought by the medieval reader:

> The literal sense refers to the events and realities of Jewish history. The other three are spiritual senses: the allegorical, which reveals the Christian or theological meaning of the text; the moral or tropological, which applies the text to the individual Christian's practice; and the anagogical, which points toward eschatological fulfillment. The classic example of the fourfold interpretation is the understanding of Jerusalem as the Jewish city (literal), the church (allegorical), the soul (tropological), and the heavenly city (anagogical) (see Cassian *Conferences* 14.8).[5]

The historical question is, of course, an important one, but so too is the spiritual or existential question. In other words, the question, "How does this biblical story illumine the Christian life?" is just as important as "Did the biblical event actually happen?" As the twentieth-century theologian Henri de Lubac, S.J., remarked,

> Finally—and here again we have an important point—the spiritual meaning, understood as figurative or mystical meaning is the meaning which, objectively, leads us to the realities of the spiritual life and which, subjectively, can only be the fruit of a spiritual life. That is where it leads; for to the extent that we have not arrived at it, we have not drawn a totally Christian interpretation from the Scriptures. It is certain that the Christian mystery is not something to be curiously contemplated like a pure object of science, but is something which must be interiorized

and lived. It finds its own fullness in being fulfilled within souls.[6]

The model of Christian life being proposed concurs with de Lubac's claim that "the Christian mystery is not something to be curiously contemplated like a pure object of science, but is something which must be interiorized and lived."

The Structure of the Book

As a way of helping the student better see how theologians can shed light on the deepest questions of the Christian life, I have structured the book along the lines of the biblical narrative. I have paired a major theologian with one of nine moments in the biblical narrative. Thinkers are not treated chronologically or grouped by "schools of thought." The book is not intended to be an exhaustive survey of the leading voices in twentieth-century theology. Particularly noteworthy in their absence are theologians from Asia or Africa. Nor do I purport to feature the nine most important theologians of the twentieth century. There are, for instance, no chapters dedicated to Paul Tillich, Charles Hartshorne, or Karl Barth. Depending on one's theological preferences, the omission of any one of them is inexcusable. The chapters themselves are usually focused on a single work by the theologian, so this is not an introduction to each thinker's entire body of work.

The approach I have taken, however, allows us to meet the three goals stated at the beginning of this Introduction. First, these theologians ably demonstrate how theology is done. There is no better way to learn theology than by listening to some of the most respected voices in the tradition and engaging them in critical dialogue. Second, the narrative structure allows us to see how theological writings can provide invaluable assistance to us as we attempt to understand the meaning of Christianity in our own lives. The key moments of the biblical narrative that are discussed theologically are also the primary categories through which Christians are able to understand the events of their own lives. Seen from this perspective, the theologians serve not only as experts in their fields, but as spiritual guides as well. Third, we can learn much about twentieth-century thought by taking notice of the issues that occupied the thinkers of that time. In this way, the narrative approach includes the theological, spiritual, and historical elements necessary to an adequate understanding of twentieth-century theology. In addition to that, the thinkers whose works we explore are some of most influential thinkers of the twentieth century. They have in many ways set the agenda for contemporary theology. A knowledge and understanding of their work is invaluable to those doing theology in the twenty-first century.

Tapestry-Making and Twentieth-Century Theology

The third goal stated in the opening paragraph of the Introduction is to acquaint students with some of the leading thinkers and movements in twentieth-century theology. We examine nine of those thinkers in the following chapters, but we must first situate their work in the context of the twentieth-century thought. For purposes of this study, three movements in twentieth-century theology are highlighted: the historical-critical method of biblical interpretation, existentialism, and narrative theology.

The Historical-Critical Method of Biblical Interpretation

For most of Christian history, the Bible was regarded as a unique, divinely inspired, literal account of salvation history. Unlike authors of other pieces of literature from the ancient world, the biblical authors, it was believed, were under the direct inspiration of the Holy Spirit. The biblical writings were in effect written *by* God *through* the particular authors. Since God would not deceive us, the biblical record was undoubtedly true. These interrelated beliefs created a consistent view of the Bible as the inerrant Word of God.

Beginning in the seventeenth century, however, scholars began to employ the historical-critical method of biblical interpretation, which sees the biblical texts as profoundly influenced by the thought patterns of the era in which they were produced. In order to properly understand the message of the biblical writings, we must first place them in the historical context in which they were composed. This is why the approach is "historical." Having placed the text in its historical context, the interpreter must next determine whether the author intended the writing to be interpreted literally, symbolically, morally, or by some other framework. This is why the approach is "critical." The term *critical* simply means "judgment." Judgments are made regarding the historical accuracy of the biblical text and the meaning intended by the author.

This historical-critical approach to the Bible directly or indirectly challenged the presumption that the Bible was unique, divinely inspired, and literally true. First, the biblical texts were examined in the same way that one would examine other texts from antiquity. Attention was given to the literary forms that were prevalent in that culture at the time of the writing. In Roman Catholic circles, this critical approach was endorsed by Pope Pius XII in his encyclical letter *Divino Afflante Spiritu* in 1943. In that encyclical, Pius XII writes that the biblical interpreter "must, as it were, go back wholly in spirit to those remote centuries of the East and with the aid of history, archaeology, ethnology, and other sciences, accurately determine what modes of writing, so to speak, the authors of that ancient period would be likely to use, and in fact, did use."[7] Second, when comparing the biblical writings with other documents from the ancient world, if it were discovered that (1) the biblical authors borrowed from other sources, or that (2) the stories were reworked during a period of oral transmission before they were actually recorded in the biblical writings, or that (3) the biblical writings themselves passed through the hands of several editors before reaching their final form, then divine authorship becomes a more complicated issue. God's inspiration is not eliminated, but the traditional belief that God's spirit moved the hand of the biblical author seems far less tenable. Third, given the common use of hyperbole and legend in stories from the ancient world, a modern reader of the Bible could legitimately ask whether Jonah was literally in the belly of the whale for three days, or Daniel was literally thrown into the lions' den, or the walls of Jericho suddenly collapsed at the sounding of the trumpets.

Given the wide acceptance of the historical-critical method, Christians might wonder, "What then becomes of the idea that the Bible is inerrant?" Scholars insist that to answer that question requires drawing an important distinction. The Bible may be in error regarding certain historical references, scientific claims, or other factors reflecting the thought patterns of that day and age, but the Bible as God's Word can not be in error regarding truths concerning our salvation. Regarding this distinction, Joseph Blenkinsopp notes that

> we read in Judith 1.2 that Nebuchadnezzar was king of the Assyrians, which he was not, in Tobit 1.15 that Sennacherib was son of Shalmaneser, which he was not, in 1 Samuel 7.13 that the Philistines never again entered Israelite territory after the victory of Samuel, which is contradicted by the subsequent narrative....This suggests that it might be useful to make a distinction between what pertains to salvation, the religious message of the Scriptures, on the one hand, and things not pertaining to salvation on the other.[8]

The Bible may err on matters of no real consequence to the faith, but it does not err on the essential religious message that God intends to convey to the readers of the Bible. Even if one accepts as valid the distinction between non-essential and essential biblical teaching, it does not resolve the problem of knowing which passages fall into which category.

Modern historical-critical study of the Bible, therefore, raises two sets of questions. As Tom Deidun notes,

> If we are to apply "what the Bible says" to our own ethical concerns (that is, if we are to pass from text to life), then we must first do our best to establish "what the Bible says." This prior task involves trying to discover what a given biblical writer understood himself to be saying. There are two distinct steps, therefore, in any attempt to apply biblical material in Christian ethics: interpretation of biblical texts and some kind of appropriation or contemporization.[9]

The first set of questions centers on how we arrive at a correct interpretation; the second on our application of that biblical teaching. First, is the correct interpretation of a biblical passage determined by reconstructing the actual event described in the Bible, discerning the intended meaning of the author, accepting the passage as literally true, or by testing it against other beliefs we accept as true? On what basis do we label an interpretation (a) correct; (b) different, but complementary to the correct interpretation; or (c) incorrect? Second, when should the Christian community continue to promote the original teaching, qualify the teaching in some fashion, or even perhaps reject the original teaching as set forth in the Bible? How do we know we are not simply dismissing teachings that we find hard to follow? All of this suggests that the act of biblical interpretation may be a more complex affair than it ordinarily appears to us as we read a text.

Existentialism

The second prominent intellectual movement in the twentieth century that continues to profoundly influence Christian theology is existentialism. As Richard Tarnas writes,

> Nowhere was the problematic modern condition more precisely embodied than in the phenomenon of existentialism, a mood and philosophy expressed in the writings of Heidegger, Sartre, and Camus, among others, but ultimately reflecting a pervasive spiritual crisis in modern culture. The anguish and alienation of twentieth-century life were brought to full articulation as the existentialist addressed the most fundamental, naked concerns of human existence—suffering and death, loneliness and dread, guilt, conflict, spiritual emptiness and ontological insecurity, the void of absolute values or universal contexts, the sense of cosmic absurdity, the frailty of human reason, the tragic impasse of the human condition.[10]

While the roots of existentialism are to be found in the nineteenth century, its widespread acceptance did not occur until the twentieth century. It was attuned to the problems of those who had experienced war, economic collapse, and the threat of nuclear annihilation. It is for this reason that the scope of existentialism's influence extends beyond the philosophical realm into literature, cinema, and theology.

Existentialism was appealing to twentieth-century theologians for three reasons. First, existentialism, by definition, was focused on human existence, not abstruse questions of philosophy. Those twentieth-century theologians who felt that theology needed to address more directly the actual lived experience of Christians in the modern world naturally felt drawn to existentialist philosophy.

Although they felt that theoretical questions have their proper place in any system of thought, these questions, they argued, should never overshadow the more immediate need to explore how a given idea impacts people's lives. Existentialism spoke directly to that sentiment. Second, existentialism emphasized the need for the individual to find meaning in his or her individual existence. Existentialism protests against collectivism of any kind. Philosophies that focus on broad movements in history or social classes or immutable essences too often neglect the individual's struggle for meaning and purpose in his or her life. In order to live authentically, people need to step apart from what Søren Kierkegaard referred to as "the herd" and make their own decisions. Through our choices we define who we are. As Jean-Paul Sartre wrote, "Man is nothing else but what he makes of himself. Such is the first principle of existentialism."[11] Third, existentialism did not turn away from the darker moments of human existence. Concepts of dread, anguish, anxiety, and fear figure prominently in the movement. Existentialism excluded no aspect of human experience and gave voice to the threat of meaninglessness and despair. Paul Tillich wrote, "Immanuel Kant once said that mathematics is the good luck of human reason. In the same way, one could say that existentialism is the good luck of Christian theology. It has helped to rediscover the classical Christian interpretation of human existence."[12] While Christian theology needs to offer a message of hope and joy, argued Tillich, it must also address the present forces of disintegration at work in the world and in our consciousness.

Narrative Theology

A third trend in twentieth-century theology was the emergence of "narrative theology." The first and most obvious point of emphasis noted by narrative theologians is that the Bible is a narrative beginning with the creation of the world and concluding with the end of human history. In the same way, our lives have a beginning and an end. Both are narratives. While there are messages, themes, or principles to be abstracted from the biblical narrative, the primary category in which the Bible must be classified is that of story. Narrative theologians, in the most general terms possible, attempt to place the individual's "story" in the wider Christian narrative. Stanley Hauerwas writes, "Not only is knowledge of self tied to knowledge of God, but we know ourselves truthfully only when we know ourselves in relation to God. We know who we are only when we can place our selves—locate our stories—within God's story."[13] Second, narrative theologians insist that the stories that shape our lives profoundly affect our motivations, our reactions, our very view of the world. Stanley Hauerwas argues that "we can only act in the world we see, a seeing partially determined by the kind of beings we have become through the stories we have learned and embodied in our life plan."[14] Stories shape our experience. Edward Schillebeeckx succinctly states this point as follows: "Experience is always interpreted experience."[15] Third, narrative theology has reminded us that human thought is historically conditioned. The thought patterns of a culture or a single interpreter may be radically unlike our own thought patterns. For example, the early and medieval church theologians were deeply influenced by Plato's and Aristotle's philosophy. In our own day and age, we need to acknowledge the different presuppositions and expectations brought to bear on the interpretation of texts, especially the Bible.

These insights of narrative theology, however, raise larger questions. The narrative theologians have accentuated the point that all assertions are conditioned by the categories of thought prevalent in the culture or within an individual's own outlook on the world. How then can we know which perspective or story most accurately reflects reality? Is it possible to arrive at an indubitable truth by which we can judge the truthfulness of all assertions? How would we know if our own outlook on the world is perfectly coherent, yet wrong? What should Christians do when they encounter a scriptural passage or medieval treatise that seems to be simply incompatible with a modern scientific perspective? When, for example, the crowds bring Jesus a boy whom they declare to have an unclean spirit, explaining "whenever it seizes him, it dashes him down; and he foams and grinds his teeth and becomes rigid" (Mark 9:18), are we as modern readers justified in diagnosing the problem not as demonic possession, but epilepsy?

The problem of how to interpret the story of Jesus curing the boy in Mark's Gospel arises because Christians in the twenty-first century live in a pluralistic world that offers a number of plausible explanations for any given occurrence. Visions could be communications from God or the result of a chemical imbalance in the brain. Rainfall after a prolonged drought could be an answered prayer or a change in the jet stream, or both. While this plurality of explanations is a blessing in that we are able to assume a number of vantage points from which to understand the events of our lives, we are also left with a very unsettling feeling: "How can we know which things we assume to be true in our day and age are in fact true?" Especially in matters of faith, how do we know what is the correct belief? Should we be skeptics who deny that we ever can know the truth, or relativists who deny that such truths even exist? These nagging questions linger in the back of the minds of many Christians beginning the twenty-first century of Christian history.

The Use of This Text in the Classroom

I envision this text being used primarily in a "Theology in the Modern Age" course. However, professors teaching systematic theology may find the chapters as helpful ways of introducing students to the following categories:

> Rosemary Radford Ruether: Creation and Theological
>   Anthropology
> Gustavo Gutiérrez: The Exodus and the Relationship
>   Between the Church and the World
> Reinhold Niebuhr: The Conquest and the Problem of Sin
> Dietrich Bonhoeffer: The Exile and the Question of God
> Karl Rahner: The Incarnation and Modern Christology
> Jürgen Moltmann: The Crucifixion and the Meaning of
>   Salvation
> Hans Küng: The Resurrection and the Critical Study of
>   Scripture and Tradition
> Yves Congar: Pentecost and the Nature and Mission of
>   the Church
> Wolfhart Pannenberg: The End of Time and Christian
>   Eschatology

The authors of the classic works in theology imparted to their readers a vision of the Christian life that is both theologically sound and spiritually compelling. It is for that reason that their works continue to challenge and enrich readers long after the authors have passed from this earth. The reader will judge whether the theologians under consideration in this present study have achieved this lofty goal, but, in any event, I hope this study provides a useful survey of twentieth-century theology. More important, I hope the work of each theologian offers some assistance to the readers as they attempt to understand the events of their lives in light of the mystery of God.

Notes

1. See "Tapestry," *New Encyclopaedia Britannica,* vol. 11, 15th ed. (Chicago: Encyclopaedia Britannica Inc., 1998), p. 553.
2. Ibid.
3. See Walter F. Bartsch, "Tapestry," *Collier's Encyclopedia* (New York: Macmillan, 1991), p. 67.
4. George Lindbeck, *The Nature of Doctrine* (Philadelphia: Westminster Press, 1984), p. 117.
5. Sandra M. Schneiders, "Scripture and Spirituality," in *Christian Spirituality: Origins to the Twelfth Century,* ed. Bernard McGinn and John Meyendorff (New York: Crossroad, 1985), p. 15.
6. Henri de Lubac, S.J., *The Sources of Revelation* (New York: Herder and Herder, 1968), pp. 20–21.
7. Pope Pius XII, *Divino Afflante Spiritu, The Papal Encyclicals,* vol. 4, ed. Claudia Carlen, I.H.M. (Wilmington, NC: McGrath Publishing Co., 1981), p. 73.
8. Joseph Blenkinsopp, *A Sketchbook of Biblical Theology* (New York: Herder and Herder, 1968), pp. 34–35.
9. Tom Deidun, "The Bible and Christian Ethics," in *Christian Ethics: An Introduction,* ed. Bernard Hoose (Collegeville: Liturgical Press, 1998), p. 4.
10. Richard Tarnas, *The Passion of the Western Mind* (New York: Harmony Books, 1991), pp. 388–89.
11. Jean-Paul Sartre, *Existentialism and Human Emotions* (New York: Philosophical Library, 1957), p. 15.
12. Paul Tillich, *Systematic Theology,* vol. 2 (Chicago: University of Chicago Press, 1957), p. 27.
13. Stanley Hauerwas, *The Peaceable Kingdom* (Notre Dame: University of Notre Dame Press, 1983), p. 27.
14. Stanley Hauerwas, "The Self as Story," in *Vision and Virtue* (Notre Dame: University of Notre Dame Press, 1974), p. 69.
15. Edward Schillebeeckx, *Christ* (New York: Crossroad, 1980), p. 31.

Discussion Questions

1. Offer your own description of "theology" and "a good Christian life."
2. Which historical events most shaped twentieth-century world history?
3. What are some of the most urgent social problems confronting humanity at the present time?
4. Which intellectual movements are exerting a profound influence on twenty-first-century thought?
5. Before the rise of the historical-critical method, the Bible was interpreted in a variety of "pre-critical" ways. Following are two examples. Discuss the plausibility of each interpretation.
    a. Read Genesis 22:1–19. Is the wood placed on Isaac's shoulder (v. 6) a foreshadowing of Christ carrying the cross?
    b. Read 2 Peter 3:18–22. Was the story of Noah's ark a foreshadowing of Christian baptism?

Suggested Readings

For treatments of individual theologians of the twentieth century, see *A Handbook of Christian Theologians,* enlarged ed. (Nashville: Abingdon, 1984), ed. Martin E. Marty and Dean Peerman, and *A New Handbook of Christian Theologians* (Nashville: Abingdon, 1996), ed. Donald W. Musser and Joseph L. Price; *The Modern Theologians,* 2nd ed. (Oxford: Blackwell, 1997), ed. David F. Ford; *Twentieth-Century Theology* (Downers Grove: InterVarsity Press, 1992) by Stanley J. Grenz and Roger E. Olson; *Modern Christian Thought* (New York: Macmillan, 1971) by James Livingston, now in a second edition co-authored with Francis Schüssler Fiorenza in two volumes.

Three very solid introductions written in a more casual style that would be especially helpful to students in introductory courses in theology are *Fortress Introduction to Contemporary Theologies* (Minneapolis: Fortress Press, 1998), by Ed. L. Miller and Stanley J. Grenz; *Contemporary Theologians* (Chicago: Thomas More Press, 1989) by James J. Bacik; and *Introducing Contemporary Theologies* (Newtown: E. J. Dwyer, 1990) by Neil Ormerod.

For a topical or systematic approach, see *Christian Theology,* ed. Peter C. Hodgson and Robert H. King (Philadelphia: Fortress Press, 1982); Richard P. McBrien, *Catholicism,* new ed. (San Francisco: HarperCollins, 1994); and Alister McGrath, *Christian Theology: An Introduction* (Cambridge, MA: Blackwell, 1994).

For trends in both philosophy and theology, see *Twentieth Century Religious Thought,* rev. ed. (New York: Charles Scribner's, 1981) by John Macquarrie.

For trends in Christology, see *Is Jesus Unique?* (Mahwah: Paulist, 1996) by Scott Cowdell.

For the understandings of God in twentieth-century Protestant thought, see *The Question of God* (New York: Harcourt, Brace, and World, 1969) by Heinz Zahrnt.

For theology and social issues, see *The Twentieth Century: A Theological Overview* (Maryknoll: Orbis Books, 1999), ed. Gregory Baum.

1

Creation and
Rosemary Radford Ruether's
Sexism and God-Talk

The opening chapters of the Bible introduce us to the narrative world that we will explore throughout our present investigation. The great Protestant theologian Karl Barth once asked, "What sort of house is it to which the Bible is the door? What sort of country is spread before our eyes when we throw the Bible open?"[1] Barth's own reply was that we enter "a strange new world." The first three chapters of Genesis seem to confirm Barth's suggestion. The Bible opens with a pair of creation stories (1:1–2:4a, 2:4b–25). In the first, a majestic God creates the world by command alone ("Then God said, 'Let there be light'; and there was light") in an orderly six-day progression from chaos to order, concluding with a seventh day of rest. In the second story, God is portrayed in a more anthropomorphic fashion. God forms a man from the clay of earth and plants a garden in Eden. In this garden stand various trees, among them the tree of knowledge of good and evil, and at the center of the garden, the tree of life. God forms the various wild animals, birds of the air, and cattle, and completes the creation by forming a woman from the man's rib. In the third chapter, the story takes an even stranger turn. A talking serpent tempts the woman to eat the forbidden fruit from the tree of knowledge, and she shares the fruit with the man. In the course of an afternoon stroll through the garden, the Lord learns of the couple's disobedience. After punishing the serpent, the woman, and the man, the Lord banishes them from the garden, denying them access to the tree of life. Cast east of Eden, the man and woman enter an uncertain world of hostility, toil, and death.

In these opening chapters of the Bible we confront some of most fundamental questions of human existence: Who is God? Who

are we? What is this world in which in live? For nearly two millennia
Christian thinkers have drawn upon the available religious, philosophical, political, scientific, and literary traditions to articulate their
understanding of God, humans, and the world. It is fitting, then, that
we pair these opening chapters of Genesis with a theologian who has
dedicated her professional career to challenging many of the deeply
held traditional Christian beliefs about the nature of God, the identity of humans, and the structure of society. Rosemary Radford
Ruether's feminist theology has generated vigorous debate and pas-
sionate responses of both support and opposition. Our study of
Ruether's work begins by situating her theology both in the social
thought of the twentieth century and in the framework of Christian
theology. We then examine her treatment of the issues raised in
Genesis 1–3 in her work *Sexism and God-Talk*. In the final sections of
the chapter we hear from Ruether's critics and offer a general summary of her spiritual theology.

Introduction to
Rosemary Radford Ruether's Theology

Ruether deliberately allows her own academic training and research,
personal life experience, and participation in various social causes to
direct the course and content of her writings. For example, Ruether
describes her undergraduate years at Scripps College in Claremont as
"years of dramatic intellectual awakening."[2] Reflecting on those years,
Ruether writes,

> One might almost speak of them as years of conversion, from
> being an object to being a subject of education, years of being
> galvanized into a process of continual, self-motivated search
> for enlarged understanding, not as a means of "winning"
> something from others, but as a way of developing and locat-
> ing myself, my own existence. Those years of education also
> laid a solid base of historical consciousness, of awareness of
> the whole Western historical experience and a methodology
> for expanding that awareness that continues to undergird
> the way I ask and answer questions.[3]

As Ruether completed her graduate work and began to raise a family with her husband Herbert, the United States was deepening its involvement in the war in Vietnam, and at home the civil rights movement was making strides. The bishops at Vatican II were updating the beliefs and practices of the Roman Catholic Church, but the controversy concerning the use of artificial contraception continued to spark dissent among church members. The civil rights movement and the process of renewal within the Roman Catholic Church, "the one questioning American society and the other questioning the Catholic church," writes Ruether, "were the matrix in which my theology developed. From my first writings I became concerned with the interconnection between theological ideas and social practice."[4] In 1965 Ruether joined the faculty of the School of Religion of Howard University in Washington, D.C., and in "the late sixties...began formal research on attitudes toward women in the Christian tradition."[5] In 1976 Ruether moved to Garrett-Evangelical Seminary near Chicago, where she remains to this day. During that time she has tackled questions of "racism, religious bigotry, especially anti-semitism, sexism, class hierarchy, colonialism, militarism, and ecological damage,"[6] but has earned the reputation of being "the most widely-read and influential articulator of the emerging feminist movement in theology."[7]

We also see in Ruether's theology the influence of the three movements of twentieth-century thought discussed in the Introduction to this book: the historical-critical method of biblical interpretation, existentialism, and narrative theology. Ruether's study of the Bible did not begin in earnest until her time at Scripps. She recalls,

> With one of my best friends, a Jewish girl of Orthodox background, I arranged our first course in Hebrew scriptures as an independent study. Gradually I began to integrate work in late Judaism, the intertestamental period, the New Testament, and early Christianity into my studies, drawing on the resources of the Claremont Theological School. There seem to me certain advantages in moving in this way from classical humanism to biblical thought. First of all, it meant that when I read the Bible for the first time I did so with the apparatus of historical-critical thought.

After certain initial shocks to my inherited model of Christ, this came to seem the natural way to decipher the Bible. I had relatively little baggage of a precritical biblical schooling to discard. Secondly, it meant that biblical thought, rather than being a drag from an alienating past, could open up to me a world of critical and prophetic vision beyond classical humanism.[8]

Second, Ruether acknowledges the existential quality of her theology.

My intellectual questions and research have never been purely theoretical. I have in every case dealt with existential questions about how I was to situate my life, my identity, my commitments. I have never taken up an intellectual issue which did not have direct connections with clarifying and resolving questions about my personal existence, about how I should align my existence with others, ideologically and socially.[9]

Finally, narrative theology's reminder that the stories of a culture or religion shape both a person's self-understanding and a society's view of acceptable social roles for its citizens will be an important theme in Ruether's social critique. Ruether's theology also calls for an expansion in the number of sources from which to draw these stories. Writings that were deemed heretical or movements that were suppressed are reexamined, and often incorporated by Ruether into her theology. Ruether also emphasizes the historically conditioned nature of human thought, including biblical thought. The proposals advanced by Ruether call into question the two sources of Christian theology: scripture and tradition. If either one or both of them prove unreliable, then on what should we base a Christian theology? We will take that question as the starting point for our investigation of Ruether's work *Sexism and God-Talk*.

Sexism and God-Talk

In *Sexism and God-Talk* Ruether offers a work of "systematic theology" from a feminist perspective. According to Richard P. McBrien, systematic theology "seeks to understand and articulate the Christian whole by examining each of its parts in relation to one another and to the whole."[10] The task of systematic theology is twofold: to articulate an understanding of each of the major Christian beliefs (God, Christ, church, and so on) and, to demonstrate how one category of Christian belief relates with other categories. In our present study, we will concern ourselves primarily with Ruether's "theological anthropology" or understanding of the human person from a theological (rather than a purely philosophical or psychological) perspective. But before tackling that question, we need to set the ground rules: On what should we base our theological positions? In chapter 1 of *Sexism and God-Talk,* Ruether deals with that very question.

The sources upon which theologians usually base their positions are scripture and tradition. These are regarded as two reliable means through which God has communicated to us. Many a theological controversy has been spawned over the question of how exactly scripture conveys God's revelation or in what that revelation consists, but essentially the problem comes down to knowing what comes from God (and therefore should be the standard for Christian belief and action) and what comes from humans (and therefore can be changed). We can begin to identify Ruether's response to that question by examining her understanding of revelation and its relation to scripture and tradition.

Ruether states, "By *revelatory* we mean breakthrough experiences beyond ordinary consciousness that provide interpretive symbols illuminating the whole of life."[11] By this definition, revelation is understood primarily to be experience, not the writings in the Bible or church doctrine. More specifically, revelatory experience consists of "breakthrough" moments in which we arrive at a new understanding of our lives. Scripture and tradition function as the customary means through which most Christians connect with that revelatory experience, but scripture and tradition can also block that experience. In that event, states Ruether, the choice is clear: "If a symbol does not speak authentically to experience, it becomes dead or must be altered to provide a new meaning."[12] The experience is what is important. Scripture and tradition are primary connections to the Christian revelatory experience, but ultimately they are subject to reinterpretation or alteration.

Ruether brings her historical perspective to bear on her understanding of the dynamic between experience and what she refers to as "codified experience" in scripture and tradition. In general terms, Ruether sees in Christian history a recurring situation in which the original revelatory experience becomes transmitted through a historical community that over time domesticates the experience, defines its content, and saps it of its original power. More specifically, the history of determining the canon (the list of accepted books of the Bible) illustrates for Ruether this deterioration of revelation into rigid codification.

> At a certain point a group consisting of teacher and leaders emerges that seeks to channel and control the process, to weed out what it regards as deviant communities and interpretations, and to impose a series of criteria to determine the correct interpretive line. This group can do this by defining an authoritative body of writings that is then canonized as the correct interpretation of the original divine revelation and distinguished from other writings, which are regarded either as heretical or of secondary authority. In the process the controlling group marginalizes and suppresses other branches of the community, with their texts and lines of interpretation. The winning group declares itself the privileged line of true (orthodox) interpretation. Thus a canon of Scripture is established.[13]

A similar process occurs when believers perceive the leaders of their religion (or perhaps the entire religious tradition itself) to be out of touch with the spirit of the original revelatory experience. As Ruether insists, "A religious tradition remains vital so long as its revelatory pattern can be produced generation after generation and continues to speak to individuals in the community and provide for them the redemptive meaning of individual and collective experience."[14] It is in this context that we can best understand reform movements within the church (for example, Francis of Assisi) or movements that break away from the dominant authority (for example, the Protestant Reformation).

We are now ready to consider the proposal advanced by Ruether concerning the role of scripture and tradition in Christian theology. This can also be seen as the guiding principle of Ruether's thought:

The critical principle of feminist theology is the promotion of the full humanity of women. Whatever denies, diminishes, or distorts the full humanity of women is, therefore, appraised as not redemptive. Theologically speaking, whatever diminishes or denies the full humanity of women must be presumed not to reflect the divine or an authentic relation to the divine, or to reflect the authentic nature of things, to be the message or work of an authentic redeemer or a community of redemption.[15]

More specifically, in terms of scripture, a commitment to "the promotion of the full humanity of women," requires that we recover what Ruether labels "the prophetic-liberating tradition of Biblical faith." Ruether elevates this biblical tradition and assesses all other biblical ideas by its standards. "Feminist readings of the Bible can discern a norm within Biblical faith by which the Biblical texts themselves can be criticized. To the extent to which Biblical texts reflect this normative principle, they are regarded as authoritative. On this basis many aspects of the Bible are to be frankly set aside and rejected." Ruether continues,

Four themes are essential to the prophetic-liberating tradition of Biblical faith: (1) God's defense and vindication of the oppressed; (2) the critique of the dominant systems of power and their powerholders; (3) the vision of a new age to come in which the present system of injustice is overcome and God's intended reign of peace and justice is installed in history; and (4) finally, the critique of ideology, or of religion, since ideology in this context is primarily religious. Prophetic faith denounces religious ideologies and systems that function to justify and sanctify the dominant, unjust social order. These traditions are central to the Prophets and to the mission of Jesus.[16]

With regard to tradition, Ruether argues for expanding the number of historical sources that inform our theology. Ruether identifies the following as being particularly valuable:

I draw "usable tradition" from five areas of cultural tradition: (1) Scripture, both Hebrew and Christian (Old and

New Testament); (2) marginalized or "heretical" Christian traditions such as Gnosticism, Montanism, Quakerism, Shakerism; (3) the primary historical theological themes of the dominant stream of classical Christian theology— Orthodox, Catholic, and Protestant; (4) non-Christian Near Eastern and Greco-Roman religion and philosophy; and (5) critical post-Christian world views such as liberalism, romanticism, and Marxism.[17]

Employing the prophetic norm in scriptural interpretation and drawing upon a wide variety of traditions, Ruether addresses a number of traditional areas of theological inquiry in the next chapters of *Sexism and God-Talk*. We limit our investigation to Ruether's discussion of theological anthropology.

Ruether's Theological Anthropology

The creation stories that begin Genesis contain two of the most important teachings about humans: first, we are created in the image of God; and second, we are sinners. A theological understanding of the human person must hold both aspects in a creative tension if it is to preserve continuity with the biblical tradition. Ruether's approach to the question of theological anthropology is fairly traditional. She begins,

> Christian theological anthropology recognizes a dual structure in its understanding of humanity. This dual structure differentiates the essence from the existence of humanity. What humanity is potentially and authentically is not the same as what humanity has been historically. Historically, human nature is fallen, distorted, and sinful. Its original and authentic nature and potential have become obscured. The *imago dei*, or image of God, represents this authentic humanity united with God. It is remanifest in history as Christ to reconnect us with our original humanity. The question for feminist theology is how this theological dualism of *imago dei*/fallen Adam connects with sexual duality, or humanity as male and female.[18]

The nontraditional dimension of Ruether's theology is that the sinful fallen world is one characterized by patriarchy, by which she "means not only the subordination of females to males, but the whole structure of Father-ruled society: aristocracy over serfs, masters over slaves, kings over subjects, radical overlords over colonized people."[19]

Ruether asserts that the traditional teachings on theological anthropology have perpetuated a distorted, patriarchal vision of human nature. The tendency has been "to correlate femaleness with the lower part of the human nature in a hierarchical scheme of mind over body, reason over passions."[20] Coupled with this is the persistent claim that Eve caused the Fall, and that consequently, women must now bear the punishment for her offense. "Within history, woman's subjugation is both the reflection of her inferior nature and the punishment for her responsibility for sin."[21] Patriarchy is defended, therefore, by insisting that it reflects "the natural order" or "the will of God."

While the dominant tradition has preserved and promoted the patriarchal view of humanity, Ruether sees three marginalized traditions as offering an egalitarian view of humanity. First, the "eschatological feminism" of early Christianity, found also in the theology of the Shakers and Quakers, viewed the church as anticipating the final redemption of humanity and restoration to its original equality. While the larger social world may operate according to patriarchal rules, the church is governed by the countercultural vision of the equality of men and women. Second, "liberal feminism," arising during the eighteenth-century Enlightenment, argued for the equal rights of all human beings, regardless of gender. Unlike eschatological feminism, the focus is on transforming the social, political, and economic institutions of this world. Third, "romantic feminism stresses the differences between male and female as representative of complementary opposites: femininity and masculinity. In contrast to patriarchal anthropology, romantic feminism takes its definition of femaleness not from carnality and sin but from spiritual femininity, that is, intuitive spirituality, altruism, emotional sensitivity, and moral (sexual) purity."[22] Ruether subdivides romanticism into three versions. In its conservative form, romantic feminism sees the home as the woman's domain and the world of politics and commerce as the man's domain. In its reformist version, romantic feminism sees the need for a social reform based on woman's virtues of peace and love rather than war and egoism. In radical romanticism, women separate from the male culture and develop independent communities governed by feminist ideals.

Ruether argues that we need to find a "creative synthesis" between liberalism and romanticism. She advocates the equality of persons, regardless of gender, race, or class, but hesitates to embrace the view that men and women have equal, yet complementary natures. For this reason, Ruether does not fully endorse the recent use of the category of "androgyny" in some recent feminist writings.

> *Androgyny* has been used in recent feminist thought to express the human nature that all persons share. *Androgyny* refers to the possession of both male and females of both halves of the psychic capacities that have been traditionally separated as masculinity and femininity. The word *androgyny* is misleading, however, since it suggests that males and females possess both "masculine" and "feminine" sides to their psychic capacity. The term thus continues to perpetuate the ideas that certain psychic attributes are to be labeled masculine and others are to be labeled feminine and that humans, by integrating these "masculine" and "feminine" sides of themselves, become "androgynous."[23]

All humans, contends Ruether, are called to integrate the rational and relational capacities. "We need to affirm not the confusing concept of androgyny but rather that all humans possess a full and equivalent human nature and personhood, as *male and female*."[24] While Ruether stresses the commonality of the essential human nature of both men and women, other thinkers differentiate between "women's nature" and "men's nature."

This debate over whether there are different natures for women and men is one of the most intriguing elements in the current study of theological anthropology. Serene Jones poses the question in the following manner: "Is being a 'woman' the product of nature or nurture? Put another way, does 'womanhood' express an inborn, natural, female disposition or follow from socially learned behavior?"[25] The "nature-nurture debate" asks whether our personalities result from nature (that is, our genetic or biological makeup) or nurture (that is, influence of family, culture, or personal experience). Most, but not all, thinkers would argue that both have a determinative role in our development, but in the context of feminist thought, the question centers on the issue of gender. Is it true to say that women are more nurturing and intuitive than men? If so, is that a result of socialization, evolution, or biology? Do women and men have different psychological makeups that result in them having fundamentally different views of human relationships, concepts of morality, and approaches in spirituality? Reporting on the work of Mary Aquin O'Neill, Anne E. Carr summarizes the challenges of these questions for Christian theology:

> O'Neill concludes by pointing to the challenge of feminism to Christian theological anthropology: what vision of humanity, what goal for human life is proposed in Christian revelation? Is it the same for both men and women? Would it be sinful to cultivate certain ways of being human? How does salvation in Christ relate to the traditional dominance of men in Western society? And what does such salvation offer to women?[26]

The role of gender in human identity and social roles extends into questions ranging from women's ordination to child development. It demonstrates anew the centrality of the concept of *imago dei* to Christian thought and practice, yet indicates as well the degree of controversy that such a concept generates.

Assessment of Ruether's Theology

There are any number of controversial proposals in Ruether's theology that could be identified and discussed, but we limit our discussion to the question of method. How to do theology is a foundational question that resurfaces in each succeeding chapter of this book. Before moving into that discussion, however, I suggest that the following three types of questions may be useful when assessing Ruether's (or any theologian's) position. First, is her assessment of the current cultural and theological situation accurate? Does patriarchy exist? Is it as pervasive a problem as Ruether indicates? Second, is her historical reconstruction of how we arrived at the current cultural and theological situation convincing? Does she overemphasize certain teachings by individual theologians or overlook other influential movements? Third, are Ruether's proposals for the future of either Western culture or the Christian Church compelling? Is she pointing us in the direction of a more just society or church, or is she introducing (or reintroducing) concepts that would be detrimental to Christianity?

In her address to the American Academy of Religion on the future of feminist theology, Ruether writes,

> The community of the good news against patriarchy needs the courage of its convictions, the confident trust that they are indeed in communion with the true foundations of reality, the true divine ground of Being, when they struggle against patriarchy, despite all claims of authority. This faith lies first of all not in the Church, its tradition, or its Scripture. The patriarchal distortion of all tradition, including Scripture, throws feminist theology back upon the primary intuitions of religious experience itself, namely, the belief in a divine foundation of reality which is ultimately good, which does not wish evil nor create evil, but affirms and upholds our autonomous personhood as women, in whose image we are made.[27]

Because both scripture and tradition suffer from "patriarchal distortion," Ruether insists that teachings derived from either source should be assessed in light of "the primary intuitions of religious experience." Critics charge that such an approach does not provide adequate standards by which competing ideas can be judged. Ed. L. Miller and Stanley J. Grenz contend,

> The heart of the debate over feminist theology lies in its appeal to the feminist consciousness as its highest authority, as well as the use of women's experience to determine what is and what is not normative in Scripture and the Christian tradition. Critics fear that if we draw our "critical principle" solely from the consciousness of a particular

group—such as women—we have effectively eliminated any other criterion for engaging in self-criticism. As a result, feminist theologians run the risk of merely replacing an old ideology with a new one.[28]

Others fear that the Christian identity of feminist thought is being endangered when experience is given priority over scripture and tradition. Linda Hogan voices the following concern:

> To what extent can a theologian who gives priority to women's experience and praxis over against texts and traditions, considered to be foundational and thereby pre-eminent, be considered Christian? Would not the identity of Christianity be too fragmented if each group claimed priority for their experiences, over Scripture and tradition, and yet called themselves Christian? Is there not a core which must remain, regardless of experience, if one wishes to call oneself Christian?[29]

This discussion raises foundational questions about Christian theology. Are scripture and tradition hopelessly patriarchal? If so, what replaces them in a theology that identifies itself as Christian? If not, by what standards are teachings judged? Is there one proper interpretation of scripture or tradition, or is there a limited range of possible interpretations? Are some beliefs properly labeled heretical and therefore to be rejected by any serious Christian thinker? Which person or persons have the authority to offer definitive judgments on such matters? These questions will also be in the background of our discussions in the following chapters.

Ruether's Spiritual Theology

The concept of *imago dei* is the basis for Ruether's account of the desired state of affairs toward which we as a church and a society should strive. This future state of personal integration and social reconstruction represents the realization of the potential with which humans were originally endowed when we were created in the image of God. Ruether writes,

Thus the recovery of holistic psychic capacities and egalitarian access to social roles point us toward the lost full human potential that we may call "redeemed humanity." Redeemed humanity, reconnected with the *imago dei*, means not only recovering aspects of our full psychic potential that have been repressed by cultural gender stereotypes, it also means transforming the way these capacities have been made to function socially. We need to recover our capacity for relationality, for hearing, receiving, and being with and for others, but in a way that is no longer a tool of manipulation or of self-abnegation. We need to develop our capacities for rationality, but in a way that makes reason no longer a tool of competitive relations with others. Recovering our full psychic potential beyond gender stereotypes thus opens up an ongoing vision of transformed, redeemed, or converted persons and society, not longer alienated from self, from others, from the body, from the cosmos, from the Divine.[30]

The dynamic here is the very one we found in the first three chapters of Genesis. We are created in the image of God, yet we are sinners who live in a fallen world.

Redemption is the recovery and reintegration of the human self according to the original creation. Ruether writes, "The working assumption of a [liberationist] feminist theology has been the dynamic unity of creation and redemption....We must recognize sin precisely in the splitting and deformation of our true relationships to creation and to our neighbor and find liberation in an authentic harmony with all that is incarnate in our social, historical being."[31] This liberation was embodied by Christ who, "though he was in the form of God, did not regard equality with God as something to be exploited, but emptied himself, taking the form of a slave, being born in human likeness..." (Phil 2:6–7a). The Greek word for "emptying" is *kenosis*. Ruether states that Christ, "the representative of liberated humanity and the liberating Word of God, manifests the *kenosis of patriarchy*, the announcement of the new humanity through a lifestyle that discards hierarchical câste privilege and speaks on behalf of the lowly."[32]

Today's Christians, insists Ruether, should recapture the spirit and practice of first-generation Christianity, in which there was "widespread participation of women in leadership, teaching and ministry." Ruether continues,

> This participation of women in the early church was not an irregular accident, but rather the expression of an alternative world-view. Women were seen equally as the image of God. The equality of women and men at the original creation was understood as restored through Christ. The gifts of the Spirit of the messianic advent were understood (in fulfillment of the prophet Joel) and poured out on the "menservants" and "maidservants" of the Lord alike (Acts 2:17–21). Baptism overcomes the sinful divisions that divide men from women, Jew from Greek, slave from free, and make us one in Christ (Gal. 3:28). The inclusion of women in early Christianity expressed a theology in direct contradiction to the theology of patriarchal subordination of women.[33]

Christ's message of equality, mutuality, and harmony thrived in the generation immediately following the resurrection, but that message has been suppressed over the course of Christian history. Ruether calls for a rediscovery of the original teaching of *imago dei,* the teaching proclaimed by Jesus. This requires an exodus from the tyranny of patriarchy to the promised land of liberation. She writes, "Feminist theology needs to affirm the God of Exodus, of liberation and new being...."[34] In our next chapter, we will examine how another theologian, one generally credited with being "the father of liberation theology," also affirms the need for contemporary Christians to heed the call of "the God of Exodus."

Notes

1. Karl Barth, "The Strange New World Within the Bible," in *The Word of God and the Word of Man* (New York: Harper and Brothers Publishers, 1957), p. 28.

2. Rosemary Radford Ruether, *Disputed Questions* (Nashville: Abingdon, 1982), p. 17.

3.   Ibid., pp. 17–18.
4.   Rosemary Radford Ruether, "The Development of My Theology," *Religious Studies Review* 15(1), 1989, p. 1.
5.   Ruether, *Disputed Questions*, p. 118.
6.   Ruether, "Development of My Theology," p. 2.
7.   Ed. L. Miller and Stanley J. Grenz, *Fortress Introduction to Contemporary Theologies* (Minneapolis: Fortress Press, 1998), 162.
8.   Ruether, *Disputed Questions*, pp. 29–30.
9.   Rosemary Radford Ruether, "Asking the Existential Questions," in *Theologians in Transition,* ed. James M. Wall (New York: Crossroad, 1981), p. 161.
10. Richard P. McBrien, *Catholicism,* new ed. (San Francisco: HarperCollins , 1994), p. 52.
11. Rosemary Radford Ruether, *Sexism and God-Talk: Toward a Feminist Theology* (Boston: Beacon Press, 1983), p. 13. Hereafter *SGT.*
12. Ibid., pp. 12–13.
13. Ibid., p. 14.
14. Ibid., pp. 15–16.
15. Ibid., pp. 18–19.
16. Ibid., p. 24.
17. Ibid., pp. 21–22.
18. Ibid., p. 93.
19. Ibid., p. 61.
20. Ibid., p. 93.
21. Ibid., p. 95.
22. Ibid., p. 104.
23. Ibid., pp. 110–11.
24. Ibid., p. 111.
25. Serene Jones, *Feminist Theory and Christian Theology* (Minneapolis: Fortress Press, 2000), p. 23.
26. Anne E. Carr, *Transforming Grace: Christian Tradition and Women's Experience* (San Francisco: Harper and Row, 1988), p. 124.
27. Rosemary Radford Ruether, "The Future of Feminist Theology in the Academy," *Journal of the American Academy of Religion* 53 (1985), p. 710.
28. Miller and Grenz, *Contemporary Theologies*, p. 175.
29. Linda Hogan, *From Women's Experience to Feminist Theology* (Sheffield, England: Sheffield Academic Press, 1995), p. 107.
30. *SGT,* pp. 113–14.
31. Ibid., pp. 215–16.
32. Ibid., p. 137.

33.   Ruether, *Disputed Questions,* p. 123.
34.   *SGT,* p. 70.

Discussion Questions

1.   What impact has the feminist movement had on college-age men and women today?
2.   What does it mean to say that humans are created in "the image of God"? What does it mean to say that humans are "fallen"?
3.   Are scripture and tradition God's revelation? Do scripture and tradition reflect patriarchal patterns of thought? What implications for Christian theology follow from your answer?
4.   Do men and women have different natures? Are women by nature more nurturing? Are men by nature more aggressive?
5.   What are the strengths and weaknesses of Ruether's theology?

Suggested Readings

For short introductions to Catholic feminist theologians, see Susan A. Ross, "Catholic Women Theologians of the Left," in *What's Left?: Liberal American Catholics,* ed. Mary Jo Weaver (Bloomington: Indiana University Press, 1999). For American feminism, see Sarah Chappell Trulove and James Woelfel, "The Feminist Re-Formation of American Religious Thought," in vol. 2 of *Religion and Philosophy in the United States of America* (Essen: Die Blaue Eule, 1987), ed. Peter Freese. For a short critique of feminism, see Stanley J. Grenz and Roger E. Olson, *Twentieth-Century Theology* (Downers Grove: InterVarsity Press, 1992), pp. 224–36.

For brief overviews of Ruether's theology, see Mary Hembrow Snyder, "Rosemary Radford Ruether," in *A New Handbook of Christian Theologians* (Nashville: Abingdon, 1996), ed. Donald W. Musser and Joseph L. Price; the chapter on Ruether in James J. Bacik, *Contemporary Theologians* (Chicago: Thomas More Press, 1989); and William M. Ramsay, *Four Modern Prophets* (Atlanta: John Knox Press, 1986). Also helpful is the retrospective on Ruether's theology in *Religious Studies Review* 15(1), 1989.

For a scholarly engagement with Ruether's theology, see Nicholas John Ansell, *"The Woman Will Overcome the Warrior": A Dialogue with the Christian/Feminist Theology of Rosemary Radford Ruether* (Lanham: University Press of America, 1994).

For a discussion of theological method in feminist theology, see Anne E. Carr, "The New Vision of Feminist Theology," in *Freeing Theology* (San Francisco: HarperSanFrancisco, 1993), ed. Catherine Mowry LaCugna.

For feminist discussions of theological anthropology, see chap. 4 of Lynn Japinga, *Feminism and Christianity: An Essential Guide* (Nashville: Abingdon Press, 1999), and chap. 6 of Anne E. Carr, *Transforming Grace* (San Francisco: Harper and Row, 1988).

For a summary of Ruether's spiritual theology, see her "Feminist Theology and Spirituality," in *Christian Feminism: Visions of a New Humanity* (San Francisco: Harper and Row, 1984), ed. Judith L. Weidman.

2

The Exodus and Gustavo Gutiérrez's *A Theology of Liberation*

In the final cycle of stories in Genesis, we follow the trials and tribulations of Joseph. Thrown into a pit by his jealous brothers, he is taken to Egypt, where he is imprisoned on false charges, summoned before the Pharaoh, appointed supervisor of the grain distribution program after correctly interpreting the Pharaoh's dreams, and finally reunited with his father and brothers in Egypt. In the opening verses of Exodus, however, a significant change of fortune is noted: "Now a new king arose over Egypt, who did not know Joseph" (Exod 1:8). The Israelites are enslaved, but God commissions Moses to lead the people forth from slavery and guide them to a land flowing with milk and honey. It is this exodus event that serves as the focal point for our next theological investigation.

In this chapter we examine *A Theology of Liberation* by the Peruvian priest and father of liberation theology, Gustavo Gutiérrez. We focus on four topics. First, we follow Gutiérrez as he situates his own work in the history of Christian thought. Second, we investigate his understanding of liberation and salvation. We then turn our attention to the spirituality he advocates. Finally, we review the major criticisms leveled against him by his critics.

Situating Gutiérrez's Theology

Gustavo Gutiérrez's groundbreaking work *A Theology of Liberation,* which appeared in English translation in 1973, is at the same time both a traditional and a revolutionary work of theology. Gutiérrez grounds his work in both scripture and the traditional teaching of the

Catholic Church, especially the teachings contained in the documents of the Second Vatican Council. He sees in his work a continuity with the teachings found in those sources, yet he also gives voice to a new type of theology emerging from the struggles of the poor in Latin America. Both features of Gutiérrez's theology—his rootedness in the tradition and his radical proposals for the future—are evident in his discussion of the role of theology, his understanding of the relationship between church and state, and his views on Latin American economic development. It is interesting to note that all three avenues of inquiry will lead to a discussion of the concept of liberation.

Gutiérrez believes his own approach incorporates many of the traditional tasks assigned to theology, while at the same time moving beyond them. In the early church, Gutiérrez points out, theology was linked to the spiritual life. While often removed from worldly concerns, this spiritual theology consisted, in large part, of meditation on the Bible. In the twelfth century, theology became regarded as a science, as an intellectual discipline that produced wisdom. A product of the union of faith and reason, this wisdom was treated by some later theologians as a list of revealed truths to be systematically presented and defended. Such presentations often seemed removed from the struggles of living a Christian life. Gutiérrez proposes a new understanding of theology as "critical reflection on praxis." He writes, "Theology as critical reflection on Christian praxis in the light of the Word does not replace the other functions of theology, such as wisdom and rational knowledge; rather it presupposes and needs them."[1] Theology, for Gutiérrez, is "critical" in that it makes judgments—judgments regarding Christians beliefs, theological proposals, as well as economic and social issues. Theology is also grounded in "praxis." As Robert McAfee Brown explains, the word *praxis* "is not quite the equivalent of 'practice.' It points to *the ongoing interplay of reflection and action.* When we act, reflect on the action, and then act in a new way on the basis of our reflection (or when we reflect, and then act, and then reflect in a new way on the basis of our action) we are illustrating praxis."[2] Theology arises out of, and contributes to, the life of the Christian community and the struggle of all people to be liberated from oppression. Gutiérrez concludes,

> Theology as critical reflection on historical praxis is a liberating theology, a theology of the liberating transformation

of the history of humankind and also therefore that part of humankind—gathered into *ecclesia*—which openly confesses Christ. This is a theology which does not stop with reflecting on the world, but rather tries to be part of the process through which the world is transformed.[3]

The church consequently plays the vital role of interpreting social and political movements in light of the gospel.

When discussing the role of the church in the world, Gutiérrez again offers a historical perspective on his work. For most of Christian history, Gutiérrez contends, the church operated with a "Christendom" mentality regarding its own role in the world. In this view, temporal or earthly affairs fell under the control of the church: for the Christian, work in the world had value only to the degree that it benefited the church. The church understood its role to be the exclusive means by which souls could be saved. In the "New Christendom" model, proposed by the twentieth-century thinker Jacques Maritain, the church and world operate in two autonomous spheres. In this model, Christians are called upon to create a just society based on Christian principles. The Catholic Church does not directly intervene in temporal affairs; rather, it concentrates on its primary mission of the salvation of souls. It is suggested that laypeople join Christian organizations aimed at creating a society based on Christian principles. In a third model, one very similar to New Christendom, which Gutiérrez calls the "Distinction of Planes" model, the spiritual and temporal realms are totally separate and autonomous. As Leslie Griffin notes,

> This does not mean that Christians should not act in the temporal world, but it does discourage participation in the organized Christian parties of New Christendom. The opinion of the Distinction of Planes supporters is that these parties are an attempt to mold Christianity into an ideology for political reform. This is not the task of Christianity; instead, Christianity must be concerned with the heart of the individual, with the individual's spiritual relationship with God. This relationship takes precedence

over any false attempt to establish the Kingdom of God on earth.[4]

This model, advocated by the twentieth-century theologian Yves Congar and present in many of the documents of Vatican II, clearly distinguishes between the church and the world and insists on the dual responsibility of laypeople to build a more just society and to participate actively in the life of the church. Gutiérrez, however, criticizes an underlying assumption at work in the Distinction of Planes model.

Gutiérrez sees in the Distinction of Planes model a rigid separation of natural and supernatural realities (or nature and grace). While this may at first appear to be a quibble over some esoteric point of theology, this assumption results, according to Gutiérrez, in a deficient understanding of human nature, a distrust of the world, and a limited view of God's grace. By contrast, when the natural and supernatural are "intimately unified," humans are seen as possessing an innate desire to see God, the world is seen as imbued with God's presence, and the church is no longer the sole depository of God's grace. This "integral" understanding of the relationship between nature and grace creates a far different understanding of the discipleship. Gutiérrez writes, "This affirmation of the single vocation to salvation, beyond all distinctions, gives religious value in a completely new way to human action in history, Christian and non-Christian alike. The building of a just society has worth in terms of the Kingdom, or in more current phraseology, to participate in the process of liberation is already, in a certain sense, a salvific work."[5]

Gutiérrez contends that all theology, like politics, is local. More precisely, all theology begins as a local affair of reflecting on the Word of God in a particular set of circumstances existing at a particular time and place. For Gutiérrez, this means reflecting on the gospel in light of the "material insufficiency and misery"[6] of the poor in Latin America. Gutiérrez lays much of the blame for this situation on failed economic policies. "Latin America in the '50s was characterized by great optimism regarding the possibility of achieving self-sustained economic development."[7] These policies did not achieve their lofty goals. As Gutiérrez notes, "A change of attitude occurred in the '60s. A pessimistic diagnosis of economic, social, and political realities replaced the preceding optimism. Today it is evident that the developmentalist

model suffered from grave problems of perspective. It did not sufficiently take into account political factors, and worse, stayed on an
abstract and ahistorical level."[8] These policies generated economic
dependency on "the great capitalist countries" whose economic
development came at the expense of the poor countries. As a result,
the gap between the wealthier and poorer nations of the world actually widened. For this reason, Gutiérrez sees "development" as insufficiently critical of the status quo. In place of "development,"
Gutiérrez calls for "liberation." Unlike "development," liberation
begins with an empowerment of the people, not with seeking assistance from outside the nation, and focuses on liberation in all forms,
not merely from material poverty.

All three inquiries have led us to the same point. Theology (critical reflection on praxis), ecclesiology (an understanding of the
church), and sociology (an understanding of forces at work in society)
all lead to the topic of liberation. It is Gutiérrez's clarion call to liberation that is at the heart of his theology, and it is to that aspect of his
thought that we now turn.

Liberation and Salvation

Gutiérrez speaks of "three reciprocally interpenetrating levels of
meaning of the term *liberation*." He writes,

> In the first place, *liberation* expresses the aspirations of
> oppressed peoples and social classes, emphasizing the con-
> flictual aspect of the economic, social, and political process
> which puts them at odds with wealthy nations and oppres-
> sive classes....
>
> At a deeper level, *liberation* can be applied to an under-
> standing of history. Humankind is seen as assuming con-
> scious responsibility for its own destiny....
>
> In the Bible, Christ is presented as the one who brings
> us liberation. Christ the Savior liberates from sin, which is
> the ultimate root of all disruption of friendship and of all
> injustice and oppression. Christ makes humankind truly
> free, that is to say, he enables us to live in communion with
> him; and this is the basis for all human fellowship.[9]

Liberation encompasses all three levels and is not reducible to any one meaning. These three meanings emerge from Gutiérrez's integral understanding of the natural and supernatural and his reading of the scriptures.

Gutiérrez sees in the transition from a Distinction of Planes model to an integral understanding of the natural and supernatural planes a shift from a "quantitative" to a "qualitative" understanding of salvation. In the former, the problems that deserve the most attention are "the number of persons saved, the possibility of being saved, and the role which the Church plays in this process."[10] Salvation, in this view, is a cure for sin in this life and consists in heavenly reward after death. The present life is a test; salvation is given to those who pass the test. By contrast, in a qualitative view of salvation, Gutiérrez notes, "Salvation is not something otherworldly, in regard to which the present life is merely a test. Salvation—the communion of human beings with God and among themselves—is something which embraces all human reality, transforms it, and leads it to its fullness in Christ...."[11] Sin is not merely a personal affair; there are sinful social structures that prevent the communion between God and humanity or between humans and their neighbors. God's grace is at work in all people's lives, and people are saved when they open themselves to both God and neighbor. Salvation is, therefore, available to all people. Human action in this world is not seen as a test; it is not simply a means to an end, but it has value in itself. "One looks then to this world, and now sees in the world beyond not the 'true life,' but rather the transformation and fulfillment of the present life. The absolute value of salvation—far from devaluing this world—gives it its authentic meaning and its own autonomy, because salvation is already latently there."[12] In this view, all history is one. In other words, there is not a sacred history juxtaposed with human history. Rather, Gutiérrez argues, "The history of salvation is the very heart of human history."[13] This theme, claims Gutiérrez, runs throughout the biblical writings.

The scriptures speak to us of a God who acts on behalf of the poor to liberate them from oppression. This theme runs throughout the entire scriptures, but is seen most clearly and dramatically in the exodus from Egypt. Robert McAfee Brown notes,

> There are a number of passages that are central to Gustavo's response to the Bible, but his theology is not

based on a few proof-text passages, a game everybody can play. The Exodus story, for example is central, but for him the truth that God acts *for* "slaves" and *against* oppressive rulers is not limited to the book of Exodus, but is central to the prophets, the gospels and the epistles. It *is* "the biblical story."[14]

The exodus account illustrates God's intention for humanity (that is, liberation from all forms of oppression), but this intention was present at the very beginning of creation and stands at the end of history as its final goal.

Gutiérrez writes, "The Bible establishes a close link between creation and salvation. But the link is based on the historical and liberating experience of the Exodus."[15] Creation is the beginning of "the salvific adventure of Yahweh." Gutiérrez continues, "The liberation from Egypt—both a historical fact and at the same time a fertile Biblical theme—enriches this vision and is moreover its true source. The creative act is linked, almost identified with, the act which freed Israel from slavery in Egypt."[16] God entrusted to humans the responsibility for building a just society. Gutiérrez speaks of humans continuing the act of creation.

> Consequently, when we assert that humanity fulfills itself by continuing the work of creation by means of its labor, we are saying that it places itself, by this very fact, within an all-embracing salvific process. To work, to transform the world, is to become a man and to build the human community; it is also to save. Likewise, to struggle against misery and exploitation and to build a just society is already to be part of the saving action, which is moving towards its complete fulfillment.[17]

The exodus event not only illumines the initial act of creation; it forms the basis of hope for the future.

The scriptures not only speak of God's past acts in history, but project forward to the consummation of "the salvific adventure of Yahweh." These passages in the Bible are called "eschatological" because they deal with the end-time. Gutiérrez notes that "the Bible presents eschatology as the driving force of salvific history radically oriented toward the future. Eschatology is thus not just one more element of Christianity, but the very key to understanding the Christian faith."[18] The prophets summoned their listeners to change their ways, to respond to God's call. They announced God's intention to intervene directly in history on behalf of the cause of justice. Again the exodus figures prominently in this strain of biblical teaching. "The Exodus is a favorite theme of the prophets; what they retain of it is fundamentally the break with the past and the projection toward the future."[19] The prophets announced a future age characterized by peace, justice, and freedom from oppression. This promise reveals God's intention for humanity that was begun in the act of creation. The future therefore impacts how believers act in the present. Believers anticipate God's coming kingdom of peace and justice by eliminating violence and injustice in their society. They act in the present in ways that anticipate the future state of humanity. This way of living in hopeful expectation and active anticipation forms the core of Gutiérrez's spirituality.

Gutiérrez's Account of Christian Spirituality

Gutiérrez sees human history as the key to understanding God's nature. Human history is God's means of revelation, the pinnacle of that revelation being Christ. In reference to God, Gutiérrez writes, "Human history, then, is the location of our encounter with God, in Christ....Both God's presence and our encounter with God lead humanity forward, but we celebrate them in the present in eschatological joy."[20] If Christ is the key to understanding human history in general and biblical history in particular, then what does that history reveal to us? How do we encounter God now? On what do we base our joy in the midst of human suffering? The answer to these questions will help us arrive at a fuller understanding of Gutiérrez's vision of the Christian life.

Gutiérrez sees in biblical history a progressive revelation about the nature of God. He writes, "The active presence of God in the midst of the people is a part of the oldest and most enduring Biblical promises."[21] The form this awareness takes, however, evolves throughout the scriptures. In the earliest manifestation, the Israelites located this presence in a particular place—the tent or dwelling place, Mount Sinai, the ark of the covenant, and the temple. There emerged in the biblical writings, however, a sense that no temple or earthly structure could contain Yahweh. God dwells everywhere. The prophets added another element in the tradition. Their cry of complaint was lodged against those who participated in the external worship practices of Israel, yet who had within them a heart of stone. The prophets begin to foresee an age in which God will be present in the heart of every person. In Christ, these traditions reach their fulfillment. Gutiérrez writes,

> What we have here, therefore, is a twofold process. On the one hand, there is a universalization of the presence of God: from being localized and linked to a particular people, it gradually extends to all peoples of the earth....On the other hand, there is an internalization, or rather, an integration of this presence: from dwelling in places of worship, this presence is transferred to the heart of human history; it is a presence which embraces the whole person. Christ is the point of convergence of both processes. In him, in his personal uniqueness, the particular is transcended and the universal becomes concrete. In him, in his Incarnation, what is personal and internal becomes visible. Henceforth, this will be true, in one way or another, of every human being.[22]

The biblical progressive revelation discloses the truth that Jesus embodied: God's loving presence extends to all people and is encountered in the heart of each individual.

How do we encounter God in our hearts? Gutiérrez insists that God's intentions for the human race that are embodied in Christ—the essence of the gospel message—are seen most clearly in the parable of the final judgment in Matthew 25. Gutiérrez identifies three themes in the parable: "The stress on communion and fellowship as the ultimate meaning of human life; the insistence on a love which is manifested in concrete actions, with 'doing' being favored over simple 'knowing'; and the revelation of the human mediation necessary to reach the Lord."[23] The parable teaches us that "the least of our brothers and sisters" are our neighbors and that loving our neighbor involves concrete actions—feeding the hungry, giving drink to the thirsty, and so on. It is in those moments that we encounter God. "We find the Lord in our encounters with others, especially the poor, marginated, and exploited ones."[24] Gutiérrez later writes, "Our encounter with the Lord occurs in our encounter with others, especially in the encounter with those whose human features have been disfigured by oppression, despoliation, and alienation and who have 'no beauty, no majesty' but are the things 'from which men turn away their eyes' (Isa 53:2–3)."[25] Given the magnitude of the oppression, despoliation, and alienation, on what does Gutiérrez base his confidence for ultimate victory?

The struggle for liberation in solidarity with the poor requires much from those who have committed themselves to that way of life. For this reason, conversion is at the heart of Gutiérrez's vision of the Christian life. "To be converted is to commit oneself to the process of the liberation of the poor and oppressed, to commit oneself lucidly, realistically, and concretely."[26] We must be converted from indifference to a life of faith. Gutiérrez sees this way of life as possessing two defining characteristics. The first is gratitude—the awareness that communion with God and neighbor is a gift from God that elicits from the receiver an eagerness to do the will of God. The second characteristic is joy. Given the oppression and injustice in the world, on what is this joy based? Why not cynicism or despair?

> This joy ought to fill our existence, making us attentive both to the gift of integral human liberation and history as well as to the detail of our life and the lives of others. This joy ought not to lessen our commitment to those who live in an unjust world, nor should it lead us to a facile, low-cost conciliation. On the contrary, our joy is paschal, guaranteed by the Spirit (Gal. 5:22; 1 Tim. 1:6; Rom. 14:17); it passes through the conflict with the great ones of this world and through the cross in order to enter into life. This is why we celebrate our joy in the present by recalling the passover of the Lord. To recall Christ is to believe in him. And this celebration is a feast (Apoc. 19:7), a feast of the Christian community, those who explicitly confess Christ to be the Lord of history, the liberator of the oppressed.[27]

In a later work Gutiérrez returns to this theme of Easter joy. "The daily suffering of the poor and the surrender of their lives in the struggle against the causes of their situation have given new power to the Easter message. The deaths of so many in Latin America, whether anonymous individuals or persons better known, have made possible a deeper understanding of the Lord's resurrection. Joy springs therefore from the hope that death is not the final word of history."[28]

Christian hope, therefore, is grounded in the assurance that the Lord of history raised from the dead a victim of injustice who suffered death on a cross at the hands of the politically powerful. In doing so, God demonstrated definitively that injustice and misery do not have the final word in human history—the final word rests with the liberating God.

Criticisms of Gutiérrez's Work

In his survey of liberation theology, Deane William Ferm devotes a chapter to the five criticisms typically leveled against it. The charges are that liberation theologians: (1) de-emphasize the gospel, (2) over-emphasize action and neglect reflection, (3) politicize the faith, (4) endorse Marxism, and (5) support violence.[29] Some of these charges are more typically directed at Gutiérrez than others, but this list provides a fair representation of the charges leveled against Gutiérrez's work.

The first charge is that liberation theologians are actually dealing with social or political theory and simply fitting into that theory the passages from scripture that support their revolutionary ideas. Ferm believes Gutiérrez is innocent of this charge. While it is certainly true that any theologian could be charged with reading into the Bible meanings that are congenial to his or her theological positions, acknowledges Ferm, "Gutiérrez grounds his call for the liberation of the oppressed in scripture; he sees the exodus and resurrection events as pivotal points in the action of the liberator God."[30] In order to evaluate the relevance of this criticism, one might ask whether the theme of liberation is a dominant, continuous thread running throughout the entire tapestry of the biblical narrative or merely one element among many.

The second charge is that liberation theology is not sufficiently reflective. In their pursuit of social and political goals, liberation theologians, it is charged, neglect the larger questions of philosophy and theology. Ferm makes the following observation: "The role and significance of the transcendent remains a troubling issue for liberation theologians. Although appreciating their genuine concern over idolatry, the question must still be raised, vis-à-vis some forms of liberation theology, Where is God in all this? What happened to the Lord of history? Is eschatology strictly a human enterprise?"[31] Gutiérrez, his critics argue, needs to specify with greater precision the relationship between the human struggle to establish a just society (which Gutiérrez regards as a salvific act) and the final divine salvation of humanity (which is exclusively the work of God). Dennis McCann raises the problem in the following way.

> If liberation is "a gift of God," in what sense must it be won in a struggle? As we have seen, this is the major difficulty in correlating the themes of "salvation" and "liberation." Gutiérrez does, however, provide a rule for interpreting this correlation. In describing the Exodus experience as "paradigmatic," he characterized it as a process governed "by the twofold sign of the overriding will of God and the free and conscious consent of men." But this rule raises as many questions as it answers.[32]

This suggests that further work may need to be done by liberation theologians in terms of tackling questions such as the proper relationship between human and divine causality, especially as it relates to questions of salvation.

The third criticism is that liberation theologians politicize the Christian faith and reduce liberation to freedom from political, social, or economic oppression. Ferm dismisses this charge as a misreading of Gutiérrez. He contends that "although these (liberation) theologians emphasize political involvement, this does not mean that they reduce the meaning of liberation to its political, economic, and social components. To make this accusation is to misread them. Gustavo Gutiérrez emphasizes the necessary spiritual component of liberation."[33]

The fourth criticism is one of the most frequent accusations leveled against Gutiérrez and other liberation theologians. Critics ask, "Is liberation theology Marxism clothed in a theological mantle?"

Ferm admits that liberation theologians often favor socialism and oppose capitalism. He writes, "This is not really surprising. After all, as many observers agree—regardless of whether or not they are advocates of liberation theology—capitalism and its twin, colonialism (or neocolonialism), have caused many of the social inequalities found throughout the Third World."[34] Whether it is fair to designate them as Marxists is for Ferm a more complicated question. First, there is no single clear definition of Marxism. Is a supporter of unions and minimum wage by definition a socialist? Second, is the incorporation of Marxist categories into one's social, political, or economic analysis sufficient to be labeled a Marxist, or is Marxism part of the marketplace of ideas that twentieth-century Western thinkers had at their disposal? The 1984 "Instruction on Certain Aspects of the 'Theology of Liberation'" issued by the Congregation for the Doctrine of the Faith expressed concern over the "deviations and risks of deviation, damaging to the faith and to Christian living, that are brought about by certain forms of liberation theology which use, in an insufficiently critical manner, concepts borrowed from currents of Marxist thought."[35] Supporters of liberation theology often make the comparison to Thomas Aquinas's incorporation of Aristotle's philosophy into his theology in the thirteenth century. Aristotle's work was deemed "pagan philosophy" and hence unsuitable for inclusion into a Christian work, but Aquinas found it extremely helpful in explicating Christian belief.

The fifth criticism deals with the use of violence to achieve social goals. Are liberation theologians promoting the class struggle advocated by Marxism? Ferm sees little advocacy for violence in the work of Third World liberation theologians. He also mentions that violence takes many forms, and those who criticize violence should oppose the "institutionalized violence" perpetrated against the poor. Interestingly, Ferm notes that one thinker, Pablo Richard "believes that violence is inevitable and notes that the book of Exodus is itself a book of violence."[36]

How is the exodus best understood and incorporated into Christian thought and practice? Michael Walzer concludes his work *Exodus and Revolution* with the following observation:

So pharaonic oppression, deliverance, Sinai, and Canaan are still with us, powerful memories shaping our perceptions of the political world. The "door of hope" is still open; things are not what they might be—even when what they might be isn't totally different from what they are. This is a central theme in Western thought, always present though elaborated in many different ways. We still believe, or many of us do, what Exodus first taught, or what it has commonly been taken to teach, about the meaning and possibility of politics and about its proper form:

—first, that wherever you live, it is probably Egypt;

—second, that there is a better place, a world more attractive, a promised land;

—and third, that "the way to the land is through the wilderness." There is no way to get from here to there except by joining together and marching.[37]

We now march on to the promised land in this study, where we turn our attention from the cries for liberation to the battle cries of conquest.

Notes

1. Gustavo Gutiérrez, *A Theology of Liberation* (Maryknoll: Orbis Books, 1988), p. 11. (Hereafter *TL*).
2. Robert McAfee Brown, *Gustavo Gutiérrez* (Atlanta: John Knox Press, 1980), pp. 33–34.
3. *TL*, p. 12.
4. Leslie Griffin, *The Integration of Spiritual and Temporal: Roman Catholic Church-State Theory from Leo XIII to John Paul II* (New Haven: Yale University Ph.D. dissertation, 1984), p. 348.
5. *TL*, p. 46.
6. Ibid., p. 14.
7. Ibid., p. 49.
8. Ibid., p. 51.
9. Ibid., pp. 24–25.
10. Ibid., pp. 83–84.
11. Ibid., p. 85.
12. Ibid.
13. Ibid., p. 86.
14. Brown, *Gustavo Gutiérrez*, p. 58. For a contrasting view, see Jeffrey S. Siker, "Uses of the Bible in the Theology of Gustavo Gutiérrez:

Liberating Scriptures of the Poor," *Biblical Interpretation* 4(1), 1996. Siker argues that the exodus story is not "the crucial biblical story or theme underlying Gutiérrez's liberation theology" (p. 44).

15. *TL*, p. 86.
16. Ibid., p. 87.
17. Ibid., p. 91.
18. Ibid., p. 93.
19. Ibid.
20. Ibid., p. 106.
21. Ibid.
22. Ibid., p. 109.
23. Ibid., p. 113.
24. Ibid., p. 115.
25. Ibid., p. 116.
26. Ibid., p. 118.
27. Ibid., p. 120.
28. Gustavo Gutiérrez, *We Drink from Our Own Wells* (Maryknoll: Orbis Books, 1984), pp. 117–18.
29. Deane William Ferm, *Third World Liberation Theologies: An Introductory Survey* (Maryknoll: Orbis Books, 1986), chap. 5.
30. Ibid., p. 102.
31. Ibid., p. 103.
32. Dennis P. McCann, *Christian Realism and Liberation Theology* (Maryknoll: Orbis Books, 1981), p. 194.
33. Ferm, *Third World Liberation Theologies*, p. 105.
34. Ibid., p. 107.
35. "Instruction on Certain Aspects of the 'Theology of Liberation,'" in Alfred Hennelly, S.J., *Liberation Theology: A Documentary History* (Maryknoll: Orbis Books, 1990), p. 394. This Instruction also appears in *Origins* 14(13), 1984, pp. 193–204.
36. Ferm, *Third World Liberation Theologies*, p. 116.
37. Michael Walzer, *Exodus and Revolution* (New York: Basic Books, 1985), p. 149.

Discussion Questions

1. What does it mean to be saved? Does salvation refer to something that happens to us only after we have died, or is salvation in any way a this-worldly concept?
2. Should the church make statements directly related to the political or economic life of a nation? What is the proper role of the church in terms of its relationship to the government?

3. Does God favor the poor? What did Christ mean when he taught, "Blessed are you who are poor, for the kingdom of God is yours" (Luke 6:20)?
4. How important a theme is the "liberating power of God" in the Bible?
5. Should a new church being built today have expensive ornamentation? Do you believe that churches should be very plainly decorated and that the money that would have been used for stained glass should be given to the poor?

Suggested Readings

For a theological reflection on the exodus, see David Tracy, "Exodus: Theological Reflection," in his *On Naming the Present* (Maryknoll: Orbis Books, 1994).

Gustavo Gutiérrez's most influential work is *A Theology of Liberation* (Maryknoll: Orbis Books, 1973). The introduction to fifteenth anniversary edition of this work is reprinted in *Expanding the View: Gustavo Gutiérrez and the Future of Liberation Theology* (Maryknoll: Orbis Books, 1990), ed. Marc H. Ellis and Otto Maduro. For a fuller πent of Guitierrez's spirituality, see his work *We Drink from Our Own Wells* (Maryknoll: Orbis Books, 1984).

For an introduction to Gutiérrez's work, see *Gustavo Gutiérrez* by Robert McAfee Brown (Atlanta: John Knox Press, 1980), and *From the Heart of the People: The Theology of Gustavo Gutiérrez* (Oak Park, IL: Meyer-Stone Books, 1988) by Curt Cadorette. See also the Introduction in *Gustavo Gutiérrez: Essential Writings*, ed. James B. Nickoloff (Minneapolis: Fortress Press, 1996). Shorter summaries can be found in chap. 3 of Denis Edwards's *What Are They Saying About Salvation* (Mahwah: Paulist Press, 1986) and chapter 2 of Deane William Ferm's *Third World Liberation Theologies: An Introductory Survey* (Maryknoll: Orbis Books, 1986). A useful resource is *Liberation Theology: A Documentary History* (Maryknoll: Orbis Books, 1990), ed. Alfred T. Hennelly, S.J.

3

The Conquest and Reinhold Niebuhr's *Moral Man and Immoral Society*

The exodus was an overwhelming experience of emancipation. During the desert sojourn that followed, the Israelites struggled with their new status as liberated slaves. Fearing for their physical survival, some Israelites clamored for a return to Egypt, where they could take strange comfort in knowing that their slavery also assured them of their fill of bread and meat. Others faced trials of a more spiritual nature. They longed for a god they could see, and they celebrated when they saw the golden calf glistening in the sun. The desert, that place in which the Israelites received the Law from God and in which they wandered for forty years for their unfaithfulness, has long been regarded as a place of spiritual tension and testing. As we move from the Torah to the first of the Historical Books (or Former Prophets), the Israelites are poised to cross the Jordan River and enter the promised land, the land of Canaan. It is the conquest of that land that serves as our next point of consideration, as the Israelites exercise brute force to take the city of Jericho.

The taking of the city of Jericho is one of the most dramatic events in the entire Bible.[1] After sending spies into the city, Joshua leads the Israelites into the land of Canaan with a miraculous crossing of the Jordan River that is meant to recall the parting of the Red Sea. Angelic forces gather to assist in the taking of Jericho. God then places the city under the "ban," which consists in nothing less than the total annihilation of all living creatures there (Josh 6:21). As Lawrence Boadt explains,

The people responsible for carrying on the ancient traditions of the conquest emphasized that the victories came from God and that Joshua and the tribes followed God's directions carefully and always dedicated their military victories as a sacrifice to God in thanksgiving for his aid. This is the terrible custom of the "ban," called in Hebrew a *herem,* in which the Israelites were to slay everyone in the defeated towns. It was practiced to show that Israel put all its trust in God alone during the war and sought nothing for itself.

Modern people are shocked by such brutality, but it is necessary to remember that the ancient world did not share our outlook.[2]

Our revulsion at the brutality of the ban also leads to confusion when the Son of God teaches us to turn the other cheek and pray for our persecutors. It is fitting, therefore, that we pause and reflect on the exercise of power in the Christian life. The most prominent twentieth-century theologian who faced the problem of the use and abuse of power was Reinhold Niebuhr. After a brief biographical sketch of Niebuhr, we focus attention on his work *Moral Man and Immoral Society.* We then explore criticisms of Niebuhr's discussion of power.

The Life and Times of Reinhold Niebuhr

Reinhold Niebuhr was born in Wright City, Missouri, on June 21, 1892.[3] His mother, Lydia Hosto, was a preacher's daughter, and his father was an ordained minister in the Evangelical Synod (now part of the United Church of Christ). He attended Elmhurst College, and in 1912 enrolled in his father's alma mater Eden Theological Seminary. After graduation from Eden, Niebuhr studied at the Yale Divinity School for two years, receiving his M.A. in 1915. As Niebuhr later writes, "Family needs (my father had died just before my entrance into Yale) and my boredom with epistemology prompted me to foreswear graduate study and the academic career to which it pointed, and to accept a parish of my denomination in Detroit."[4]

The Detroit experience was, in the words of Larry Rasmussen, "theologically decisive." Rasmussen writes,

On the anvil of harsh industrial reality in Detroit, the trauma of the First World War, and the onset of the world-wide Depression, Niebuhr tested the alternatives he would find wanting—religious and secular liberalism and Marxism—even when he remained a sobered and reformed liberal and a socialist (albeit one who, beguiled by Franklin Roosevelt, came to embrace a mixed economy and gradualist reform). Detroit kindled the Christian indignation that would fire Niebuhr, as well as the restless quest to theologically illumine the events of the day and thereby render them meaningful. It was the prophet's intensity and clarity that Detroit evoked from Niebuhr—or perhaps better said, invoked, since the signs of volcanic activity were already present. Detroit was Niebuhr's entry into the world of his day.[5]

During his thirteen years in Detroit, Niebuhr served as a member and chair of the mayor's Commission on Interracial Relations; represented the Evangelical Synod at the Federal Council, a Protestant interdenominational group that later merged into the National Council of Churches; spoke frequently at conferences and colleges; and began his career as a prolific writer of articles for a variety of religious and secular journals.[6] It was Niebuhr's contact with the workers in the Ford auto plants, however, that would sear in his mind a lasting impression of the dehumanizing effect of both modern industry and capitalism. As D. R. Davies reports,

Mr. Seebohm Rowntree, after a visit which he paid to the Ford works, said that it was the nearest thing to hell he had ever seen. That was the aspect of it which impinged on Niebuhr. All this triumph of organization, with its efficient and it alleged benefits to the worker, was a vast mechanism which dehumanized and depersonalized the worker at the same time. It was all built up on the principle of a scientific reduction of physical movement to a minimum and of adapting the worker, the human agent, to the remorseless continuity of the machine. It was the worker, enslaved by the conveyor belt, who paid the price for this in nervous tension.[7]

Niebuhr saw firsthand the inequity in power between owner and worker, the human toll of decisions made on upper levels of corporate management, and the complicity of the church in maintaining the status quo.

Niebuhr's parish ministry also put him in touch with ordinary people involved in the daily struggles of life and of faith. Later in his life, Niebuhr described his experience of ministering to two elderly ladies in his congregation shortly after he arrived at his parish. Both were dying. The first woman faced her death with great fear and resentment. The second woman had both raised a family and worked outside the home to support them, since her husband suffered periodic bouts of insanity. When she could finally enjoy the benefits of her labor, she was diagnosed with cancer. Niebuhr later recalls, "I stood weekly at her bedside while she told me what passages of Scripture, what Psalms and what prayers to read to her; most of them expressed gratitude for all the mercies of God which she had received in life. She was particularly grateful for her two daughters and their love; and she faced death with the utmost peace of soul. I relearned the essentials of the Christian faith at the bedside of that nice old soul."[8] William E. Hordern relates another episode from Niebuhr's ministry that seems to have exerted an influence on Niebuhr's theology. He writes,

> Niebuhr told in his classes a story which no doubt had a considerable effect upon his thought and which illustrates his position. In his Detroit pastorate, while he still held a liberal theology, he was teaching a Sunday-school class about the Sermon on the Mount. Having expounded eloquently upon turning the other cheek, he was challenged by one of the boys in the class. This boy made a living for his widowed mother and family by selling papers. Each day, he said, there was a fight among the newsboys to see which one would get the best corner upon which to sell papers. Was he, as a Christian, to turn the other cheek, allow another boy to take his corner, and thus reduce the

support that he could give to his family? Niebuhr found that his theology had no answer.[9]

Niebuhr said he entered parish life with reluctance and left parish life with reluctance, but in 1928 he accepted an offer from Union Theological Seminary on Broadway at 120th Street in New York City, now known as Reinhold Niebuhr Place.

The late 1920s were tumultuous times. The country was in the throes of the Depression; Union was divided over the appointment of this Detroit pastor who did not hold a Ph.D.; and Niebuhr was struggling to find a relevant political and theological voice.

About student life at Union Seminary in the late 1920s and early 1930s, J. King Gordon writes,

> For those of us who came to Union in 1929, Niebuhr's apocalyptic lectures in Christian Ethics seemed to be documented by the events headlined in the daily press or encountered in the streets of New York—the Wall Street Crash in October, the reassuring words of Mr. Hoover from the White House, the confident announcement of Mr. John D. Rockefeller Sr. that he and his sons were buying up sound stocks at bargain prices, the lengthening breadlines, the apple sellers on the street corners, the protest meetings of the unemployed in Union Square, broken up by Grover Whalen's club-swinging police.[10]

John Bennett offers the following similar assessment.

> In 1932 Niebuhr published a book entitled *Moral Man and Immoral Society*. This book was landmark. It was the first major attack from within the ranks of liberal Christianity upon the optimistic idealism of the liberalism of that period and upon the dominant faith among intellectuals, especially among social scientists, in a coming rational control of history. In the year 1932 the United States was in the depth of the great Depression and Hitler was close to power in Germany. The results of the First World War seemed to be little more than steps toward another world conflict. It was a dark period of history, and yet the liberal

theologians and the people whom Niebuhr likes to call "the wise men" had not really begun to face the depth and the stubbornness of evil in the world.[11]

It was during this dark period of history that the young Detroit pastor moved to New York City to begin his long academic career at Union Theological Seminary.

Niebuhr's appointment to Union Seminary was not without its controversy. The president of Union, Henry Sloan Coffin, was impressed by Niebuhr's preaching and invited him to join the faculty of the seminary. A Niebuhr supporter, Sherwood Eddy, had offered to pay Niebuhr's salary, which he did for the first two years of Niebuhr's tenure at Union. Nevertheless Niebuhr's appointment was narrowly approved by the faculty. Rasmussen reports, "Despite the president's strong endorsement and windfall solution to the money matter, the faculty nonetheless approved Niebuhr's appointment by only one vote. After all, he not only did not hold a Ph.D., he had done no doctoral studies whatsoever; and he was a preacher, not a scholar."[12] Niebuhr's entrance into academic life did not, however, spell a departure from his involvement in political life.

Niebuhr was always active politically. Nathan A. Scott, Jr., explains,

> In the autumn of 1928 Niebuhr took up residence in New York City as a member of the faculty of Union Theological Seminary, where, despite the many prestigious university chairs that were later to be offered, he chose to remain until his retirement in 1960. Though his removal from the pressures of an urban pastorate to a professional berth brought new opportunities for systematic research that were to make for a great deepening of his thought, he seems never to have intended, however, that an academic career should foreclose political engagement. He remained a decisive figure in the Fellowship for a Christian Social Order, and after its absorption in 1928 into the leading pacifist organization of the period, the Fellowship of Reconciliation, he became the Fellowship's national chairman. By 1929, with John Dewey and Paul Douglas, he was

sitting on the Executive Committee of the League for Independent Political Action. In 1930 he was the Socialist's Party candidate for Congress in the Morningside Heights community on New York's upper west side. Moreover, in the same year, he was founding the Fellowship of Socialist Christians.[13]

Originally a Socialist Party supporter, Niebuhr cast his vote for Franklin D. Roosevelt in 1940 and 1944 and by the late 1940s supported the left wing of the Democratic Party.[14]

Niebuhr was also grappling with theological issues and the adequacy of his training in liberal theology to address the complex realities of life in the modern age. His commitment to pacifism also began to waver. In his personal life, things were also changing. "While Niebuhr was grappling, in the early thirties, with the problems of justice in the collective realm, he was learning a thing or two in the personal realm about the problems of love."[15] In 1930 he met Ursula Keppel-Compton, an Oxford theology graduate and first woman to be awarded the "English fellow" scholarship at Union. They were engaged the following spring and were married in December 1931.[16] In the midst of those changing times, Niebuhr "published the volume that launched his scholarly career and immediately established him both as a formidable thinker and a public intellectual. He wrote *Moral Man and Immoral Society* in the course of one summer, and it has been in print continuously since its publication in 1932."[17]

An Analysis of Moral Man and Immoral Society

Paul Merkley argues that *"Moral Man* is meant to be Niebuhr's parting blast at liberalism."[18] Niebuhr wastes no time firing the first shot. The opening line of the Introduction sets forth the central thesis of the work: "The thesis to be elaborated in these pages is that a sharp distinction must be drawn between the moral and social behavior of individuals and of social groups, national, racial, and economic; and that this distinction justifies and necessitates political policies which a purely individualistic ethic must always find embarrassing."[19] In the 1960 preface to the work, Niebuhr reaffirms his conviction of the truth of the book's central thesis: "The central thesis was, and is, that

Liberal Movement both religious and secular seemed to be uncon-
scious of the basic difference between the morality of individuals and
the morality of collectives, whether races, classes or nation."[20] The
passage of time seemed only to further corroborate for Niebuhr the
truth of this insight. As Robert McAfee Brown notes, "In a late book,
Man's Nature and His Communities, Niebuhr commented ruefully, as
his recognition of the pervasiveness of human sin deepened, that the
thesis of the early book could have been more accurately communicated by the title *The Not So Moral Man in His Less Moral
Communities.*"[21] Niebuhr contends that individuals are able to consider the interests of others, to experience sympathy for others in
need, and to cultivate a sense of justice that compels them on occasion to act in the interest of the other at the expense of their own self-
interest. "But," argues Niebuhr, "all these achievements are more
difficult, if not impossible, for human societies and social groups. In
every human group there is less reason to guide and check impulse,
less capacity for self-transcendence, less ability to comprehend the
needs of others and therefore more unrestrained egoism than the
individuals, who compose the group, reveal in their personal relationships."[22] For example, heads of state, business executives, or owners
of professional sports franchises may act in ways they would never act
toward family or friends, if they believed that such actions promoted
the interests of the nation, company, or team. Niebuhr takes the liberals, both secular and religious, to task for failing to truly appreciate
the radically dissimilar ways individuals and groups behave. Because
they overlook that critical distinction, liberals fail to see the real
causes of social injustice and offer solutions to those problems that
are misguided and doomed to failure.

Religious and secular liberals of the nineteenth and early twentieth centuries shared a basic optimism about the human potential.
While religious liberals looked to the preacher to unleash this potential, secular liberals pinned their hopes on the teacher, but both
believed the hope for a better tomorrow for the human race could be
realized if the human spirit was properly directed and motivated. The
signs of the times seemed to confirm this hopeful intuition. As Clyde
Crews notes, the nineteenth century brought significant developments in technology that offered immense practical benefits to the
average person living in the Western world.

Technologically, the century was a marvel. The steamboat, the steam locomotive, telegraph and telephone revolutionized travel and communication. Advances in electricity, photography, phonography, medicine, surgery; the growth of industry, cities, transatlantic immigration—all these changed lives drastically for the millions.

The century soon began to identify itself as the "Age of Progress," especially after the Crystal Palace Exhibition in London in 1851 and the Centennial Exhibition in Philadelphia in 1876. Perhaps most incredible and melancholy of all, the century even began to think of itself as wonderfully progressive in human relations. From the Congress of Vienna (1815) to the onset of the First World War (1914) there was little by way of global warfare as earlier centuries had known. In fact, the Crimean War for Britain (1853–1856) and the Civil War for the United States (1861–1865) were among the few really massive and extended battle situations of the age. There were those thinkers who began to think that serious wars were part of humanity's past, swept aside by the drive of inevitable progress.[23]

The great Protestant liberal theologian Adolf von Harnack captured the optimism of that movement in his work *What Is Christianity?* He states,

> But in connexion with this message of his, Jesus opens up to us the prospect of a union among men, which is held together not by any legal ordinance, but by the rule of love, and where a man conquers his enemy by gentleness. It is a high and glorious ideal, and we have received it from the very foundation of our religion. It ought to float before our eyes as the goal and guiding star of our historical development. Whether mankind will ever attain to it, who can say? but we can and ought to approximate to it, and in these days—otherwise than two or three hundred years ago—we feel a moral obligation in this direction. Those of us who possess more delicate and therefore more

prophetic perceptions no longer regard the kingdom of love and peace as a mere Utopia.[24]

For many Christians, Niebuhr included, who were raised with a liberal faith, that outlook died on the battlefields of World War I; it is for that reason that many people speak of 1914 as the beginning of the twentieth century. *Moral Man and Immoral Society* was Niebuhr's attempt to rally the troops to a new cause, a new theological and political outlook, one equipped to deal with the complexities and ambiguities of the modern world. As for liberalism, well, let the dead bury the dead.

Niebuhr takes aim at educators and religious moralists who assume that the problems of social injustice will be solved either by developing a greater awareness of these problems or by generating a greater sense of religious goodwill. Niebuhr regards both strategies as equally naive. "What is lacking among all these moralists, whether religious or rational, is an understanding of the brutal character of the behavior of all human collectives, and the power of self-interest and collective egoism in all inter-group relations."[25] Niebuhr's more realistic hard-nosed approach insists that "when collective power, whether in the form of imperialism or class domination, exploits weakness, it can never be dislodged unless power is raised against it."[26] Social change, in other words, does not result from a more perfect education or a purer religion. Rather, the "relations between groups must...always be predominantly political rather than ethical, that is, they will be determined by the proportion of power which each group possesses at least as much as by any rational and moral appraisal of the comparative needs and claims of each group."[27] In plotting a strategy for social change, Niebuhr prefers to speak of justice rather than love, to emphasize coercion more than cooperation, to assume selfishness, not selflessness, and to approximate goals rather than attain them.

This approach to social problems, which Niebuhr refines in later writings, becomes known as "Christian Realism." Robin W. Lovin, a sympathetic critic of Niebuhr's work, offers the following assessment: "*Moral Man and Immoral Society* was by all measures a major achievement of modern religious social thought, but the idea of Christian Realism that emerges at the end of its pages lacks the synthetic perspective that Niebuhr's writings as a whole offers to the task of Christian ethics."[28] Even in its nascent stage of development in *Moral Man*, however, Niebuhr's Christian Realism struck his liberal colleagues as, in the words of Alan Richardson, an "outpouring of a cynical and perverse spirit, very far removed from the benevolent and sanguine serenity which was held to be the hallmark of a truly Christian mind."[29] Niebuhr's defenders, by contrast, see in Christian Realism a method of assessing situations and plotting strategy that identifies the actual causes and remedies of social injustice. Lovin, for example, offers the following defense.

> The reality in question is the multiplicity of forces that drive the decisions that people actually make in situations of political choice. The desire to reward one's friends and punish one's enemies, convictions about the justice of a cause, the hope to advance one's own interests through the success of one's group or party, the need to demonstrate one's powers over events, and the wish to acquire more of it, fear of the loss of power, fear of the consequences of failure—all of these, and more, shape the responses of individuals and groups to choices about use of public resources and about institutions that serve public purposes. To be "realistic" in this context is, Niebuhr suggests, to take all of these realities into account. None should be overlooked, and each should be assigned a weight that reflects its real effect on the course of events, rather than its place in our own scale of values.[30]

The most helpful conceptual tool for realistic social analysis according to the Niebuhr of *Moral Man* is Marxism, and it is Marxism that provides the framework for much of Niebuhr's social analysis in the second half of his book.

Niebuhr contrasts the ethical attitudes of the privileged classes and the proletarian (that is, working) class. "The moral attitudes of dominant and privileged groups are characterised by universal self-deception and hypocrisy."[31] Niebuhr asserts with equal bravado that "it is a fact that Marxian socialism is a true enough interpretation of what the industrial worker feels about society and history, to have become the accepted social and political philosophy of all self-conscious and politically intelligent industrial workers."[32] The Niebuhr of *Moral Man* confidently predicted that "the full maturity of American capitalism will inevitably be followed by the emergence of the American Marxian proletarian."[33]

Niebuhr saw in Marxism a quasi-religious interpretation of history as a march to a classless society in which humans worked according to their abilities and received according to their needs. While Niebuhr does not explicitly propose a spirituality in *Moral Man*, he does, nonetheless, speak of a "proletarian spirituality" that is grounded in "a promise of a just society, a promise which the proletarian makes and believes with such fervor and religious feeling."[34] Niebuhr continues,

> There are other redemptive forces in society beside those of proletarian spirituality. There are eyes which see clearly, other than those which have been clarified by his suffering; and there are wills which are resolute beside those which have been fortified by his bitter personal experience. Yet their number is restricted by the limits of the human imagination which permit only a few to see what they do not personally experience.[35]

Because "only a few" in the privileged classes see the need for social change, most of them will resist the Marxist restructuring of the economic and political order.

Marxism was upfront about how to dislodge the privileged classes who strained to maintain their economic clout. "The distinctive feature of the Marxian dream is that the destruction of power is regarded as the prerequisite of its attainment. Equality will be established only through the socialisation of the means of production, that is, through the destruction of private property, wherever private property is social power."[36] Niebuhr further insists that the Marxist "is not cynical but only realistic, in maintaining that disproportion of power in society is the real root of social injustice. We have seen how inevitably social privilege is associated with power, and how ownership of the means of production is the significant power in modern society. The clear recognition of that fact is the greatest ethical contribution which Marxian thought has made to the problem of social life."[37] As we have seen in our earlier discussion of liberation theology, one of the most controversial features of Marxist thought is the inevitability of the class struggle and the need for violent revolution to effect social change.

Niebuhr's discussion of violence in *Moral Man* signals a complete break with his former commitment to pacifism. In its pages, he explicitly rejects the intrinsic immorality of violence and revolution. Niebuhr admits that "Western civilisation will not be ripe for proletarian revolutions for many decades, and may never be ripe for them, unless one further condition of the Marxian prophecy is fulfilled, and that is, that the inevitable imperialism of the capitalistic nations will involve them in further wars on a large scale."[38] For that reason, Niebuhr suggests that justice might have to be secured through political means. If revolution is unlikely, "it would become necessary to abandon the hope of achieving a rational equalitarian social goal, and be content with the expectation of its gradual approximation."[39] Nevertheless, "if violence can be justified at all, its terror must have the tempo of a surgeon's skill and healing must follow quickly upon its wounds."[40]

Niebuhr's suggestion that the use of violence may be necessary in order to secure a just society is not his final word on pacifism. He takes the offensive and challenges the validity of the pacifists' distinction between violent and nonviolent coercion. Coercion, whether it is violent or nonviolent, harms either people or property, insists Niebuhr. The refusal to pay taxes or the boycotting of certain industries causes harm; consequently, both violent and nonviolent forms of coercion are forms of aggression. It is interesting to note Niebuhr's assessment of Gandhi's work in India:

> The cotton spinners of Lancashire are impoverished by Gandhi's boycott of English cotton, though they can hardly be regarded as the authors of British imperialism....
>
> Non-co-operation, in other words, results in social consequences not totally dissimilar from those of violence. The differences are very important; but before considering them it is necessary to emphasise the similarities and to insist that non-violence does coerce and destroy. The more intricate and interdependent a social process in

which non-co-operation is used, the more certainly is this the case. This insistence is important because non-resistance is so frequently confused with non-violent resistance. Mr. Gandhi, the greatest modern exponent of non-violence, has himself contributed to that confusion.[41]

Once the distinction between violent and nonviolent coercion has been obliterated, a strategy using either form of coercion must be crafted to achieve a greater balance of power within society.

Niebuhr addresses himself to the racial issues of his day. He writes that "non-violence is a particularly strategic instrument for an oppressed group which is hopelessly in the minority and has no possibility of developing sufficient power to set against its oppressors."[42] Niebuhr continues,

> The emancipation of the Negro race in America probably waits upon the adequate development of this kind of social and political strategy. It is hopeless for the Negro to expect complete emancipation from the menial social and economic position into which the white man has forced him, merely by trusting in the moral sense of the white race. It is equally hopeless to attempt emancipation through violence rebellion.[43]

Niebuhr's writings exerted an incalculable influence on American intellectual and political life, but one cannot help but wonder what impact Niebuhr's work had on a young divinity school student named Martin Luther King, Jr. Kenneth L. Smith and Ira G. Zepp, Jr., make the following report:

> King studied Reinhold Niebuhr for the first time in "Christian Social Philosophy II." He also returned to the study of Rauschenbusch, but this time around he saw Rauschenbusch in juxtaposition to Niebuhr. Although King would vacillate back and forth in reaction to certain aspects of Niebuhr's thought, it is not going too far to say that King was never again comfortable with certain emphases of liberalism after his introduction to the thought of Reinhold

Niebuhr. He admitted readily that his first encounter with Niebuhr's *Moral Man and Immoral Society*, one of the few books mentioned by title in King's writings and the only one mentioned more frequently than Rauschenbusch's *Christianity and the Social Crisis*, left him "confused" and later on that he "began to question some of the theories that had been associated with so-called liberal theology." Finally, he confessed that he "became so enamored of his [Niebuhr's] social ethics that I almost fell into the trap of accepting uncritically everything he wrote." In short, Niebuhr burst like a bombshell into King's liberal theological-ethical world view.[44]

Niebuhr's realism surfaces in his discussion of civil rights. Violent revolution would be unsuccessful and counterproductive. Boycotting banks and stores that discriminate against African Americans are measures that will produce some gains, but larger social strategies need to be devised.

Niebuhr concludes *Moral Man* with a call to accept a "frank dualism in morals." "Such a dualism," writes Niebuhr, "would have two aspects. It would make a distinction between the moral judgments applied to the self and to others; and it would distinguish between what we can expect of individuals and of groups."[45] While an individual is able to transcend his or her selfishness and act according to disinterested motives, society will act along selfish lines. The individual strives to love; the society aims to be just. The religious individual may submit to injustice, the social group seeks to throw off its yoke. Any attempt to build a more just society needs to recognize this frank dualism if it is to respond realistically to the complexities of life in modern society.

Criticisms of Niebuhr's Work

We focus on two of the most common criticisms of Niebuhr's work. The first is that Niebuhr's Christian Realism amounts to a defense of the status quo. The second is that Niebuhr's theology is insufficiently developed in certain key areas.

It may seem odd that the radical, Marxist author of *Moral Man* would be accused of supporting the status quo, but this is perhaps the most common criticism of Niebuhr's Christian Realism. In an article, "Christian Realism: Ideology of the Establishment," Ruben A. Alves writes, "Realism and pragmatism are words dear to American ears, hearts, and brains. If this is so, anyone involved who is involved in social analysis should suspect at once that realism is functional to the system, contributes to its preservation and gives it ideological and theological justification."[46] In an article with an equally provocative title, "Apologist of Power: The Long Shadow of Reinhold Niebuhr's Christian Realism," Bill Kellermann reviews two books dealing with Reinhold Niebuhr: one by Richard Fox and the other by Robert McAfee Brown. Kellermann charges that Niebuhr's position

> means that the morally responsible are to be freed from their arrogant pretensions, but also from the squeamishness that holds them back from the exigencies of, say, military necessity. Fox writes of a telling description of Niebuhr's import to the inner circle policy-makers of the Kennedy administration: "He helped them maintain faith in themselves as political actors in a troubled—what he termed sinful—world. Stakes were high, enemies were wily, responsibility meant taking risks: Niebuhr taught that 'moral men had to play hardball.'" Call it justification.[47]

Finally, Stanley Hauerwas and Michael Broadway level the following charge: "Claims of 'realism,' such as those of Niebuhr, provide the perfect setting for the development of a severe case of ideological blindness. The eventual convergence of Reinhold Niebuhr's 'realism' with accepted doctrine of American foreign policy in the 1950s and 1960s further confirms the suspicion that many theologians had accepted a version of reality that was easily compatible with the views of the dominant groups of society."[48]

Robin W. Lovin defends Niebuhr against the charge that his approach to social problems can be reduced to a systematic defense of the prevailing interests of the social and political elite. Lovin comments on the following observation by Hans Morgenthau: "Reinhold Niebuhr has shown that...this relationship between a concealed political reality and a corrupted ethic is the very essence of politics; that, in other words, political ideologies are an inevitable weapon in the struggle for power which all participants must use to a greater or lesser extent."⁴⁹ Lovin remarks,

> Niebuhr was puzzled by this accolade, and he found Morgenthau's analysis one-sided. Ideology is inevitably an element in political controversy, but it is not the only element. The moral ambiguities of politics cannot be neglected, but the terms of moral evaluation are not simply reducible to individual and group interests. The political reality to which Niebuhr wants to be attentive thus includes both the "established norms" and the "factors of self-interest and power" which offer resistance to them.⁵⁰

John C. Bennett's observation may prove helpful. He recalls the debates between Niebuhr and Henry Pitney Van Dusen in the Union Seminary chapel. Bennett writes, "Dr. Van Dusen felt that Niebuhr put too little stress on moral discipline and the formation of character. I always felt that they talked past each other because they were interested in different things. Dr. Niebuhr was concerned about the sins of the strong who were often too well disciplined. Dr. Van Dusen was concerned about the sins of the weak who were in danger of being lost as persons through lack of discipline."⁵¹ Niebuhr's theology was geared toward those who held power rather than those for whom power was a distant dream. As Larry Rasmussen notes, "He was utterly clear-eyed about the sins of those who, holding power, extend and abuse it, rather than surrender or share it. He was less clear about the social-psychological dynamics of relatively powerless people who must proudly claim power in order to experience pride in a strongly self-affirming, constructive, freeing, life-giving and self-empowering sense."⁵²

It is precisely on the question of the proper exercise of power that we can begin to speak of Niebuhr's spirituality. In *Moral Man* he speaks of a "proletarian spirituality" that seeks the promise "of a just society, a promise which the proletarian makes and believes with such fervor and religious feeling. The vision of a classless world gives moral dignity to the dream of the victory of his class."⁵³ Larry Rasmussen, however, offers the following observation:

Niebuhr himself had, and he teaches, a profound spirituality for risky and ambiguous but justice-directed uses of power in a season when the reigning paradigm of growth and social progress is itself on the rocks. His utter honesty about the beauty and terror of life, not least in changing and convulsive times, an honesty grounded in his theology of the cross and suffering divine love, is at the heart of this spirituality of boldly exercising precarious power.[54]

The second criticism leveled against Niebuhr is that his positions are not sufficiently developed theologically. Two features of Niebuhr's writings contribute to this impression. First, in his "Intellectual Autobiography," Niebuhr himself disavowed the designation "theologian." He claimed no competence to deal with the "nice points of pure theology." Second, as Larry Rasmussen notes,

> Niebuhr was at his very best in his ability to render a theological interpretation of events as a basis for common action for a wide audience. But precisely because of the audience's diverse beliefs, Niebuhr often cast his case in ways which left his Christian presuppositions and convictions unspoken. His theology was always the controlling framework, but his public discourse did not require knowledge of it, much less assent to it, in order to solicit response.[55]

Because his Christian convictions remained unspoken, critics quickly cite their absence. Certain essential strands of the biblical tapestry, critics charge, are overlooked by Niebuhr. Hauerwas complains that "Niebuhr simply provided no place for the church as a political alternative to the ways of nations and empires."[56] Bill Kellermann mentions that "a number of commentators have noticed that Niebuhr had little or no doctrine of the resurrection."[57] Kellermann reserves his most stringent criticism for later in the piece. He writes,

> This is ultimately the theological and political crux of the matter. For all the gifts of Niebuhr's thought—his comprehension of the complex ambiguities of every human decision, his contagious biblical appreciation of irony and

paradox, his identification of collective sin, his relentless critique of self-righteousness, and his passion for justice— not to mention his lucid rhetoric and epigrammatic one-liners—he lacks one thing: a faith that begins and ends in divine grace.[58]

Critics charge that Niebuhr did not sufficiently recognize his own theological liberalism while he was attacking it in others. They insist that Niebuhr's Jesus is irrelevant for social ethics; his Jesus is the passive, otherworldly Jesus of liberalism. Lovin again defends Niebuhr on this point. "In a realistic Christian ethics, biblical resources help us to pick out, among a range of forces that have been clearly differentiated and accurately understood, those that move in directions that are compatible with the hope for justice, and to distinguish them from those which do not. The first task of ethical reflection is to establish the connections between human experience, social fact, and biblical symbol that make those judgments possible."[59] In other words, biblical and theological concepts play a determinative role in Niebuhr's ethics even when they are not explicitly stated.

Of the many students whose lives were impacted by Niebuhr, one of the most famous was a young German student who studied at Union Seminary in 1930–1931 named Dietrich Bonhoeffer. Larry Rasmussen reports that "an important relationship developed, and Bonhoeffer, on a trip largely arranged by Niebuhr, found himself back at Union in 1939, making the most important decision of his life—to return to Germany where, before long, he joined family members and others in the conspiracy to overthrow Hitler."[60] It is to that momentous decision that we now turn.

Notes

1. It is important to recall that a historical-critical study of this event would necessitate asking questions that are not pursued here. For a summary of some of the important historical questions regarding the conquest of Canaan, see Bernhard W. Anderson, *Understanding the Old Testament,* 4th ed. (Englewood Cliffs: Prentice-Hall, 1986), pp. 131–37.
2. Lawrence Boadt, *Reading the Old Testament: An Introduction* (Mahwah: Paulist Press, 1984), p. 197.

3. I am relying on Dennis P. McCann, *Christian Realism and Liberation Theology* (Maryknoll: Orbis Books, 1981), chap. 1, and Stanley J. Grenz and Roger E. Olson, *Twentieth-Century Theology* (Downers Grove: InterVarsity Press, 1992), pp. 99–101, for biographical information on Niebuhr.

4. Reinhold Niebuhr, "Intellectual Autobiography," in *Reinhold Niebuhr: His Religious, Social, and Political Thought*, ed. Charles W. Kegley (New York: Pilgrim Press, 1984), p. 4.

5. Larry Rasmussen, "Introduction," *Reinhold Niebuhr: Theologian of Public Life* (London: Collins, 1989), p. 7. Hereafter "Introduction."

6. See Donald B. Meyer, *The Protestant Search for Political Realism, 1919–1941* (Berkeley: University of California Press, 1960), p. 218

7. D. R. Davies, *Reinhold Niebuhr: Prophet from America* (New York: Macmillan, 1948), pp. 18–19.

8 . Niebuhr, "Intellectual Autobiography," p. 6.

9. William E. Hordern, *A Layman's Guide to Protestant Theology* (New York: Macmillan, 1968), p. 161.

10. Quoted in Rasmussen, *Reinhold Niebuhr*, p. 287, fn. 21.

11. John C. Bennett, "The Contribution of Reinhold Niebuhr," *Union Seminary Quarterly Review* XXIV (1), 1968, pp. 6–7.

12. Rasmussen, "Introduction," p. 9.

13. Nathan A. Scott, Jr., "Introduction," *The Legacy of Reinhold Niebuhr* (Chicago: University of Chicago Press, 1975), p. xi–xii.

14. See Rasmussen, "Introduction," p. 11.

15. June Bingham, *Courage to Change* (New York: Charles Scribner's Sons, 1972), p. 182.

16. See Rasmussen, "Introduction," p. 12.

17. Ibid., p. 10.

18. Paul Merkley, *Reinhold Niebuhr: A Political Account* (Montreal: McGill-Queen's University Press, 1975), p. 83.

19. Reinhold Niebuhr, *Moral Man and Immoral Society* (New York: Charles Scribner's Sons, 1932), p. xi. I am using the 1960 edition of the work. Hereafter *Moral Man*.

20. Ibid., p. ix.

21. Robert McAfee Brown, *The Essential Reinhold Niebuhr* (New Haven: Yale University Press, 1986), p. xv.

22. *Moral Man*, pp. xi–xii.

23. Clyde F. Crews, *Ultimate Questions: A Theological Primer* (Mahwah: Paulist Press, 1986), p. 50.

24. Adolf von Harnack, *What Is Christianity?* (Gloucester, MA: Peter Smith, 1978), pp. 113–14.

25. *Moral Man,* p. xx.

26. Ibid., p. xii.

27. Ibid., p. xxiii.

28. Robin W. Lovin, *Reinhold Niebuhr and Christian Realism* (Cambridge: Cambridge University Press, 1995), p. 98.

29. Alan Richardson, "Reinhold Niebuhr as Apologist," in *Reinhold Niebuhr: His Religious, Social, and Political Thought* ed. Charles W. Kegley (New York: Pilgrim Press, 1984), p. 218. Quoted in Scott, "Introduction," p. xiii.

30. Lovin, *Reinhold Niebuhr and Christian Realism,* p. 4.

31. *Moral Man,* p. 117.

32. Ibid., p. 144.

33. Ibid.

34. Ibid., pp. 162, 161.

35. Ibid., p. 162.

36. Ibid., p. 163.

37. Ibid.

38. Ibid., p. 190.

39. Ibid., p. 219.

40. Ibid., p. 220.

41. Ibid., pp. 241–42.

42. Ibid., p. 252.

43. Ibid.

44. Kenneth L. Smith and Ira G. Zepp, Jr., *Search for the Beloved Community* (Valley Forge: Judson Press, 1974), p. 71.

45. *Moral Man,* p. 271.

46. Ruben A. Alves, "Christian Realism: Ideology of the Establishment," *Christianity and Crisis* (September 17, 1973), p. 176.

47. Bill Kellermann, "Apologist of Power: The Long Shadow of Reinhold Niebuhr's Christian Realism," *Sojourners* (March 1987), p. 17.

48. Stanley M. Hauerwas with Michael Broadway, "The Irony of Reinhold Niebuhr: The Ideological Character of 'Christian Realism,'" in *Wilderness Wanderings* (Boulder: Westview Press, 1997), p. 50.

49. Hans Morgenthau, "The Influence of Reinhold Niebuhr in American Political Life and Thought," in *Reinhold Niebuhr: A Prophetic Voice in Our Time* (Greenwich: Seabury Press, 1962), pp. 108–9.

50. Lovin, *Reinhold Niebuhr and Christian Realism,* p. 10.

51. Bennett, "Contribution of Reinhold Niebuhr," p. 11.

52. Larry Rasmussen, "Niebuhr on Power: Assessment and Critique," in *Reinhold Niebuhr (1892–1971): A Centenary Appraisal,* ed. Gary A. Gaudin and Douglas John Hall (Atlanta: Scholars Press, 1984), p. 175.

53. *Moral Man,* p. 161.
54. Rasmussen, "Niebuhr on Power," pp. 182–83.
55. Rasmussen, "Introduction," p. 3.
56. Stanley Hauerwas, *Against the Nations* (San Francisco: Harper & Row, 1985), p. 123.
57. Kellermann, "Apologist of Power," p. 18.
58. Ibid., p. 20.
59. Lovin, *Reinhold Niebuhr and Christian Realism,* p. 105.
60. Rasmussen, "Introduction," p. 12.

Discussion Questions

1. Would God command the Israelites to kill all living beings in the city of Jericho? What does your answer imply about how we should read the Bible?

2. Was Lord Acton right when he said, "Power tends to corrupt, and absolute power corrupts absolutely"?

3. Do honorable, morally upright individuals do things in their roles as public officials or as corporate executives that they would never do in their private lives?

4. Offer your assessment of one of Niebuhr's most famous lines: "Man's capacity for justice makes democracy possible; but man's inclination to injustice makes democracy necessary." (From *The Children of Light and the Children of Darkness,* New York: Charles Scribner's Sons, 1944, p. xiii.)

5. Is nonviolent protest morally better than violent protest? Why? Why not? If violent action would produce a more just society, should Christians endorse violence action?

6. How relevant are Jesus' teachings to the complexities of modern life?

7. Could a pro-life Christian vote for a pro-choice candidate that endorses every other cause that the voter supports?

Suggested Readings

For a biography of Niebuhr, see Richard Wightman Fox, *Reinhold Niebuhr: A Biography* (New York: Pantheon Books, 1985). For introductions to Niebuhr's thought, see the Introduction by Larry Rasmussen to *Reinhold Niebuhr: Theologian of Public Life* (London: Collins, 1989); the Introduction to *The Legacy of Reinhold Niebuhr,* ed. Nathan A. Scott, Jr. (Chicago: University of Chicago Press, 1975); and chap. 15 of *Modern Christian Thought* (New York: Macmillan, 1971) by James Livingston. For longer critical introductions, see Robin W. Lovin, *Reinhold Niebuhr and Christian*

Realism (Cambridge: Cambridge University Press, 1995), and Dennis P. McCann, *Christian Realism and Liberation Theology* (Maryknoll: Orbis Books, 1981). For discussions of Niebuhr's view of power, see Kenneth Durkin, *Reinhold Niebuhr* (Harrisburg: Morehouse Publishing, 1989), pp. 41–50; Langdon Gilkey's essay, "Reinhold Niebuhr as Political Theologian" in *Reinhold Niebuhr and the Issues of Our Time,* ed. Richard Harries (Grand Rapids: Eerdmans, 1986); and Larry Rasmussen's article, "Niebuhr's Theory of Power: Social Power and Its Redemption," in *Reinhold Niebuhr (1892–1971): A Centenary Appraisal,* ed. Gary A. Gaudin and Douglas John Hall (Atlanta: Scholars Press, 1984). See also Paul Jersild, "Reinhold Niebuhr: Continuing the Assessment," in *Dialog,* Fall 1983. For an interesting reflection on the significance of *Moral Man and Immoral Society,* see Matthew Berke's piece in "A Century of Books: An Anniversary Symposium" in *First Things,* March 2000, pp. 41–42.

4

The Exile and Dietrich Bonhoeffer's *Letters and Papers from Prison*

In 587 B.C.E. the Babylonians destroyed the Temple in Jerusalem, and in doing so, they shattered the religious, political, and social world of God's chosen people. As John Bright observes,

> The destruction of Jerusalem and the subsequent exile mark the great watershed of Israel's history. At a stroke her national existence was ended and, with it, all the institutions in which her corporate life had expressed itself; they would never be re-created in the precisely the same form again. The state destroyed and the state cult perforce suspended, the old national-cultic community was broken, and Israel was left for the moment an agglomeration of uprooted and beaten individuals, by no external mark any longer a people. The marvel is that her history did not end altogether. Nevertheless, Israel survived the calamity and, forming a new community out of the wreckage of the old, resumed her life as a people. Her faith, disciplined and strengthened, likewise survived and gradually found the direction that it would follow through all the centuries to come. In the exile and beyond it, Judaism was born.[1]

Out of the exile, new life emerged, as foretold by the prophet Ezekiel in his famous vision of the dry bones (Ezek 37). Judaism was born, but first came the horror, the dislocation, and the questioning.

Jews in the twentieth century experienced their own horror, dislocation, and questioning. The haunting images of emaciated faces peering from the crowded bunks of the concentration camps, and film footage of mass burials for those exterminated by their captors stand as horrific reminders to modern Jews of the enduring threat of anti-Semitism. For modern Christians too, questions abound. As John Gager writes, "The experience of the Holocaust reintroduced with unprecedented urgency the question of Christianity's responsibility for anti-Semitism: not simply whether individual Christians had added fuel to modern European anti-Semitism, but whether Christianity itself was, in its essence and from its beginnings, the primary source of anti-Semitism in Western culture."[2] One theologian who struggled with questions such as these was a young German pastor named Dietrich Bonhoeffer, who was himself executed by the Nazis on April 9, 1945.[3] After a brief overview of Bonhoeffer's life, we turn our attention to an examination of the central themes in his letters from prison, and conclude with an investigation of the spirituality suggested by Bonhoeffer's provocative aphorisms.

Bonhoeffer's Biography

Dietrich Bonhoeffer was born into a comfortable upper-middle-class family in Breslau, Germany, on February 4, 1906. His father was a prominent physician and eventually became professor of psychiatry at the University of Berlin; his mother was a descendant of Karl van Hase, a distinguished nineteenth-century German church historian. After completing his university studies, Bonhoeffer served a German-speaking congregation in Barcelona, Spain. Returning in 1929 to Berlin, he began work on his "inaugural dissertation, a requisite for being permitted a faculty position in theology. In 1930, after completing *Act and Being: Transcendental Philosophy and Ontology in Systematic Theology*, he was given a position teaching systematic theology."[4] Before beginning his teaching career, however, Bonhoeffer attended Union Theological Seminary for one year, where he struck up a friendship with Reinhold Niebuhr. In 1931 he returned to Germany. In addition to his teaching responsibilities, Bonhoeffer continued his ministry and became involved in the ecumenical movement.

The Nazis came to power in Germany in 1932. This was the first of a series of events that culminated in Bonhoeffer's death at age thirty-nine. The young preacher delivered a radio address in early 1933 that the Nazis cut off the air before its completion. At that time the Protestant churches in Germany were divided over the question of loyalty to the Führer. Some supported the nationalism of the Nazis—these became known as the "German Christians." Others protested what they saw as a threat to church independence—these became known as "the Confessing Church." In the fall of 1933 Bonhoeffer moved to London to serve as the minister of two German-speaking congregations. In London, the young German pastor met G. K. A. Bell, the bishop of Chichester, who would play a critical role in a decisive moment later in Bonhoeffer's life. In 1935 Bonhoeffer returned to Germany to head an illegal seminary for the Confessing Church. Despite the Nazi prohibition against the ordination of ministers for the Confessing Church, Bonhoeffer organized a seminary first in Zingst and then in Finkenwalde near Stettin. In 1936 Bonhoeffer was no longer permitted to teach at the University of Berlin. In 1937 the Gestapo closed down the seminary. In 1939 Bonhoeffer accepted an invitation from Reinhold Niebuhr to conduct a lecture tour in the United States. He stayed in the United States for less than a month and returned to Germany. His reasoning was simple. "I must live through this difficult period of our national history with the Christian people of Germany. I will have no right to participate in the reconstruction of Christian life in Germany after the war if I do not share the trials of this time with my people."[5]

Upon his return, Bonhoeffer was forbidden to preach. "Convinced now that submission to the state in the name of conscience unsullied by violence made one an accomplice in the 'great masquerade of evil,' he decided to join the anti-Nazi underground. Its center was the *Abwehr,* the German military intelligence organization."[6] His job was ostensibly to gather intelligence through his ecumenical contacts. His position, however, exempted him from the draft and provided him with ample opportunities to leave the country.

At a fateful meeting with the Bishop of Chichester at Sigtuna, Sweden, in May, 1942, Bonhoeffer presented to the bishop for conveyance to the British government detailed information on the plans for overthrowing the Nazi regime, together with proposals for the subsequent establishment of peace. The proposals reached British foreign secretary Anthony Eden but were summarily rejected; "unconditional surrender" was to be the Allied policy.[7]

On April 5, 1943, three months after he was engaged to Maria von Wedemeyer, two men from the Gestapo arrived at his house and brought him to Tegel Military Prison in Berlin, where he would spend the next eighteen months. During his confinement he read voraciously and wrote numerous letters to his parents, fiancée, friends, and Eberhard Bethge, the husband of his niece. These letters, smuggled out of Tegel Prison and hidden by Bethge in tin cans buried in his garden, eventually were published under the title *Letters and Papers from Prison*. In July 1944 an assassination attempt on Hitler failed. The Gestapo's discovery of the secret files of the Abwehr in Zossen in September 1944 confirmed Bonhoeffer's role in the assassination plot. He was soon transferred from Tegel to a Gestapo prison on Prinz Albrecht Street, where he was tortured. In February 1945 he was moved to Buchenwald, then to Flossenburg. There he was court-martialed and hanged on April 9, 1945, just days before Allied forces reached the camp.

Dietrich Bonhoeffer's life and theology testify to the ongoing relevance of "exile" as a category of Christian experience. First, he was physically exiled from his native land. An unwelcomed prophet, he put himself in self-imposed exile in London and then, briefly, in the United States. His estrangement, however, was not merely geographical. Bonhoeffer was an exile culturally. He experienced a profound sense of disconnection with the prevailing attitudes of the German nation. Describing Bonhoeffer's growing sense of alienation during the early years of the Third Reich, Eberhard Bethge comments,

> Bonhoeffer's initial position placed him in a difficult dilemma. His personal vitality, the sense of public responsibility which he had inherited, combined with his successful start in an academic career, made it impossible for him

simply to submerge silently. If there was no prospect of his still belonging to that society in which he lived, then he had to find a suitable form of exile. Although the term "inner exile" does not completely cover the phenomenon, it would still be fairly accurate to apply it to Bonhoeffer's passage into the Church, where he looked for a kind of legitimate exile. Yet each time his exile took shape, his restless wandering would begin anew.[8]

Bonhoeffer's cultural exile culminated in his decision to join the plot to assassinate Hitler. As Robert Coles notes,

> To stand outside the gates of money and power and rank and approved success and applause, to be regarded as irregular or odd or "sick" or, that final exile, as a traitor—such an outcome, in this era, carries its own special burdens and demands: the disapproval, if not derision, of colleagues, neighbors, the larger world of commentators who meticulously fall in line with reigning authority, but perhaps most devastating of all, the sense of oneself that is left in one's mind at the end of a day. What *am* I trying to do—and is this, after all, not only futile, but evidence that I have gone astray? In that regard, those of us who have been granted the right to decide what is "normal" or "abnormal" ought to be nervous, indeed, by the likes of a...Bonhoeffer...."[9]

Finally, Bonhoeffer's theology is filled with the urgent zeal of the biblical prophets, such as Jeremiah announcing the coming destruction of Jerusalem and the exile that was sure to follow. Bonhoeffer frequently quotes the short but powerful forty-fifth chapter of Jeremiah in his letters. Bonhoeffer speaks of his own time as one in which we must live *etsi deus non daretur:* even if there were no God. He writes, "And we cannot be honest unless we recognize that we have to live in the world *etsi deus non daretur*....God would have us know that we must live as men who manage our lives without him....God lets himself be pushed out of the world on to the cross."[10] We live, in other words, in exile from God, or more provocatively stated, God is exiled from the world. The letters are filled with intriguing thoughts such as these; we concentrate on three of them.

Three Themes in the Letters *and Papers from Prison*

Bonhoeffer's letters from prison have sparked widely varying interpretations. This is due in large part to the nature of the writings themselves. They were not theological treatises intended for public scrutiny. As Charles Marsh notes, "Bonhoeffer's final book, *The Letters and Papers from Prison,* illustrates not only textual but theological fragmentariness as well. Yet the power of the book lies precisely in its 'trial combinations' and 'lightning flashes' of theological insight."[11] The bulk of the letters are written to his faithful friend Eberhard Bethge, who served as a sounding board for his theological musings. It is also important to remind ourselves that Bonhoeffer composed these letters while facing an uncertain future, suffering the constant monotony and frustration of more than a year's time in prison. In addition to the burden of confinement, there were air raids, medical problems, and the despondency of some of his fellow prisoners weighing on Bonhoeffer. It should also be noted, however, that Bonhoeffer—because of his family's prominence and his own celebrity—enjoyed certain privileges not accorded other prisoners. We, of course, will never know what a mature Bonhoeffer living in postwar Germany would have made of the various theological thoughts he recorded in his prison correspondence. As we read these letters decades after Bonhoeffer's death, we can only speculate about the direction in which his thought was headed. We will glean three provocative expressions scattered throughout his letters—to borrow an image from the German fairy tale "Hansel and Gretel"—like bread crumbs sprinkled on the forest floor. We will follow them, not knowing where they will lead us—perhaps deeper into the dark woods or perhaps to a place we never knew existed.

The category of exile serves as the organizing principle for our investigation of Bonhoeffer's letters. Exile involves a loss of a former way of life, a present state of uncertainty, and a proposed course of action for the future. The loss is summarized best by Bonhoeffer's comment that "Jesus calls men, not to a new religion, but to life."[12]

The state of uncertainty following the loss of "religion" is described by Bonhoeffer as "the world come of age." He writes, "The question is: Christ and the world that has come of age."[13] Finally, for the future, Bonhoeffer makes the following clarion call: "Man is summoned to share in God's sufferings at the hands of a godless world."[14] In these three thought-provoking sentences we find some of the most enduring concepts in Bonhoeffer's theological legacy, and we turn now to a closer examination of each of them.

"Jesus calls men, not to a new religion, but to life."

Bonhoeffer contends that the age of religion has ceased to exist. He does not, however, mourn its passing. Clifford Green explains, "In Bonhoeffer's judgment, religion has been a garment that Christianity has worn in various modes throughout its history; and while this garment may have been warm, comfortable, flattering to the wearer, and even according to the finest pattern of its type, it must now be discarded."[15] What, then, did Bonhoeffer mean by "religion"? Larry Rasmussen offers the following summary:

> To characterize religion he uses pejoratively such terms as *deus ex machina* (the God-of-the-gaps); provinciality (religion as a separated sector of one's life); metaphysics (thinking in two realms, the supernatural completing the natural); individual inwardness (pietism or other forms of ascetic escape); indispensability (a religious a priori as constitutive of human nature); and sanction (religion as the protector of privilege).[16]

Bonhoeffer launches his assault on the concept of "religion" in his April 30, 1944, letter. He writes,

> What is bothering me incessantly is the question [of] what Christianity really is, or indeed who Christ really is, for us today. The time when people could be told everything by means of words, whether theological or pious, is over, and so is the time of inwardness and conscience—and that means the time of religion in general. We are moving towards a completely religion-less time; people as they are

now simply cannot be religious any more. Even those who honestly describe themselves as "religious" do not in the least act up to it, and so they presumably mean something quite different by "religious."[17]

While Bonhoeffer does not treat this topic in any systematic fashion, he does seem to propose two arguments in his letters: one historical, the other theological.

The first line of argumentation is historical: that is, Bonhoeffer reads the history of Christianity, politics, and science as a movement away from "religion." In his letter of July 16, 1944, Bonhoeffer writes,

> Now for a few more thoughts on our theme. I'm only grad-ually working my way to the non-religious interpretation of biblical concepts; the job is too big for me to finish just yet.
>
> On the historical side: There is one great development that leads to the world's autonomy. In theology one sees it first in Lord Herbert of Cherbury, who maintains that reason is sufficient for religious knowledge. In ethics it appears in Montaigne and Bodin with their substitution of rules of life for the commandments. In politics Machiavelli detaches politics from morality in general and founds the doctrine of "reasons of state." Later, and very differently from Machiavelli, but tending like him towards the autonomy of human society, comes Grotius, setting up his natural law as international law, which is valid *etsi deus non daretur*, "even if there were no God." The philoso-phers provide the finishing touches: on the one hand we have deism of Descartes, who holds that the world is a mechanism, running by itself with no interference from God; and on the other hand the pantheism of Spinoza, who says that God is nature. In the last resort, Kant is a deist, and Fichte and Hegel are pantheists. Everywhere the thinking is directed towards the autonomy of man and the world.[18]

Bonhoeffer insists that an honest reading of the intellectual tradition of the West will lead the reasonable person to acknowledge the cultural fact that "God as a working hypothesis in morals, politics, or science, has been surmounted and abolished; and the same thing has happened in philosophy and religion (Feuerbach!)."[19]

Bonhoeffer's second line of argumentation is theological. Here he insists that not only does the history of the Western world bear witness to the loss of religion, but that theologians need to face that challenge head on. He writes, "Anxious souls will ask what room there is left for God now; and as they know of no answer to the question, they condemn the whole development that has brought them to such straits."[20]

Before turning to Bonhoeffer's proposal for the future course of Christian theology, we first clear away two theological options that Bonhoeffer explicitly identifies and rejects in the letters. First, he opposes any attempt to turn back the theological clock and have believers accept certain ideas that they simply can no longer—as a matter of intellectual honesty—hold to be true. He writes, "Barth was the first theologian to begin the criticism of religion, and that remains his really great merit; but he put in its place a positivist doctrine of revelation which says, in effect, 'Like it or lump it': virgin birth, Trinity, or anything else; each is equally significant and necessary part of the whole, which must simply be swallowed as a whole or not at all."[21] Second, Bonhoeffer is equally critical of the liberal Protestant theology of Rudolf Bultmann. Bultmann's project dealt with "demythologizing" the New Testament, that is, extracting the existential message from the New Testament (which is still meaningful and relevant to modern Christians) from the mythological categories of thought in which that message is embedded (which modern Christians cannot accept). Referring to Bultmann's demythologization, Bonhoeffer writes,

> My view of it today would be, not that he went "too far," as most people thought, but that he didn't go far enough. It's not only the "mythological" concepts, such as miracle, ascension, and so on (which are not in principle separable from the concepts of God, faith, etc.), but "religious" concepts generally, which are problematic. You can't, as Bultmann supposes, separate God and miracle, but you must be able to interpret and proclaim both in a "non-

religious" sense. Bultmann's approach is fundamentally still a liberal one (i.e. abridging the gospel), whereas I'm trying to think theologically.[22]

Bonhoeffer's own proposal for speaking about God, the one which "ultimate honesty" requires, is a paradoxical one. He writes,

> And we cannot be honest unless we recognize that we have to live in the world *etsi deus non daretur.* And this is just what we do recognize—before God! God himself compels us to recognize it. So our coming of age leads us to a true recognition of our situation before God. God would have us know that we must live as men who manage our lives without him. The God who is with us is the God who forsakes us (Mark 15.34). The God who lets us live in the world without the working hypothesis of God is the God before whom stand continually. Before God and with God we live without God.[23]

The loss of religion is a welcomed development for Bonhoeffer, therefore, because it signals a new awareness of God. As Geffrey Kelly notes, Bonhoeffer "opposed all efforts to make God the postulated answer to human weakness, a *deus ex machina* hovering over the stage of life, ready to descend to the rescue. God becomes thus only a 'working hypothesis' foisted on people as substitute for their own autonomy in and responsibility to the world."[24] The understanding of God as the One who calls us to turn our gaze from this world, to seek our own personal salvation, and to focus on our own personal weaknesses is replaced with an understanding of God as the One who turns our eye to our neighbor, to concern ourselves with the welfare of others and share in the suffering of God in this world. This is, for Bonhoeffer, an affirmation about the painful process of Christian maturation. The loss of religion is a transition from an earlier, more confident, yet magical understanding of God's activity in the world to an admittedly more awkward, yet ultimately more responsible understanding of God by the "world come of age."

"The question is: Christ and the world that has come of age."

This leads to the second of Bonhoeffer's thought-provoking ideas: "Christ and the world that has come of age." Larry L. Rasmussen offers the following explanation.

> Bonhoeffer designates the increase of human autonomy by various forms of the German *"muendig."* The person who is *"muendig"* is one who "speaks for himself." The reference is to the passage from adolescence to adulthood. One is no longer a minor but is on his own. He has "come of age." He is now fully responsible for his actions. The reader of Bonhoeffer in English should note carefully that *"muendig"* is thus a reference to moral *accountability* and not moral maturity. That is, Bonhoeffer is saying that man is fully responsible for his actions whether he acts childishly, immaturely, irresponsibly, or whatever. The world's adulthood is in part, then, Bonhoeffer's designation of man's irrevocable responsibility for his answers to life's questions, together with all the consequences. Man can no longer return to an adolescent dependence upon a father to whom final responsibility falls.[25]

Bonhoeffer correlates his understanding of Jesus with "the world come of age." The loss of religion signals the close of one era in Christian history, "the world come of age" signals the transition into a new era, one which Bonhoeffer suggests may actually be in greater accordance with the gospel than the "religion" preached throughout most of Christian history.

"Religion" offered God as a source of comfort to people experiencing doubt and trouble and of assurance to people confronting the painful riddle of death. Bonhoeffer regards the continued attempt to speak of God in this way as a misguided endeavor. Such an effort rests on assumptions about God and the world that "the world come of age" will no longer accept. Bonhoeffer insists that "man has learnt to deal with himself in all questions of importance without recourse to the 'working hypothesis' called 'God.'"[26] People do not expect God to act unilaterally to bring about a desired state of affairs here on Earth. The failure of much of modern Christian theology consists in its attempt to convince the world that it needs the God of "religion." Bonhoeffer argues that this approach removes God from the center of people's day-to-day existence and speaks of God only in terms of "boundary situations" or "ultimate questions" of life. As William Kuhns explains,

> The man come of age is one whose work, family, education, and awareness of the world have made daily recourse to God unnecessary. He attempts no conscious movement of atheism and would not admit he was an atheist; very possibly he attends church on Sunday mornings. Yet he does not think that he needs God; and the preaching he hears, the books he may read, the sin he is told surrounds him—these do not summon the whole man, in complete involvement, as do his family, his work, his friendships. In short, he is a man able to live a human relatively complete life in the midst of a secular culture and with an immense confidence in that culture—without God.[27]

This failure on the part of many modern Christians to grasp the new situation presented by the world come of age compounds itself by proposing a view of Christ that is outmoded. Bonhoeffer writes,

> The attack by Christian apologetic on the adulthood of the world I consider to be in the first place pointless, in the second place ignoble, and in the third place unchristian. Pointless, because it seems to me like the attempt to put a grown-up man back into adolescence, i.e. to make him dependent on things on which he is, in fact, no longer dependent, and thrusting him into problems that are, in fact, no longer problems to him. Ignoble, because it amounts to an attempt to exploit man's weakness for purposes that are alien to him and to which he has not freely assented. Unchristian, because it confuses Christ with one particular stage in man's religiousness, i.e. with human law.[28]

What, then, is the proper understanding of Jesus in the world come of age?

Bonhoeffer's answer to that crucial question is that "Christ takes hold of man at the centre of his life"[29] and that Jesus is "the man for others."[30] Christ does not call us away from the world, but into the world. Bonhoeffer writes,

> During the last year or so I've come to know and understand more and more the profound this-worldliness of Christianity. The Christian is...simply a man, as Jesus was a man—in contrast, shall we say, to John the Baptist. I don't mean the shallow and banal this-worldliness of the enlightened, the busy, the comfortable, or the lascivious, but the profound this-worldliness, characterized by discipline and the constant knowledge of death and resurrection.[31]

In his "Outline for a Book" which he includes in a letter to Bethge, Bonhoeffer writes,

> Encounter with Jesus Christ. The experience that a transformation of all human life is given in the fact that "Jesus is there only for others." His "being there for others" is the experience of transcendence. It is only this "being there for others," maintained till death, that is the ground of his omnipotence, omniscience, and omnipresence. Faith is the participation in this being of Jesus (incarnation, cross, and resurrection).[32]

Christ participates in the world and Christians participate in Christ. We participate not only in Christ's ultimate victory, but also in Christ's suffering. Bonhoeffer summarizes this point as follows:

> By this-worldliness I mean living unreservedly in life's duties, problems, successes and failures, experiences and perplexities. In doing so we throw ourselves completely into the arms of God, taking seriously, not our own sufferings, but those of God in the world—watching with Christ in Gethsemane. That, I think, is faith; that is *metanoia;* and that is how one becomes a man and a Christian (cf. Jer. 45!).[33]

We are now able to move to our consideration of the third theme in Bonhoeffer's letters.

"Man is summoned to share in God's sufferings at the hands of a godless world."

Like Jesus in the Garden of Gethsemane, Christians are called to partake in the suffering of God. William Hamilton explains, "God may have withdrawn from the world, but he has not withdrawn from us. As Bonhoeffer had said earlier, and which we are now prepared to understand, 'God allows himself to be edged out of the world and on to the cross.' (16 July 1944). The world come of age is now seen as the world in which God suffers."[34]

Bonhoeffer sees participation in God's suffering as the most appropriate understanding of the divine–human relationship in a world come of age, an understanding that is, in Bonhoeffer's eyes, closer to the one proclaimed by Jesus than the one preached in churches for most of Christian history. He writes,

> Here is the decisive difference between Christianity and all religions. Man's religiosity makes him look in his distress to the power of God in the world: God is the *deus ex machina*. The Bible directs man to God's powerlessness and suffering; only the suffering God can help. To that extent we may say that the development towards the world's coming of age outlined above, which has done away with a false conception of God, opens up a way of seeing the God of the Bible, who wins power and space in his world by his weakness.[35]

In a letter written two days later, Bonhoeffer continues his discussion of this theme. "Jesus asked in Gethsemane, 'Could you not watch with me one hour?' That is a reversal of what the religious man expects from God. Man is summoned to share in God's sufferings at the hands of a godless world....It is not the religious act that makes the Christian, but participation in the suffering of God in the secular life."[36] The Christian is called to suffer with God in Christ, to put Christ at the center of his or her life, and to affirm the world, not flee from it.

Bonhoeffer's Spirituality

We conclude first with a brief examination of Bonhoeffer's own personal spirituality, and second, with the spiritual vision developed in a fragmentary way in the prison letters.

We get hints of Bonhoeffer's spirituality early in his career when he served as director of the underground seminary and later in the scattered references to his own devotional practices contained in his prison letters. Geffrey B. Kelly notes,

> In a Germany geared for war, Bonhoeffer's seminary was described as an oasis of peace and spiritual freedom. The community began each morning with prayer and meditation. Their life together included daily prayers, personal confession, Bonhoeffer's own lectures, and discussions on preaching and the spiritual life.
>
> It was a regimen considered by some of the seminarians as a bit strict.[37]

James W. Woelfel offers the following account of Bonhoeffer's devotional practices while in prison. He writes,

> Bonhoeffer's own life of prayer, meditation, liturgical observance, and pastoral work while in prison is the most impressive testimony of all to the "secret discipline" which is the inner foundation and sustenance of "religionless Christianity…."
>
> He experienced "arid" periods which he mentioned quite frankly, when he was unable to make himself read the Bible, but daily reading and meditation following the *Losungen* was at the heart of his spiritual discipline. In the letter which initiated his remarks on "religionless Christianity," Bonhoeffer mentions his practice of reading the Bible "every morning and evening." There can be no doubt that his continued practice of grounding his daily life in the Word of God was an incalculable source of strength to him throughout his imprisonment.[38]

Bonhoeffer's letters are filled with references to scriptural passages and German hymns. Kelly comments that "prayer in solitude and fellowship in God's Word were, in fact, the very soul of Bonhoeffer's spirituality. This was the sustenance which carried him through the years of crisis and imprisonment."[39] We turn now to the spiritual sustenance Bonhoeffer offers to the "world come of age."

Bonhoeffer offers an interesting suggestion: "The world that has come of age is more godless, and perhaps for that very reason nearer to God, than the world before its coming of age."[40] What then does the world come of age realize that draws it closer to God? The answer may be found in a line from a letter written to his fiancée. He writes, "Our marriage shall be a yes to God's earth; it shall strengthen our courage to act and accomplish something on earth. I fear that Christians who stand with only one leg upon earth also stand with only one leg in heaven."[41] "Religion" is individualistic and focused on the afterlife. By contrast, the Christian life in the world come of age is "a silent and hidden affair"[42] of human solidarity and worldly involvement. The world come of age realizes, to borrow one of Bonhoeffer's more cryptic sayings, that "God is beyond in the midst of our life."[43]

A musical image presented by Bonhoeffer nicely captures his understanding of God's involvement in the world. James Woelfel explains,

> The religionless Christian lives an integrated existence, in which the many and conflicting experiences of his life are held together by a unifying theme rather than fragmented into disjointed compartments. Bonhoeffer, a keen music lover, discusses this characteristic of the mature man of faith in terms of the musical analogy of *polyphony*....The Christian's love of God and his love of the things of earth, such as friendship, are not mutually exclusive. It is rather the case that the love of God undergirds all earthly affections as the basic melody of, say, a fugue sets the pattern for and finds infinitely varied expression in the contrapuntal themes which are developed from it. It is both together—*cantus firmus* and counterpoint—which mingle architectonically to form the whole fugue. So life is not

complete without the harmonious expression of the love of God in the love of the earth. Here is a further articulation of Bonhoeffer's lifelong theme: the inseparability and mutual relationship of the two parts of the Summary of the Law—love of God and love of neighbor.[44]

Bonhoeffer writes, "What I mean is that God wants us to love him eternally with our whole hearts—not in such a way as to injure or weaken our earthly love, but to provide a *cantus firmus* to which the melodies of life provide the counterpoint."[45] This is the challenge and the hope offered to us who must live in a godless world.

Admirers of *Letters and Papers from Prison* have enlisted Bonhoeffer as a spokesman for their various causes, from the death-of-God movement to Protestant neo-orthodoxy. Critics have berated the work as a record of Bonhoeffer's psychological and/or religious collapse under the stress and strain of confinement, bombings, and impending execution. This theological work is certainly unique in that it was in all likelihood not intended by the author to become a published work, that it makes no effort to construct a sustained, systematic argument on any traditional category of Christian theology, and that it was published posthumously. Any argument about the text, therefore, is in large part an argument from silence. For that reason, we will simply let the work stand as is and allow its provocative aphorisms to rest like hot embers that will unexpectedly flare up into flame to shed much needed light.

Exilic prophets such as Ezekiel offered hope to Jewish exiles by proclaiming that God had not abandoned them and that they would once again worship God in a new Temple in Jerusalem. In a similar vein, in a letter written on the occasion of the baptism of young Dietrich Bethge, Bonhoeffer holds out hope for the future:

It is not for us to prophesy the day (though the day will come) when men will once more be called so to utter the word of God that the world will be changed and renewed by it. It will be a new language, perhaps quite non-religious, but liberating and redeeming—as was Jesus' language; it will shock people and yet overcome them by its power; it will be the language of a new righteousness and truth, proclaiming God's peace with men and the coming of his kingdom.[46]

N. T. Wright argues that the sense of exile continued to pervade Jewish thought even until the time of Jesus. He writes,

> Babylon had taken the people into captivity; Babylon fell, and the people returned. But in Jesus' day many, if not most, Jews regarded the exile as still continuing. The people returned in a geographical sense, but the great prophecies of restoration had not yet come true. What was Israel to do? Why, to repent of the sin which had driven her into exile, and to return to YHWH with all her heart. Who would stand in her way, to prevent her return? The mixed multitude, not least the Samaritans, who had remained in the land while the people were in exile. But Israel would return, humbled and redeemed: sins would be forgiven, the covenant renewed, the Temple rebuilt, and the dead raised. What her god had done for her in the exodus—always the crucial backdrop for Jewish expectations—he would at last do again, even more gloriously. YHWH would finally become king, and would do for Israel, in covenant love, what the prophets had foretold.[47]

Christians, of course, believe that Israel's hopes were realized in the life of Jesus of Nazareth, and it is to that "good news" that we now turn.

Notes

1. John Bright, *A History of Israel,* 3rd ed. (Philadelphia: Westminster Press, 1981), p. 343.
2. John G. Gager, *The Origins of Anti-Semitism* (New York: Oxford University Press, 1983), p. 13.
3. For biographical information on Bonhoeffer, I am relying heavily on chap. 1 of *Dietrich Bonhoeffer* (Waco: Word Books, 1972) by Dallas Roark; chap. 1 of *Liberating Faith* (Minneapolis: Augsburg, 1984) by Geffrey B. Kelly; and chap. 12 of *In Pursuit of Dietrich Bonhoeffer* (Dayton: Pflaum Press, 1967) by William Kuhns.

4.   Dallas M. Roark, *Dietrich Bonhoeffer* (Waco: Word Books, 1972), p. 16.

5.   Geffrey B. Kelly, *Liberating Faith* (Minneapolis: Augsburg, 1984), p. 28.

6.   Quoted in Ibid., p. 27.

7.   Franklin Sherman, "Dietrich Bonhoeffer," in *A Handbook of Christian Theologians,* ed. Martin E. Marty and Dean G. Peerman (Nashville: Abingdon Press, 1984), pp. 465–66.

8.   Eberhard Bethge, *Bonhoeffer: Exile and Martyr* (New York: Seabury Press, 1975), p. 107.

9.   Robert Coles, "The Making of a Disciple," in *Dietrich Bonhoeffer* (Maryknoll: Orbis Books, 1998), p. 40.

10. Dietrich Bonhoeffer, *Letters and Papers from Prison,* enlarged ed. (New York: Touchstone Books, 1971), ed. Eberhard Bethge, p. 360. Hereafter *LPP.*

11. Charles Marsh, "Dietrich Bonhoeffer," in *The Modern Theologians,* 2nd ed., ed. David F. Ford (Oxford: Blackwell Publishers, 1997), p. 47.

12. *LPP,* p. 362.

13. Ibid., p. 327.

14. Ibid., p. 361.

15. Clifford Green, "Bonhoeffer's Concept of Religion," *Union Seminary Quarterly Review* 19(1), 1963, p. 11.

16. Larry L. Rasmussen, *Dietrich Bonhoeffer: Reality and Resistance* (Nashville: Abingdon Press, 1972), pp. 81–82.

17. *LPP,* p. 279.

18. Ibid., p. 359.

19. Ibid., p. 360.

20. Ibid.

21. Ibid., p. 286.

22. Ibid., p. 285.

23. Ibid., p. 360.

24. Kelly, *Liberating Faith,* p. 75.

25. Rasmussen, *Dietrich Bonhoeffer,* p. 81.

26. *LPP,* p. 325.

27. William Kuhns, *In Pursuit of Dietrich Bonhoeffer* (Dayton: Pflaum Press, 1967), p. 195.

28. *LPP,* p. 327.

29. Ibid., p. 337.

30. Ibid., p. 382.

31. Ibid., p. 369.

32. Ibid., p. 381.

33. Ibid., p. 370.
34. William Hamilton, "'The Letters Are a Particular Thorn': Some Themes in Bonhoeffer's Prison Writings," in *World Come of Age,* ed. Ronald Gregor Smith (London: Collins, 1967), p. 155.
35. *LPP,* p. 361.
36. Ibid.
37. Kelly, *Liberating Faith,* pp. 24–25.
38. James W. Woelfel, *Bonhoeffer's Theology: Classical and Revolutionary* (Nashville: Abingdon, 1970), pp. 200–201. Bethge informs us that the *Losungen* were "daily texts, published yearly since 1731" (*LPP,* p. 265). Bonhoeffer mentions the *Losungen* in the letter on Christmas Eve 1943.
39. Kelly, *Liberating Faith,* p. 144.
40. *LPP,* p. 362.
41. Ibid., p. 415.
42. Ibid., p. 300.
43. Ibid., p. 282.
44. James W. Woelfel, "Bonhoeffer's Portrait of the Religionless Christian," *Encounter* 28(4), 1967, pp. 352–53.
45. *LPP,* p. 303.
46. Ibid., p. 300.
47. N. T. Wright, *Jesus and the Victory of God* (Minneapolis: Fortress Press, 1996), pp. 126–27.

Discussion Questions

1. Which life experiences are forms of exile?
2. Was it proper for Bonhoeffer, a Christian pastor, to be involved in any way in the plot to assassinate Hitler?
3. What negative influence does religion play in society? What positive influence does it play? Is it useful to distinguish between religion and spirituality?
4. Do we as a culture no longer accept God as "a working hypothesis" when solving our problems? If so, is that a positive or negative development? Do we live in a "world come of age"?
5. Is Christ best thought of as "a man for others"? How does that understanding of Jesus relate to your own understanding of Jesus?
6. What does it mean "to share in God's sufferings"?
7. Is Bonhoeffer's theology, in your view, positive or negative?

Suggested Readings

For a study of the exile, see Peter R. Ackroyd, *Exile and Restoration* (Philadelphia: Westminster, 1968), and Ralph W. Klein, *Israel in Exile* (Philadelphia: Fortress, 1979).

For shorter introductions to Bonhoeffer's entire theology, see "Dietrich Bonhoeffer" by Charles Marsh in *The Modern Theologians* (2nd ed.), ed. David F. Ford (Oxford: Blackwell Publishers, 1997); "Dietrich Bonhoeffer" by Franklin Sherman in *A Handbook of Christian Theologians*, ed. Martin E. Marty and Dean G. Peerman (Nashville: Abingdon Press, 1984); and *Twentieth-Century Theology* by Stanley J. Grenz and Roger E. Olson (Downers Grove: InterVarsity Press, 1992), pp. 146–56. See also Issue 32 X(4) of Christian History.

For book-length treatments, see *In Pursuit of Dietrich Bonhoeffer* (Dayton: Pflaum Press, 1967) by William Kuhns; *The Theology of Dietrich Bonhoeffer* (Philadelphia: Westminster Press, 1960) by John D. Godsey; *Dietrich Bonhoeffer* (Waco: Word Books, 1972) by Dallas Roark, *Liberating Faith* (Minneapolis: Augsburg, 1984) by Geffrey B. Kelly; and *The Cambridge Companion to Dietrich Bonhoeffer*, ed. John W. de Grunchy (Cambridge: Cambridge University Press, 1999). Chap. 12 of *The Cambridge Companion to Dietrich Bonhoeffer*, "Christianity in a World Come of Age," by Peter Selby, is very helpful.

5

The Incarnation and Karl Rahner's *Theological Investigations*

In the opening chapter to his work *God Matters,* Graeme Garrett offers an interesting vantage point from which to survey the field of theology. Garrett writes,

> In his Gifford lectures of 1985 the Princeton physicist Freeman Dyson wrote: "God did not only create mountains, he also created jungles." Dyson was making a point about two types of science, two types of physics in fact. He called one the "unifying" and the other the "diversifying" type. Einstein and Maxwell are dominating examples of the first, the unifying type. Their concern is with "mountains." Throughout his life Einstein sought for a broad, rational, unified theory of the physical world and its components. His most famous shot at it was the theory of relativity. Maxwell plotted the dynamics of electromagnetism in a brief series of elegant, far-reaching equations. Both thinkers drew together vast ranges of experimental data in their theories. Their aim was to bring more and more of the observed phenomena within the scope of a few fundamental principles: in short, to discern the unity of things, how they hang together.
>
> On the other hand, Rutherford and Eddington stand for Dyson's diversifying science. The diversifiers are in love with complexity, with the myriad details of the world. They live in the "jungle." What fascinates them is the uniqueness of particular entities, the hard and messy "givenness" of

things. They don't care so much how things hang together as what they are really *like*.[1]

The Christian tradition, continues Garrett, is similarly mixed with thinkers extolling the virtues of either the unifying or the diversifying approach to theology. The former prefer theological systems that integrate the various elements of their thought into a consistent whole. Thinkers favoring the diversifying approach cast a suspicious eye toward such projects. Some of them have a nagging sense that such grand systems of thought conceal more than they reveal; others believe that such systems are built on presuppositions about the world that are no longer universally shared in today's highly pluralistic world; and still others simply believe that the Christian faith defies the neat, clean categorization such systems seem to require.

We turn our attention now to the point where the biblical narrative shifts into what Christians call the New Testament. We take as our theological guide in this moment the thinker who was arguably the most important Roman Catholic theologian of the twentieth century: Karl Rahner. We have in Rahner an example of a great unifying theological mind at work. While his writings covered an amazingly wide range of topics, he carried on those investigations in light of his unifying vision, a grand scheme in which theological questions could be, according to him, most profitably asked and answered. It will fall to the reader to determine whether Rahner simply ignored the jungle or whether he blazed a trail straight through it.

At his death in 1984, Rahner left behind a body of work that was both enormous in volume and wide ranging in scope. Stanley J. Grenz and Roger E. Olson report, "By 1984 over 3,500 books and articles had appeared in print under his name. His most important articles were collected and published in a twenty-volume set entitled *Theological Investigations,* which contains over eight thousand pages in the German edition."[2] We focus our attention on three of Rahner's essays dealing with the incarnation that appeared in his *Theological Investigations*. The incarnation, described in the opening chapter of John's Gospel, is literally the event of God taking on human flesh in the person of Jesus Christ. The reader may operate with a different understanding of Jesus' identity. In theology, one's understanding of Jesus is called a Christology. Readers may not share Rahner's particular

Christology, but they couldn't ask for a better conversation partner when formulating or identifying their own. With that goal in mind, we first examine Rahner's approach to theological questions in general and christological questions in particular. We then delve into Rahner's three essays, review the leading criticisms leveled against his position, and conclude with his spiritual vision.

A cautionary note is in order before we begin: Rahner's work is often difficult. I offer four axioms to help us understand Rahner. Three are ancient or medieval in origin, and the fourth is from Michael Polanyi. For the essay, "On the Theology of the Incarnation": "What is received is received according to the mode of the receiver." For the essay, "Christology Within an Evolutionary View of the World": "The higher order always embraces the lower." For the essay, "The Two Basic Types of Christology": "All truth is one," and for Rahner's spirituality: "We can know more than we can tell."[3]

"On the Theology of the Incarnation"

The first of the three essays by Rahner that we examine introduces us to his "transcendental method." Regarding this method, Robert Kress informs us that "the term and approach have received a definite character from Kant. His description has become normative: the investigation into the conditions presupposed by or necessary for any knowledge."[4] This seems terribly abstract at first, but it simply means that the theologian needs to engage in an orderly method of investigation. For example, suppose a valuable work of art were stolen from a prestigious museum. Investigators are called to the scene to determine how such a theft could have occurred. They will determine how the security system was bypassed, who had access to the museum, when the crime took place, and so on. The religious believer accepts on faith that certain events took place in history— for example, that God took on human flesh. Given that fact, the theologian deduces what conditions were necessary for such an event to take place. This requires formulating assumptions about humans (as receivers of God's revelation), history (as the locus of God's revelation), and Christology (as the culmination of God's revelation). Robert Kress believes, "In the long run Rahner's transcendental method is a very elaborate explanation of the old scholastic axiom,

'*What is received is received according to the mode of the receiver.*'[5] If Kress is correct, then the investigation of God's revelation and the investigation into the human reception of that revelation are two sides of the same coin.

Rahner's essay "On the Theology of the Incarnation" begins, "Let us put the simple question: what do we Christians mean when we profess our faith in the incarnation of the Word of God?"[6] Rahner stresses that his work is not to be seen as a departure from the teachings found in the church councils held in Nicaea in 325, in Ephesus in 431, and in Chalcedon in 451. Rahner asks, "The Word of God became *man*. What does it mean 'became *man*'?"[7] Using the transcendental method, the inquirer could ask, "What conditions exist within human nature that make it possible for God to become one with humanity?" Rahner's answer is simple. Humans have the capacity to know and love God. Humans are mysteries who defy definitive categorization and resolution. "Man is therefore mystery in his essence, his nature. He is not in himself the infinite fullness of mystery which concerns him, for that fullness is inexhaustible, and the primordial form of all that is mystery to us."[8] Humans are mysteries who yearn to know and love God, who is absolute mystery.

Rahner turns to the second phase of his investigation. He writes, "The Word of God has *become* man: this is the assertion which we are trying to understand better. We take the word 'become.' Can God 'become' anything?"[9] Here Rahner insists that Christian faith requires that Christ be fully human and fully divine, not divine in substance, but merely human in appearance. "We must therefore regard as heretical any concept of the incarnation which makes the humanity of Jesus only a disguise used by God to signal his challenging presence."[10] Those who enjoy mulling over a theological turn of phrase might consider the following Rahnerian summary: "If we face squarely the fact of the incarnation, which our faith testifies to be the fundamental dogma of Christianity, we must simply say: God can become something, he who is unchangeable in himself can himself become subject to change *in something else*."[11]

Combining these two phases of the investigation, we can postulate certain preliminary ideas. First, given the fact of the incarnation, we can assume theologically that human nature has the possibility of being assumed by God. There is an innate capacity for reception of

God's grace. As J. A. Di Noia, O.P., states, "The message of revelation—the divine self-communication—travels airwaves, so to speak, which are already in place. Revelation does not invade human reality as something utterly alien but as something to which human beings are already in some sense attuned."[12] Second, we can also assume that God's love is the motive for the incarnation, since God would not assume human nature in order to make up some deficiency in God's own nature. As Otto H. Hentz explains,

> To acknowledge the true becoming of God in the human is to confront the mystery of God's creative, self-giving love. Why does God do this, why does God become human? By choice, by will—that is, out of love. The only necessity for God to become in and through an other is the necessity of utterly gratuitous love. The apparently strange idea of God's becoming is really the idea of God's self-giving love.[13]

Third, the unity of two natures in one person suggests a deeper unity existing between what at first may appear to be conflicting forces. For example, Rahner situates the incarnation in the dynamic interplay between human receptivity and divine activity. Consequently, obedience to God and human fulfillment are united. "The incarnation of God is therefore the unique, *supreme,* case of the total actualization of human reality, which consists of the fact that man *is* in so far as he gives up himself."[14] Similarly, in Christ, divine and human natures are not pitted in battle. "Thus Christ is most radically man, and his humanity is the freest and most independent, not in spite of, but because of its being taken up, by being constituted as the self-utterance of God."[15] Karen Kilby notes,

> Christ can be seen, on Rahner's account, as the radicalization, the supreme case, of what is true of us all. If to be oriented towards God is what makes us human, then the one who is so oriented towards God that he is utterly given over to God, and taken over by God, is actually the one who is at the same time the most fully human. So the divinity of Christ can be conceived not as the contradiction of Christ's humanity, but as its ultimate fulfillment.[16]

In "On the Theology of the Incarnation," Rahner employs the transcendental method to argue for a fundamental compatibility among anthropology (a view of the human person), theology (view of God), and Christology (view of Christ). We turn now to Rahner's attempt to locate the incarnation in the larger scope of human history.

"Christology Within an Evolutionary View of the World"

Rahner's starting point in his essay, "Christology Within an Evolutionary View of the World," is not the mysterious subjective world of the individual, but rather the external world studied by biologist and physicists. Rahner's essay falls into four parts: an exposition of his working assumptions, observations on the course of natural history, Christology within an evolutionary worldview, and a conclusion.

Rahner identifies five working assumptions. First, the material and the spiritual both originate from God. Second, matter and spirit are not to be seen as diametrically opposed entities, but as mutually related elements. The third assumption follows from the first two: Matter is not something from which Christians should seek escape, but is what enables them to come to a reliable knowledge about the world and even some limited knowledge about God. Fourth, the interplay between matter and spirit is not static; it has a history. Rahner labels this process "active self-transcendence." Furthermore, "this notion of self-transcendence includes also transcendence into what is substantially new, i.e. the leap to a higher *nature*."[17] This belief is expressed in the principle that *"the higher order always embraces the lower."*[18] Each stage of development requires the earlier stages yet moves beyond them. Fifth, the Christian sees the course of that development in history as the interplay between God's offer of grace and the free human response to that offer. Since "the freedom-history of the spirit is enveloped by the grace of God which perseveres victoriously unto the good, the Christian knows that this history of the cosmos as a whole will find its real consummation despite, in, and through the freedom of man, and that its finality as a whole will also be its consummation."[19] In other words, by plotting points along a continuum, the observer of history can offer predictions about where we are headed.

Rahner next offers a theological assessment of the course of human history. The course of human history is one in which "the cosmos gradually becomes conscious of itself."[20] Human history, then, is the history of God's self-communication. This self-communication takes place not apart from the material, but in and through the material, and decisively in the incarnation.

These preliminary observations converge in Rahner's discussion of the incarnation in the third part of his essay. He offers the following conclusion:

> God's communication of himself does not suddenly become uncosmic—directed merely to an isolated, separate subjectivity—but is given to the human race and is historical. This event of self-communication must therefore be thought of as an event which takes place historically in a specifically spatio-temporal manner and which turns to everyone and calls upon their freedom. In other words, this self-communication must have a permanent beginning and must find in this a permanent guarantee of its reality so that it can rightly demand a free decision for the acceptance of this divine self-communication.[21]

He continues, "We give the title Saviour simply to that historical person who, coming in space and time, signifies the beginning of God's absolute communication for all men as something happening irrevocably and which shows this to be happening."[22] Geffrey B. Kelly offers the following summary:

> Much of Rahner's mode of doing theology is, therefore, grounded in his conviction that all the dynamics of human life exist in unity within the cosmos and that individual history takes place in the history of Christ and in that of humanity as a whole. For him, the final result of the evolutionary, historical process is still a person's life in God— the very God with whom the people can enjoy a unique relationship in the mystery of God's oneness with them....

This attitude toward the historical process, like all of Rahner's theology, is primed by his compelling portrayal of Christ as the subjective expression of God's self-communication. To this end, Rahner declares that in the special event of Christ, "This self-communication realizes its proper nature and...breaks through."...Christ is the point at which the history of the world, viewed salvifically, the history of the church and its correlative, the history of dogma, and the evolutionary perspective all seem to come together. One makes sense of the other. Together they create a coherence in Rahner's theological reflections.[23]

In the incarnation we have the culmination of all that has gone before and the anticipation of all that will be. Modern evolutionary thought, in other words, not only does not exclude the incarnation, but it in fact provides support for this essential doctrine of Christian faith.

Rahner next argues for the compatibility of his own position with the traditional affirmations of faith. He first turns his attention to the doctrine of the "Hypostatic Union." Robert A. Krieg, C.S.C., defines the concept as "the uniting of the divine nature and the human nature of Jesus Christ in one person, or *hypostasis* (Gk.). This notion is meant to illumine the mystery of Christ's personal unity, while at the same time safeguarding the Church's insight regarding the mystery of Jesus Christ's two natures, his full divinity and full humanity."[24] In terms of the preservation of Christ's full humanity, Rahner writes,

> Seen in this light, it now becomes possible to understand what is really meant by the doctrine of the Hypostatic Union and of the Incarnation of the divine Logos and how, following quite naturally from what has been said, it fits into an evolutionist view of the world. In the first place, the Saviour is himself a historical moment in God's saving action exercised on the world. He is a moment of the history of God's communication of himself to the world—in the sense that he is a part of this history of the cosmos itself. He must not be merely God acting on the world but must be a part of the cosmos itself in its very climax. This

is in fact stated in the Christian dogma: Jesus is true man; he is truly a part of the earth, truly a moment in the biological evolution of this world, a moment of human natural history, for he is born of woman; he is a man who in his spiritual, human, and finite subjectivity is just like us, a receiver of that self-communication of God by grace which we affirm of all men—and hence of the cosmos—as the climax of development in which the world comes absolutely into its own presence and into the direct presence of God.[25]

In terms of the preservation of Christ's divinity, Rahner insists, "Hence, if the reality in which God's absolute self-communication is pledged and accepted for the whole of humanity and thus becomes 'present' for us (i.e. Christ's reality) is to be really the final and unsurpassable divine self-communication, then it must be said that it is not only posited by God but is God himself."[26] Rahner concludes his reflection on the hypostatic union as follows: "It means this, and properly speaking, nothing else: in the human reality of Jesus, God's absolute saving purpose (the absolute event of God's self-communication to us) is simply, absolutely and irrevocably present; in it is present both the declaration made to us and its acceptance—something effected by God himself, a reality of God himself, unmixed and yet inseparable and hence irrevocable."[27] In short, Rahner sees his position in complete continuity with the traditional affirmation that Christ was one person with two natures, one fully human and the other fully divine.[28]

In the final section of his essay, Rahner weighs in on the ancient theological question of whether there would have been an incarnation if there were no sin in the world. He begins, "It should be stated, first of all, that there is quite a long established school of thought among Catholic theologians (usually called the 'Scotist school') which has always stressed that the first and most basic motive for the Incarnation was not the blotting-out of sin but that the Incarnation was already the goal of the divine freedom even apart from any divine fore-knowledge of freely incurred guilt."[29] This debate will most likely strike the modern reader as an example of arcane theologizing, but Rahner believes that seeing the incarnation as a gift of divine self-communication rather than as a remedy for human sinfulness opens up a vision of human history as imbued with the presence of God. In other words, the incarnation is the *decisive*, but necessarily the *exclusive* expression of God's constant concern for the salvation of each and every human being. A second consequence is that life in this world takes on immense religious significance. "Because man cannot effect his salvation apart from his worldly task but only through it, the latter attains its highest dignity, honour, danger-point and ultimate significance by this very fact."[30]

The reader may wonder, "Where is the Jesus who overturned the money changer's tables? Where is the Jesus who suffered anguish in the garden of Gethsemane?" In other words, if we change the starting point, and begin not with the dogmatic statements of the church (that is, one person with two natures), but the stories of Jesus found in the Gospels, do we arrive at the same conclusion about Jesus?

"The Two Basic Types of Christology"

Rahner distinguishes between a "saving history" type of Christology and a "metaphysical" type of Christology in his essay, "The Two Basic Types of Christology."[31] In the former type, he writes, "the eye of the believer in his experience of saving history alights first on the man Jesus of Nazareth, and on him in his fully human reality."[32] The starting point, in other words, is Christ's humanity. The latter metaphysical type is a "descending" Christology.

> The pre-existence of the Logos, his divinity, his distinction from the Father, the predicate "Son of God" ascribed to the divine Logos as him who pre-exists in this christology, are regarded as manifestly belonging to him from the first, and assumed more or less to be statements based upon the verbal assertions and convictions of Jesus himself. This pre-existent Logos who is the Son of God descends from heaven, becomes man, i.e. assumes a human reality as his own, in such a way that this pre-existent Logos also achieves a visibly historical dimension and appears in the very history which as pre-existent he has already shaped and moulded.[33]

In this descending Christology, the starting point is Christ's divinity. Do these two approaches conflict or arrive at radically different portraits of Jesus? Not necessarily, if the principle "All truth is one" is correct. "All truth is one" means that truth discovered in one field of inquiry will not conflict with truth discovered in another field of inquiry.

Rahner argues that it is possible to combine the "saving history" type of Christology and a "metaphysical" type of Christology. He contends,

> But if we take the transcendentality and the historicity of man as constituting the two poles of our basic understanding of humanity, then, for our understanding of what is meant by Jesus Christ, there can be only one conception, in which man remains freely within his history, from which in fact he can never be separated so as to achieve a state of total transcendentality, and in which he finds his salvation, and one conception according to which man radically brings to bear his metaphysical powers in order to proceed from the question of what he is as subject and what the whole of reality is in one, and attempts once more to understand what he has initially freely experienced in history as his salvation.[34]

Rahner clears a middle ground between the two types, in which a number of christological positions may prove acceptable to the Christian community.

> These two types and their mutual interrelationship surely enable us to understand that in present-day Christian theology too there is room for a pluralism of christologies. If these christologies respect the Church's credal formulae concerning Christ where these are definitive, and constantly submit afresh to critical reappraisal by standards outside themselves, and provided that at the same time they include, and accord all due respect to, essential reference to Jesus as the bringer of eschatological salvation, the different christologies can continue to be different, and still be orthodox.[35]

Tyron Inbody regards this attempt to unite these two approaches in Christology as one of the most appealing features of Rahner's theology. He writes, "Anxious to avoid the truncation, uncertainty, and heterodoxy of much christology from below, Rahner is also anxious to avoid the abstractness and diminution of history and Christian experience, original and contemporary, characteristic of christologies from above. His effort at unifying this double strand of the christological tradition must stand as one of the high-water marks of his theology."[36]

Rahner's Spiritual Vision

What are some of the essential features of the worldview Rahner develops in the course of his christological investigations? Three of the most important features are the universality of grace, the centrality of Christ, and the sacramentality of the created order. First, God's grace is universally present. At every turn God's grace is present. The material and spiritual worlds are created out of the effusive love of God. The incarnation reveals God's intimate ongoing relationship with the world and stands as God's pledge to that world that its final consummation rests with God. God's grace overflows every boundary we humans erect (even the limits of the Christian religion itself). Rahner himself once summarized his view in the following straightforward manner: "I really only want to tell the reader something very simple. Human persons in every age, always and everywhere, whether they realize it and reflect upon it or not, are in relationship with the unutterable mystery of human life that we call God."[37] Polanyi's comment that *we can know more than we can tell*," I believe, captures nicely this element of Rahner's theology. We are in a constant, though not always conscious, relationship with God who is mystery. Language will at times fail to capture the depths of that mysterious divine–human relationship, but that does not diminish the believer's confidence that it exists.

The second feature is the centrality of Christ. Rahner's transcendental method does not begin with features about the world and then move into how Christ "fits" into those categories. The process begins with the incarnation and then proceeds to hypothesize about the conditions that must have been present for that event to have occurred. Christ is the starting point; Christ is the definitive expression of God's continuous love for the world (John 3:16); Christ is the irrevocable pledge for the future.

Third, Rahner rejects any understanding of the world that too radically separates "matter and spirit" or "nature and grace." Just as in the hypostatic union, there is a distinction but not a separation between Jesus' humanity and divinity; there is a union of the natural history of the human race and "salvation history." Richard McBrien argues that "no theological principle or focus is more characteristic of Catholicism or more central to its identity than the principle of *sacramentality*. The Catholic vision sees God in and through all things: other people, communities, movements, events, places, objects, the world at large, the whole cosmos. The visible, the tangible, the finite, the historical—all these are actual or potential carriers of the divine presence."[38] Here Rahner maintains the tradition of Ignatius of Loyola, the founder of the Jesuits, who encouraged Christians to "find God in all things."

In summary, we can say that Rahner's theology is grounded in the axiom, "What is received is received according to the mode of the receiver," guided by the beliefs that "the higher order always embraces the lower" and that "all truth is one," and permeated with a sense that "we can know more than we can tell."

Criticisms of Rahner's Christology

We focus on three criticisms of Rahner's theology: the first centers on the question of the uniqueness of Jesus; the second questions whether Rahner has given sufficient attention to the cross; and the third charges that Rahner's presuppositions are outdated.

John McDermott raises the first objection clearly and forcefully in his review of Rahner's claim for the compatibility between human freedom and the omnipotence of God. McDermott writes,

> Just as subject and predicate are unified in a sentence without surrendering their diversity, so divine omnipotence and human freedom are joined while retaining their difference. Indeed, the greater the unity, for Rahner, the clearer is the difference. Thus he saw in the full, greatest

possible actuation of Jesus' freedom the greatest possible union with God, indeed, what the word "Incarnation" intends. But does this universal principle regarding God and man mark the uniqueness of Jesus? Why is it not possible for another human being to accomplish the total surrender to God ascribed to Jesus?[39]

Denise and John Carmody, in a very favorable review of Rahner's Christology, seem inadvertently to raise the same question as McDermott: "Why is it not possible for another human being to accomplish the total surrender to God ascribed to Jesus?" They write,

> To be sure there is a uniqueness in the quality and intensity of the union that Jesus has with God his Father, and "hypostatic union" retains a worth by signaling this uniqueness, this soleness in Jesus' divinization. But what happens in the Incarnation happens, to a considerable degree, whenever any human being accepts God's love, for the dynamics of that love are such, in its incorporation of human beings into the "Body of Christ" and its bestowal of the Spirit, that it works an "assumption" of our human natures into the divine life that is at least analogous to the Logos' assumption of a human nature born of Mary.[40]

This seems to undercut the foundational claim that Christ is the absolute savior that Rahner contends he is upholding.

The second criticism concerns Rahner's treatment of the cross in his Christology. Rahner insists that the incarnation is not to be regarded as a remedy to human sinfulness, but as the highest expression of God's self-communication to the world. John McDermott comments, "In such a panhistoric view one might well ask how Jesus' death actually accomplished anything new for man in history; for everything had been determined before creation by the immutable God."[41] Harvey Egan, S.J., writes, "God is unchanging love. God loves even sinful humanity and offers himself even prior to Jesus' actual sacrifice on the cross but in view of it because creation is Christocentric from the very beginning. Because God loves the sinner and wishes to reconcile us to him (not vice versa), the cross, in

Rahner's view, is the symbol of God's irrevocable will to communicate himself to us as unconditional love."[42] Critics charge this simply does not agree with the scriptural claims that we are saved by Christ's death.

The third and final criticism is that Rahner's operating assumptions are no longer widely shared by thinkers in the Western world. J. A. Di Noia, O.P., offers a balanced summary of this objection:

> But Rahner's enthusiastic, if critical, embrace of modernity entwines the fortunes of his theological program with those of specific modern conceptualities which are themselves under attack. It was Rahner's contention that Catholic theology must appropriate the transcendental, anthropological and subjective turns characteristic of modern thought. Thus, in an intellectual climate in which philosophers and theologians are increasingly critical of precisely these elements of modern thought, Rahner's theological program will seem wedded to outmoded interests and conceptions.[43]

This criticism brings us full circle. In the opening paragraph of this chapter, we contrasted theologians who see mountains with those who see jungles. The former, like Rahner, prefer grand systems of thought that integrate and relate the various elements of Christian belief. The latter praise diversity and proceed in a more *ad hoc* manner. The great revelatory moments for the unifiers are creation and the incarnation. The decisive moment for the iconoclastic diversifiers is the crucifixion, to which we now turn.

Notes

1. Graeme Garrett, *God Matters: Conversations in Theology* (Collegeville: Liturgical Press, 1999), pp. 3–4.
2. Stanley J. Grenz and Roger E. Olson, *Twentieth-Century Theology* (Downers Grove: InterVarsity Press, 1992), p. 240.
3. Michael Polanyi, *The Tacit Dimension* (Gloucester, MA: Peter Smith, 1983), p. 4. I discovered the quotation in John S. Dunne, *The Music of Time* (Notre Dame: University of Notre Dame Press, 1996), p. 70.
4. Robert Kress, *A Rahner Handbook* (Atlanta: John Knox Press, 1982), p. 27.

5. Ibid., p. 78. Italics mine.
6. Karl Rahner, "On the Theology of the Incarnation," in *Theological Investigations*, vol. IV (Baltimore: Helicon Press, 1966), p. 105.
7. Ibid., p. 107.
8. Ibid., p. 108.
9. Ibid., p. 112.
10. Ibid., pp. 117–18.
11. Ibid., p. 113.
12. J. A. Di Noia, O.P., "Karl Rahner," in *The Modern Theologians*, 2nd ed., ed. David F. Ford (Oxford: Blackwell Publishers, 1997), p. 124.
13. Otto H. Hentz, "Anticipating Jesus Christ: An Account of Our Hope," in *A World of Grace*, ed. Leo J. O'Donovan (New York: Seabury Press, 1980), p. 117.
14. Rahner, "Theology of the Incarnation," p. 110.
15. Ibid., p. 117.
16. Karen Kilby, *Karl Rahner* (London: Fount Paperbacks, 1997), p. 19.
17. Karl Rahner, "Christology Within an Evolutionary View of the World," in *Theological Investigations*, vol. V, trans. Karl–H. Kruger (Baltimore: Helicon Press, 1966), p. 165.
18. Ibid., p. 167. Italics mine.
19. Ibid., p. 168.
20. Ibid., p. 171.
21. Ibid., p. 174.
22. Ibid., pp. 174–75.
23. Geffrey B. Kelly, "Introduction," *Karl Rahner: Theologian of the Graced Search for Meaning* (Minneapolis: Fortress, 1992), p. 55.
24. Robert Krieg, C.S.C., "Hypostatic Union," in *HarperCollins Encyclopedia of Catholicism* (San Francisco: HarperCollins, 1995), p. 647.
25. Rahner, "Christology Within an Evolutionary View," p. 176.
26. Ibid., p. 183.
27. Ibid., pp. 183–84.
28. For a helpful discussion of this particular feature of Rahner's theology, see James J. Buckley, "Karl Rahner as a Dogmatic Theologian," *Thomist* 47 (1983), pp. 364–94.
29. Rahner, "Christology Within an Evolutionary View," p. 184.
30. Ibid., p. 191.
31. Karl Rahner, "The Two Basic Types of Christology," in *Theological Investigations*, vol. XIII (New York: Crossroad, 1983), pp. 213–23.
32. Ibid., p. 215.
33. Ibid., p. 217.
34. Ibid., pp. 219–20.

35. Ibid., p. 222.

36. Tyron Inbody, "Rahner's Christology: A Critical Assessment," *St. Luke's Journal of Theology* XXV(4), 1982, p. 306.

37. *Karl Rahner in Dialogue: Conversations and Interviews,* 1965–1982, ed. Paul Imhof and Hubert Biallowons (New York: Crossroad, 1986), p. 147. I discovered this quote in Stanley J. Grenz and Roger E. Olson, *Twentieth–Century Theology* (Downers Grove: InterVarsity Press, 1992), p. 240.

38. Richard P. McBrien, *Catholicism,* new ed. (San Francisco: Harper-Collins, 1994), p. 1196.

39. John M. McDermott, "The Christologies of Karl Rahner," *Gregorianum* 67 (1986), p. 122. For a fascinating book–length survey of the question of Jesus' uniqueness, see Scott Cowdell *Is Jesus Unique?* (Mahwah: Paulist Press, 1996).

40. Denise and John Carmody, "Christology in Karl Rahner's Evolutionary World View," *Religion in Life* XLIX(2), 1980, p. 209.

41. McDermott, "Christologies of Karl Rahner II," p. 323.

42. Harvey D. Egan, S.J., *Karl Rahner: The Mystic of Everyday Life* (New York: Crossroad, 1998), p. 135.

43. Di Noia, "Karl Rahner," p. 131.

Discussion Questions

1. Is it possible to organize all Christian beliefs into a grand system in which all the various beliefs are related to each other in an orderly fashion?

2. Do you believe that Christ was one person, with two natures, one fully human and the other fully divine? Is this the standard by which all Christologies should be measured?

3. Does the modern evolutionary worldview support or undermine the traditional affirmations about Christ?

4. Would the incarnation have taken place if sin had never entered the world?

5. Do non-Christians know as much about God's grace as Christians?

6. Could another human, in theory, be equal to Christ in terms of openness to doing God's will?

7. Which is more important to Christian faith: the incarnation or the crucifixion? Why?

Suggested Readings

For a detailed introduction to the scriptural material on the incarnation, see James D. G. Dunn, *Christology in the Making* (Philadelphia: Westminster, 1980).

For shorter, yet very helpful introductions to Rahner's theology, see "Karl Rahner" by Anne Carr in *A Handbook of Christian Theologians*, enlarged ed. (Nashville: Abingdon Press, 1984), ed. Dean G. Peerman and Martin E. Marty; chap. 8 of Stanley J. Grenz and Roger E. Olson, *Twentieth-Century Theology* (Downers Grove: InterVarsity Press, 1992); J. A. Di Noia, O.P., "Karl Rahner," in *The Modern Theologians,* 2nd ed., ed. David F. Ford (Oxford: Blackwell Publishers, 1997); Geffrey B. Kelly, "Introduction," *Karl Rahner: Theologian of the Graced Search for Meaning* (Minneapolis: Fortress, 1992); the Introduction by Karl Lehmann to *The Content of Faith* (New York: Crossroad, 1992); and chap. 2 of Robert Kress, *A Rahner Handbook* (Atlanta: John Knox Press, 1982).

For shorter, yet helpful introductions to Rahner's Christology, see chap. 5 of William V. Dych, S.J., *Karl Rahner* (Collegeville: Liturgical Press, 1992); chap. 2 of Karen Kilby, *Karl Rahner* (London: Fount Paperbacks, 1997); chap. 6 of Harvey D. Egan, S.J., *Karl Rahner: Mystic of Everyday Life* (New York: Crossroad, 1998); chap. 5 of Michael Skelley, S.J., *The Liturgy of the World: Karl Rahner's Theology of Worship* (Collegeville: Liturgical Press, 1991). For a helpful article, see "Rahner's Christology: A Critical Assessment," in *St. Luke's Journal of Theology* XXV(4), 1982, pp. 294–310. Students well acquainted with Rahner's work should see John M. McDermott's two-part article, "The Christologies of Karl Rahner," in *Gregorianum* 67 (1986), pp. 87–123, 297–327.

For a brief primary source for Rahner's Christology, see his "I Believe in Jesus Christ: Interpreting an Article of Faith," in *Theological Investigations*, vol. IX, trans. Graham Harrison (New York: Herder and Herder, 1972). Robert Kress recommends *The Eternal Year* (Baltimore: Helicon Press, 1964) as an accessible introduction to Rahner's theology.

6

The Crucifixion
and Jürgen Moltmann's
The Crucified God

At the beginning of the previous chapter, we included Karl Rahner in a group of thinkers labeled "unifiers," who looked for the grand over-arching structure into which various theological beliefs could be placed, related, and ultimately joined. The contrasting approach was labeled "diversifying." Graeme Garrett writes,

> Diversifiers are also suspicious of too much consistency. Since when were things humans, especially things reli-gious, consistent? Paul's writing is full of inconsistency. "I do not understand my own actions. For I do not do what I want, I do the very thing I hate" (Rom 7:15). "My strength is made perfect in weakness" (2 Cor 12:9). It is hard to avoid this kind of oxymoron if you take seriously a *theo-logy* of the cross, that is, the essence of God revealed in the death of a criminal.[1]

We turn now to that death and its theological significance. In this moment of the biblical narrative, it seems that the diversifying approach seems the most appropriate, for at the cross we see not rationality and order, but cruelty and horror. Our investigation begins with the scriptural claims about the significance of Christ's death, then moves into a discussion of Jürgen Moltmann's work *The Crucified God,* and concludes with a critical assessment of Moltmann's text.

Biblical Background

Jesus of Nazareth was crucified at Golgotha (Calvary in Latin) by Roman authorities on charges that he claimed to be "the King of the Jews." While this teaching is an essential part of early Christian preaching, the questions that the event raises have occupied Christian thinkers for two millennia. For example, Paul writes in his letter to the Romans:

> For Christ, while we were still helpless, yet died at the appointed time for the ungodly. Indeed, only with difficulty does one die for a just person, though perhaps for a good person one might find the courage to die. But God proves his love for us that while we were still sinners Christ died for us. How much more then, since we are now justified by his blood, will we be saved through him from the wrath. Indeed, if, while we were enemies, we were reconciled to God through the death of his Son, how much more, once reconciled, will we be saved by his life. (5:6–10)

The interpreter could pursue any number of possible lines of inquiry. One could ask about Paul's understanding of the human situation prior to Christ's death. What was Paul's understanding of human sinfulness? How able are we to save ourselves from that sinfulness? A second set of questions could center around Paul's understanding of Christ's death. Did Christ have to be crucified? What does it mean to say Christ died "at the appointed time"? A third set of questions could focus on the effect of Christ's death. What does it mean to say that we are justified by Christ's blood? How does Christ's death impact those living centuries later?

The first set of questions deals with human sinfulness. Christ's death is a remedy to a problem. The most common biblical designation for that problem would be sin. Sin functions as an umbrella concept under which other problems may be discussed, including death (1 Cor 15:26), the fear of death (Heb 2:15), Satan (2 Cor 11), principalities and powers (Col 2:14), and darkness (1 John 1:7). All these are conditions of the fallen, sinful world. Christ is the solution to the problem of sin. As Paul writes in 2 Corinthians, "For our sake he made him to be sin who knew no sin, so that in him we might become the righteousness of God" (5:21).

The second set of questions deals with the role of the cross. John P. Galvin speaks of three major early Christian assessments of Jesus' death: the death of a prophet-martyr, the death of a righteous sufferer, and an atoning, redemptive death. In the first instance, Christ stands in a long line of prophets who were persecuted and/or executed for their bold proclamations. In the second portrait, the righteous one suffers persecution for the sake of the unrighteous. It is the third portrait that has occupied much of Christian theology during the past 2,000 years. The righteous one suffered for us, and in doing so, won a victory for us.

The third set of questions asks specifically about the effect of Christ's death. In the passage from Romans, Paul speaks of our justification, reconciliation, and salvation. This change was brought about by Christ's death (that is, "by his blood"). This teaching is found elsewhere in the New Testament (see, for example, 1 John 2:2, 1 Pet 3:18, and Heb 9:11–28). Paul locates this in the context of God's love. Again, this prompts a series of questions. In what sense is the crucifixion a display of God's love? Is God wrathful? Could Christ have saved us without dying on the cross?

The interpretations of other biblical passages dealing with Christ's death involve in some way these three sets of questions. For example, in Mark's Gospel, Jesus announces that "the Son of Man came not to be served but to serve, and to give his life a ransom for many" (10:45). The metaphor of "ransom" is a provocative one; it suggests Christ paid the price for our release from sin. While this is "good news" indeed, it also raises a host of questions. To whom was the ransom paid? If it was paid to the Father, did the Father sacrifice the Son? If it was paid to Satan, does that represent a victory for the devil? How did that act of ransoming effect salvation for those born centuries later?

It seems, therefore, that we have at least three elements to include in any complete biblical understanding of the death of Christ. First, it was an event that involved profound, genuine human suffering. The church has wisely resisted any effort to say that Jesus only appeared to be human and consequently only seemed to suffer. Second, Christ's suffering and death on the cross was not without benefit. It was an event of salvation for others, a decisive victory over Satan, and a reconciliation. Christ, Paul insists, "died for our sins" (1 Cor 15:3). Third, it was part of God's plan for the world. Again Paul insists that Christ died for us "in accordance with the scriptures" (1 Cor 15:3). In Luke and Acts, where we find no developed theology of the cross, there is nonetheless the sense of the necessity of Christ's death (see Luke 17:25, 24:26). In Acts, Peter announces, "This man, handed over to you according to the definite plan and foreknowledge of God, you crucified and killed by the hands of those outside the law" (2:23).

Theologians have struggled mightily to devise theories that do justice to all three aspects of the biblical proclamation. Anselm of Canterbury (1033–1109) constructed an argument that has probably generated the most attention. Most commentators see Anselm's argument as reflective of the feudal times in which he lived, with their hierarchical understanding of social orders and their respective duties and obligations. Anselm understood human sin to be a dishonor against God. Since humans were the offending party, justice required that humans make the proper satisfaction to God. Since humans already owed everything to God, they were incapable of offering the proper satisfaction. Humans *needed* to offer the satisfaction; only God *was able* to offer the satisfaction. Therefore, a "God-man" was needed to offer the perfect satisfaction for human sinfulness to God. Trevor Hart makes the following observation at the close of his discussion of Anselm's theory: "If there is a striking omission in Anselm's account of the cross, it is his failure to press beyond the categories of Creator and creature, and to read it as an event in a relationship between a Father and a Son, a dimension which would have provided his basic understanding with an even keener edge, and perhaps set it safely beyond the bounds of misconstrual in terms of a penal exaction model."[2] We turn now to a theologian who has attempted to do just that, that is, to see the cross not as an exchange required by justice, but as an event between the Father and the Son.

Biographical Background on Jürgen Moltmann

As was true with Dietrich Bonhoeffer, Moltmann's biography sheds light on his theology. He was born in Hamburg, Germany, in 1926. As a young man fighting in the German Army during World War II, he was captured and held as a prisoner of war in camps in Belgium and Scotland.[3] In a piece written more than fifty years after his capture, Moltmann compared his own time in the camp to Jacob's struggle with the angel (Gen 32). Moltmann recounts,

> In the years I spent as a prisoner of war, 1945–1948, the biblical story about Jacob's struggle with the angel of the Lord at the Jabbok was for me always the story about God in which I found again my own little human story....
>
> We were caught up in the terrors of the end of the war, and in the hopeless misery of a prisoner of war's existence. We wrestled with God in order to survive in the abysses of senselessness and guilt and we emerged from those years "limping" indeed, but blessed. The end of the war, when it at last came, found us with deeply wounded souls; but after the years in the Norton prisoner-of-war camp in Scotland many of us said: "My soul has been healed, for I have seen God."[4]

Moltmann describes the low point of imprisonment.

> And then came what was the worst of all. In September 1945, in Camp 22 in Scotland, we were confronted with pictures of Belsen and Auschwitz. They were pinned up in one of the huts, without comment. Some people thought it was propaganda. Others set the piles of bodies which they saw over against Dresden. But slowly and inexorably the truth filtered into our awareness, and we saw ourselves mirrored in the eyes of the Nazi victims. Was this what we had fought for? Had my generation, at the last, been driven to our deaths so that the concentration camp murderers could go on killing, and Hitler could live a few months longer?[5]

Moltmann's spiritual rejuvenation came from two sources: the kindness of other people, including the local Scots and English who extended hospitality to the prisoners of war, and the Bible. Moltmann's upbringing was not especially religious, but when he began to read the psalms of lament (especially Ps 39), he was struck to the core. More important for this present investigation, the passion of Christ proved particularly illuminating.

> Then I came to the story of the passion, and when I read Jesus' death cry, "My God, why have you forsaken me?" I knew with certainty: this is someone who understands you. I began to understand the assailed Christ because I felt that he understood me: this was the divine brother in distress, who takes the prisoners with him on his way to the resurrection. I began to summon up the courage to live again, seized by a great hope. I was even calm when other men were "repatriated" and I was not. This early fellowship, the brother in suffering and the redeemer from guilt, has never left me since. I never "decided for Christ" as is often demanded of us, but I am sure that then and there, in the dark pit of my soul, he found me. Christ's godforsakenness showed me where God is, where he had been with me in my life, and where he would be in the future.[6]

With this background, we now turn our attention to Moltmann's theology of the cross. It is a theology about grief, forsakenness, but ultimately liberation.

Jürgen Moltmann's The Crucified God

Our investigation of *The Crucified God* focuses on three areas: the foundational claims asserted by Moltmann, his theology of the cross, and the interpersonal and social implications of the cross.

Three Foundational Claims

Three of Moltmann's foundational claims are of particular importance to us in this investigation. The first is methodological, the second philosophical, and the third christological.

First, Moltmann believes the task confronting contemporary theologians is to construct a Christian theology that is both relevant to the lives of people, yet preserves the identity as Christians. Moltmann suggests that too often theologians choose one to the exclusion of the other. He asserts, however, that a theology of the cross captures both aspects. Moltmann writes,

> Christian theology finds its identity as such in the cross of Christ....His cross distinguishes belief from unbelief and even more from superstition. Identification with the crucified Christ alienates the believer from the religions and ideologies of alienation, from the "religion of fear" and the ideologies of revenge. Christian theology finds its relevance in hope, thought out in depth and put into practice, in the kingdom of the crucified Christ, by suffering in the "sufferings of this present time," and makes the groaning of creation in travail its own cry for God and for freedom.[7]

By keeping the crucified Christ as the "inner criterion of theology" and a theology of the cross as "the key signature for all Christian theology," Christian theologians preserve their identity as Christians while speaking meaningfully to the "despised, abandoned, and oppressed" of the world.[8]

The second foundational claim deals with epistemology—the study of knowledge. The ancient principle of "Like is known only by like" explains how humans come to knowledge of truth. For Plato, the immortal soul recognizes truth that it knew before it was joined with a human body. In that way, knowledge is actually recollection. If like is known by like, continues this line of reasoning, an analogy discloses truth by enabling us to see the similarity between the two objects in a comparison. It is what helps Christians understand the meaning of the psalmist's poetic assertion that "the Lord is my shepherd." Moltmann, however, argues that truth can also be discovered in dissimilarity.

> This analogical principle of knowledge is one-sided if it is not supplemented by the dialectic principle of knowledge. This principle derives from medicine, going back to Hippocrates, and states that *contraria contrariis curantur,* or, in Schelling's words: "Every being can be revealed only in its opposite. Love only in hatred, unity only in conflict."

Applied to Christian theology, this means that God is only revealed as "God" in his opposite: godlessness and abandonment by God. In concrete terms, God is revealed in the cross of Christ who was abandoned by God. His grace is revealed in sinners. His righteousness is revealed in the unrighteous and in those without rights, and his gracious election in the damned. The epistemological principle of the theology of the cross can only be this dialectic principle: the deity of God is revealed in the paradox of the cross.[9]

Moltmann gives the following list of contrary notions that one encounters when one studies the paradox of the cross:

In the crucified Christ the contrary is found on several levels: in the contrary to the God who revealed his will in the law and is in practice known in the works of the law. For Jesus was sentenced to death by the law as a blasphemer. Faith finds in him the contrary to, and liberation from, the so-called gods, who are venerated in the political theology of political religions. For Jesus died, rightly or wrongly, a political death as a rebel, on a cross. Finally, faith finds in him the contrary to a God who reveals himself indirectly in the creation and in history. For Jesus died abandoned by God.[10]

The cross, to repeat Paul's words, remains "a stumbling block to Jews and foolishness to Gentiles, but to those who are the called, both Jews and Greeks, Christ the power of God and the wisdom of God" (1 Cor 1:23–24).

The third foundational claim is christological in nature. Here again we find a dual focus. Just as theology must be relevant while maintaining its Christian identity, Christology must engage in historical investigation in order to better understand the biblical proclamation about Christ. Yet it must speak in a meaningful way to the situation of Christians and the world today. Moltmann concludes, "Thus the first task of christology is the critical verification of the Christian faith in its origin in Jesus and his history. The second is the critical verification of the Christian faith in its consequences for the present and the future."[11]

If attention is focused exclusively on the former goal, then the Christology may be faithful to scripture, but ineffective as an agent for social change. If attention is focused exclusively on the latter goal, then the scriptural moorings would be torn loose.

Moltmann's Theology of the Cross

In the sixth chapter of *The Crucified God*, Moltmann constructs a theology—an understanding of God—that is remarkably traditional in some aspects and utterly revolutionary in others. It is traditional in the sense that is thoroughly trinitarian. In the modern age, many theologians have minimized the role of the Trinity in their thinking. The great father of Protestant liberalism Friedrich Schleiermacher didn't deal with the Trinity until the conclusion in his *magnum opus, The Christian Faith.* Moltmann, by contrast, sees the Trinity as essential to Christian faith. We turn now to the revolutionary aspects that Moltmann includes in his discussion of the Trinity.

Moltmann's first revolutionary move is to see the crucifixion as an inner trinitarian event between Father and Son. Moltmann states that "what happened on the cross was an event between God and God. It was a deep division in God himself, in so far as God abandoned God and contradicted himself, and at the same time a unity in God, in so far as God was at one with God and corresponded to himself."[12] Moltmann explains,

> To understand what happened between Jesus and his God and Father on the cross, it is necessary to talk in trinitarian terms. The Son suffers dying, the Father suffers the death of the Son. The grief of the Father here is just as important as the death of the Son. The Fatherlessness of the Son is matched by the Sonlessness of the Father, and if God has constituted himself as the Father of Jesus Christ, then he also suffers the death of his Fatherhood in the death of the Son.[13]

By focusing on the cross as an event of salvation for humanity, theologians, charges Moltmann, have overlooked the critical question, "What does the cross of Jesus mean for God himself?"[14] Moltmann concludes,

"In the cross, Father and Son are most deeply separated in forsaken-ness and at the same time are most inwardly one in their surrender. What proceeds from this event between Father and Son is the Spirit which justifies the godless, fills the forsaken with love and even brings the dead alive...."[15] In other words, the cross is the supreme manifes-tation of the "inner-trinitarian tensions and relationships of God."[16] More provocatively stated, "Anyone who really talks of the Trinity talks of the cross of Jesus, and does not speculate in heavenly riddles."[17]

Moltmann's second revolutionary move is to speak of "the grief of the Father." For Moltmann, the concept of God's grief captures more faithfully the dynamism of the biblical language about God and provides a meaningful answer to the atheists who insist that the evil in this world disproves the existence of the Christian God. Moltmann argues that much of early Christian theology was shaped by the pre-vailing Greek patterns of thought that regarded suffering or emotion as signs of instability and imperfection. Moltmann believes that "the time has finally come for differentiating the Father of Jesus Christ from the God of the pagans and the philosophers (Pascal) in the inter-est of Christian faith."[18] The God of Jesus Christ, insists Moltmann, loves, rejoices, and grieves—in short, is a God of pathos, not apathy. This view of God, contends Moltmann, offers a more forceful coun-terpunch to the arguments commonly advanced by atheists.

> With a trinitarian theology of the cross faith escapes the dis-pute between and the alternative of theism and atheism: God is not only other-worldly but also this-worldly; he is not only God, but also man; he is not only rule, authority and law but the event of suffering, liberating love. Conversely, the death of the Son is not the "death of God," but the beginning of that God event in which the life-giving spirit of love emerges from the death of the Son and the grief of the Father.[19]

The cross does not signal the death of God, but rather that there is "death *in* God."[20]

This leads to the third of Moltmann's revolutionary concepts: the history of God. The history of the world, including its suffering, is "taken up in God."[21] Moltmann argues,

If one describes the life of God within the Trinity as the "history of God" (Hegel), this history contains within itself the whole abyss of godforsakenness, absolute death and the non-God....Because this death took place in the history between Father and Son on the cross on Golgotha, there proceeds from it the spirit of life, love and election to salvation. The concrete "history of God" in the death of Jesus on the cross on Golgotha therefore contains within itself all the depths and abysses of human history and therefore can be understood as the history of history. All human history, however much it may be determined by guilt and death, is taken up into this "history of God," i.e. into the Trinity, and integrated into the future of the "history of God." There is no suffering which in this history of God is not God's suffering; no death which has not been God's death in the history on Golgotha. Therefore there is no life, no fortune and no joy which have not been integrated by his history into eternal life, the eternal joy of God.[22]

In an earlier discussion of Moltmann's biography, we read his reaction to the pictures of Auschwitz that were posted on the walls of the camp in which he was confined as a prisoner of war. In light of that fact, the following passage is especially significant. He writes that

it must also be said that, like the cross of Christ, even Auschwitz is in God himself. Even Auschwitz is taken up into the grief of the Father, the surrender of the Son and the power of the Spirit. That never means that Auschwitz and other grisly places can be justified, for it is the cross that is the beginning of the trinitarian history of God. As Paul says in 1 Cor. 15, only the resurrection of the dead, the murdered and the gassed, only with the healing of those in despair who bear lifelong wounds, only with the abolition of all rule and authority, only with the annihilation of death will the Son hand over the kingdom to the Father. Then God will turn his sorrow into eternal joy. This will be the sign of the completion of the trinitarian history of God and the end of world history, the overcoming of the history of man's sorrow and the fulfillment of his history of hope.[23]

This endpoint is the culmination of the history of God's ongoing love relationship with the world, which evoked both joy and grief in God. Between now and that future moment, there is hope, the virtue that sustains our faith and allows us to love. We turn now to Moltmann's discussion of the Christian life in this world.

The Interpersonal and Social Implications of the Cross

Moltmann concludes *The Crucified God* with a discussion of psychological and social liberation. Christians are called to act in the present moment in ways that reflect their beliefs about the end of time. Moltmann is quite specific about what he sees as the "vicious circles of death" and what social, economic, and political commitments are needed to break through each of those circles. Moltmann includes in his list of vicious circles of death the following: poverty, force, racial and cultural alienation, industrial pollution, senselessness, and godforsakenness. By way of a concrete guide for liberation, Moltmann believes the following commitments that correspond to each of the various woes he has listed. Moltmann calls for socialism, democracy, cultural emancipation, peace with nature, and a general commitment to human welfare. He concludes,

> In the vicious cycle of poverty, it can be said: "God is not dead. He is bread." God is present as bread in that he is the unconditional which draws near, in the present sense. In the vicious cycle of force God's presence is experienced as liberation for human dignity and responsibility. In the vicious cycle of alienation his presence is perceived in the experience of human identity and recognition. In the vicious cycle of the destruction of nature God is present in joy in existence and in peace between man and nature. In the vicious circle of meaninglessness and godforsakenness,

finally, he comes forward in the figure of the crucified Christ, who communicates courage to be.[24]

Moltmann's three revolutionary concepts—the inner trinitarian dynamics, the emotion of God, and the taking up of human history in God's history—converge in his understanding of the Christian life. Moltmann ends his work with the following summary.

> Brotherhood with Christ means the suffering and active participation in the history of this God. Its criterion is the history of the crucified and risen Christ. Its power is the sighing and liberating spirit of God. Its consummation lies in the kingdom of the triune God which sets all things free and fills them with meaning.[25]

For Moltmann's critics, this description is either couched in problematic language or the means by which Moltmann arrived at it are flawed. It is to his critics that we now turn.

Criticisms of The Crucified God

We examine three criticisms of Moltmann's theology as presented in *The Crucified God.* The first deals with theology proper, that is to say, Moltmann's concept of God. The second charges that he operates with a truncated view of revelation. The final charge is that he is uncritically accepting of the biblical stories as history.

The first charge is that Moltmann makes God in some way dependent on the world for God to be the triune God. Stanley J. Grenz and Roger E. Olson offer the following observation:

> Given Moltmann's adamant insistence that Jesus' cross and resurrection as well as the sending of the Spirit to the church constitute the trinitarian life of God, his "trinitarian history of the cross" naturally raises a crucial question: Would God be trinitarian apart from the events of the world history?
>
> In *The Crucified God* Moltmann seemed to deny any eternal triune life of God already constituted apart from

the event of the cross: "Anyone who really talks of the Trinity talks of the cross of Jesus and does not speculate in heavenly riddles." This appears to be a thorough rejection of the traditional doctrine of the immanent or ontological Trinity, which views God as existing in triune heavenly perfection from all eternity.[26]

Richard Bauckham puts the matter this way:

> It seems that it would be less accurate to say that Moltmann's God is love than that he becomes love. For in a manner akin to that of process theology and in firm opposition to the aloof and self-sufficient God of philosophical theism, Moltmann so concentrates on God's involvement with his creation as virtually to make that involvement his whole being. So in the event of the cross in which God's love for the godless is enacted a *change* in God is revealed. In the process of salvation history God not only reveals himself but actually becomes himself.[27]

This concept of a change in God leads us to Moltmann's contention that God is grieved by the death of Christ.

In his treatment of "God's grief," Moltmann uses language that is reminiscent of the ancient belief known as *patripassianism*—"(Lat., 'the suffering of the Father'), the belief that, in Christ's suffering and death, God suffered and died."[28] Moltmann believes he has avoided the charge of patripassianism by making a distinction between the suffering of the Father and the suffering of the Son.

> In the forsakenness of the Son the Father also forsakes himself. In the surrender of the Son the Father also surrenders himself, though not in the same way. For Jesus suffers dying in forsakenness, but not death itself; for men can no longer "suffer" death, because suffering presupposes life. But the Father who abandons him and delivers him up suffers the death of the Son in the infinite grief of love. We cannot therefore say here in patripassian terms that the Father suffered and died. The suffering and dying of the

Son, forsaken by the Father, is a different kind of suffering from the suffering of the Father in the death of the Son.[29]

Carl Braaten takes Moltmann to task here.

> Although Moltmann wishes to give real substance to his metaphor of "the crucified God," in the end he draws away from patripassianism. But can Moltmann have it both ways, both that there is any real meaning to his chosen phrase "the crucified God"—which incidentally is an untrinitarian way of speaking—and that his teaching is not patripassianist (p. 243)? In what sense is it or is it not patripassianist when he speaks of the "infinite grief of the Father" in the death of his Son? In the traditional theism of the orthodoxy the Father could not suffer, because the divine ultimate of Hellenistic metaphysics was immutable and therefore also impassible. But that means also beyond the suffering of grief, which can be more intense than the suffering of dying. Moltmann wants to use the language about the "suffering of God," but he somehow clings to the verdict of the ancient church against the patripassianist heresy. This should have merited an explicit treatment rather than a mere assertion that the Father's suffering is of a different kind than the Son's (p. 243). Certainly it is different, but it is still real suffering. Why be afraid of patripassianism? Why not meet it head-on if one seriously hopes to challenge the old Greek philosophical concept of God that placed restrictions on the more passionate language of God in the Bible?[30]

John Macquarrie, who believes that *The Crucified God* "would have a good claim to be regarded as possibly the most important theological book to be published in the second half of the twentieth century,"[31] argues that Moltmann is locked in a contradiction. He remarks,

> But we may note a problematic area in *The Crucified God*. In spite of the tradition of the divine impassibility, Moltmann thinks of God *in* Christ or *with* Christ, even in

the passion. But as a concession to the Reformed theological tradition to which he belongs, Moltmann also wants to
speak of Jesus as abandoned by God. Jesus, it would appear
from his cry of dereliction, did subjectively *feel* himself
abandoned. But Moltmann wants to say he really was abandoned, and this is in plain contradiction to his claim that
the Father was suffering in and with Jesus.[32]

While Braaten and Macquarrie have argued that Moltmann is trying
to hold too many positions simultaneously, others believe he does not
hold enough, and this leads us to the next group of criticisms.

The second general criticism leveled against *The Crucified God*
concerns Moltmann's almost exclusive focus on the cross as the
moment of revelation. Roland D. Zimany offers the following
reminder: "We don't have to wait until Jesus is on the Cross to find
the unexpected. His life is filled with the unexpected, from his insistence on the imminence of God's reign, his eating with publicans and
sinners, his fraternization with other 'unacceptable' people, his
recognition of the 'full citizenship' of women, and his teaching of
righteousness through grace to his claim of personal authority—as
Moltmann himself recognizes."[33] Zimany's complaint reflects many
of the same complaints leveled against Rahner on the incarnation. If
a Christian theologian argues for a single moment in the life of Christ
as the decisive revelatory moment, doesn't that diminish (and possibly eliminate) the importance of other moments in the life of Christ
or of the importance of the entire life of Christ? In one of his final
comments about *The Crucified God,* Braaten raises a similar concern. He writes, "My most serious difficulty is with its overstatement.
It suffers from the occupational hazard of systematic theologians in
particular—the tyranny of the single category. We are told by
Moltmann that the cross is the criterion of *all* theology. *Only* the
cross is the test of *everything* to be called Christian. The cross is *the*
center of *all* Christian theology."[34] In fairness to Moltmann, this criticism would lose some of its force if one were to consider the entire
corpus of his work, but as a criticism specifically of *The Crucified
God,* it seems fair.

The third criticism is that Moltmann resembles ancient
Procrustes who "tied travelers to his bed and made them fit; if their

legs were too short, he stretched them; if they were too long, he cut them off."[35] If Christ is the center, then Christology should structure one's system. Moltmann is accused, however, of fitting Christ to his system rather than letting his Christology dictate the course of his thought. Scott Cowdell writes,

> Lastly, what of the historical Jesus in *The Crucified God*? On the face of it, Moltmann appears firmly committed to his importance: "The first task of christology," he writes, "is the critical verification of the Christian faith in its origin in Jesus and his history" (83). But is it to the historical Jesus, the Jesus of history, or merely to aspects of the various New Testament "Jesus portraits" that Moltmann really refers? There is not much evidence here of engagement with the niceties of historical criticism, or even awareness of their necessity.[36]

Some might argue that historical analysis of the gospel stories is not essential to Christian theology. Such pursuits, it might be argued, are inappropriate, misguided, or unprofitable. Some might argue that no amount of historical research could even confirm or deny the central fact of Christianity, namely, that Christ was raised from the dead. It is to that event that we now turn.

Notes

1. Graeme Garrett, *God Matters: Conversations in Theology* (Collegeville: Liturgical Press, 1999), p. 7.
2. Trevor Hart, "Redemption and Fall," *Cambridge Companion to Christian Doctrine*, ed. Colin Gunton (Cambridge: Cambridge University Press, 1997), p. 201. This chapter provides a very helpful introduction to the concept of salvation.
3. See Stanley J. Grenz and Roger E. Olson, *Twentieth-Century Theology* (Downers Grove: InterVarsity Press, 1992), p. 173.
4. Jürgen Moltmann, "Wrestling with God: A Personal Meditation," *Christian Century* 114(23), 1997, p. 726.
5. Ibid., p. 727.
6. Ibid.
7. Jürgen Moltmann, *The Crucified God* (San Francisco: Harper & Row, 1974), p. 24.

8. Ibid., pp. 7, 72, 24.
9. Ibid., p. 27.
10. Ibid., pp. 68–69.
11. Ibid., p. 84.
12. Ibid., p. 244.
13. Ibid., p. 243.
14. Ibid., p. 201.
15. Ibid., p. 244.
16. Ibid., p. 204.
17. Ibid., p. 207.
18. Ibid., p. 215.
19. Ibid., p. 252.
20. Ibid., p. 207.
21. Ibid., p. 277. For a discussion of the Hegelian background of this expression, see Siu-Kwong Tang, *God's History in the Theology of Jürgen Moltmann* (Berlin: Peter Lang, 1996), pp. 104–9.
22. Ibid., p. 246.
23. Ibid., p. 278.
24. Ibid., pp. 337–38.
25. Ibid., p. 338.
26. Grenz and Olson, *Twentieth-Century Theology,* p. 182. See also Ed. L. Miller and Stanley J. Grenz, *Fortress Introduction to Contemporary Theologies* (Minneapolis: Fortress, 1998), pp. 122–23.
27. Richard Bauckham, "Moltmann's Eschatology of the Cross," *Scottish Journal of Theology* 30 (1977), p. 310.
28. "Patripassianism," *HarperCollins Encyclopedia of Catholicism* (San Francisco: HarperCollins, 1995), ed. Richard P. McBrien, p. 966.
29. Moltmann, *Crucified God*, p. 243.
30. Carl Braaten, "A Trinitarian Theology of the Cross," *Journal of Religion* 56 (1976), pp. 117–18.
31. John Macquarrie, *Jesus Christ in Modern Thought* (Philadelphia: Trinity Press, 1990), p. 321.
32. Ibid., p. 323.
33. Roland D. Zimany, "Moltmann's Crucifed God," *Dialog* 16 (1977), p. 52.
34. Braaten, "Trinitarian Theology," p. 120.
35. J. E. Zimmerman, *Dictionary of Classical Mythology* (New York: Bantam Books, 1964), p. 221.
36. Scott Cowdell, *Is Jesus Unique?* (Mahwah: Paulist, 1996), p. 34.

Discussion Questions

1. Did Christ have to die on the cross? What did Christ accomplish by dying on the cross? Could Christ have accomplished all that he needed to accomplish and not have been crucified?
2. Did the Father grieve over the death of the Son? Do you find language about God suffering appealing or unappealing?
3. What do you think Moltmann means when he says that human history is taken up into God's history?
4. Does the cross define most clearly and concretely the nature of God? If so, what is revealed about God at the cross?
5. Is there a connection between the cross and social questions such as poverty or pollution? If so, what is it?
6. How do you interpret Jesus' words on the cross, "My God, my God, why have you forsaken me?" (Mark 15:34)?
7. What is the significance of the crucifixion for those of us who live 2,000 years after it occurred?

Suggested Readings

For an excellent scholarly treatment of the crucifixion, see the two-volume work of Raymond E. Brown, S.S., *The Death of the Messiah* (New York: Doubleday, 1994).

For an overview of contemporary thinking about salvation, see Trevor Hart, "Redemption and Fall," in *The Cambridge Companion to Christian Doctrine,* ed. Colin E. Gunton (Cambridge: Cambridge University Press, 1997). See also Denis Edwards, *What Are They Saying About Salvation?* (Mahwah: Paulist Press, 1986), and chap. 11 of Brennan Hill, *Jesus the Christ* (Mystic: Twenty-Third Publications, 1991).

For overviews of Moltmann's theology, see chap. 6 of Stanley J. Grenz and Roger E. Olson, *Twentieth-Century Theology* (Downers Grove: InterVarsity Press, 1992); Richard Bauckham's entry, "Jürgen Moltmann," in *The Modern Theologians,* 2nd ed., ed. David F. Ford (Oxford: Blackwell Publishers, 1997), and his *Theology of Jürgen Moltmann* (Edinburgh: T & T Clark, 1995). See also "Jürgen Moltmann" by Christopher Morse in *A Handbook of Christian Theologians,* enlarged ed. (Nashville: Abingdon Press, 1984), ed. Dean G. Peerman and Martin E. Marty. Also helpful is Ed. L. Miller and Stanley J. Grenz, *Fortress Introduction to Contemporary Theologies* (Minneapolis: Fortress, 1998).

For shorter pieces devoted almost exclusively to *The Crucified God,* see chap. 3 of Richard Bauckham's *The Theology of Jürgen Moltmann* (Edinburgh: T & T Clark, 1995), and his article, "Moltmann's Eschatology of the Cross," in the *Scottish Journal of Theology* 30 (1977), pp. 301–11; Roland D. Zimany's "Moltmann's Crucified God" in *Dialog* 16 (1977), pp. 49–57; Don Schweitzer's "Jürgen Moltmann's Theology as a Theology of the Cross" in *Studies in Religion* 24(1), 1995, pp. 95–107; and D. G. Attfield, "Can God Be Crucified?: A Discussion of J. Moltmann," in the *Scottish Journal of Theology* 30 (1977), pp. 47–57. A more difficult but helpful piece is chap. 4 of A. J. Conyers, *God, Hope, and History* (Macon: Mercer University Press, 1988).

7

The Resurrection and Hans Küng's *On Being a Christian*

The gospel that Christians proclaim does not end at the cross. The ignominy of Christ's death was surpassed by the glory of his resurrection. So central, in fact, is the resurrection that Paul insists that if Christ has not been raised from the dead, then Christianity is a fraud (cf. 1 Cor 15:13–19). Such a spectacular event is linked in this study with arguably the most controversial Catholic theologian of the twentieth century: Hans Küng. We will focus our attention on Küng's treatment of Christ's resurrection in his work *On Being a Christian*.

The Life and Times of Hans Küng

It is hard to mention Hans Küng without dealing in some way with the controversy that swirls around him. Born in 1928 in Switzerland, Küng decided to become a priest and studied at the Gregorian University in Rome.[1] He was ordained a priest in 1954. After his ordination, he moved to Paris to study for his doctorate in theology. His dissertation dealt with the compatibility between the Roman Catholic understanding of "justification"—one of the key issues in Luther's theology—and the view held by the prominent Protestant theologian Karl Barth. In 1960, Küng was appointed professor of theology at the University of Tübingen—a prestigious post to be awarded a scholar at the ripe old age of thirty-two. In the 1960s, Küng played an active role at the Second Vatican Council, where he, like Congar, served as a *peritus* (expert). His writings in the 1960s dealt primarily with the church and the changes that he believed were needed in the church. His work put him in greater and greater tension with the church hierarchy, especially the

Congregation for the Doctrine of the Faith—the office within the governing body of the church that safeguards the Catholic faith against heresy. The relationship between Küng and the Congregation for the Doctrine of the Faith grew increasingly antagonistic, until Küng's license to teach as a Catholic theologian, known as his *missio canonica,* was finally revoked in 1979. Conservatives hailed the decision as a public declaration of what they had argued for years, namely, that Küng no longer taught orthodox Roman Catholic theology. Supporters, however, saw in this a political move intended to squelch the voice of an influential critic. One of Küng's supporters, Leonard Swidler, writes,

> On December 18, 1979, Küng was the object of a previously unheard-of Vatican document, a Declaration that he "can no longer be considered a Catholic theologian or function as such in a teaching role." In the past, Catholic theologians who fell into severe disfavor with Rome were either censured, silenced, made to recant, suspended from priestly office, excommunicated, burned at the stake—or all of the above. Küng suffered none of them. Why this *novum?* To those familiar with the relationship of German universities, the German state, and Rome the answer was obvious. If authoritative evidence could be presented that Küng was not a Catholic and therefore could not function as one in teaching, then the local Catholic bishop of Tübingen, where Küng teaches, would have legal grounds to request the state to replace Küng as professor of Catholic theology at the university. This was to be done on the basis of the Concordat between the Vatican and Hitler's Germany in 1933. It was all carefully planned out and executed in a series of secret meetings by key Vatican and German hierarchs that reads like a plot of an international intrigue—which it was.[2]

Küng has remained at Tübingen, but is no longer a member of the Catholic theology faculty. Instead, he is a professor of ecumenical theology and director of the Ecumenical Institute of the university.[3] In the final two decades of the twentieth century, Küng's work dealt with dialogue among the various world religions and the development of an ecumenical theological methodology.

Küng's Approach in On Being a Christian

In *On Being a Christian,* Küng offers to those who are inquisitive about Christianity his account of the Christian message. His intended audience is wide ranging: committed believers, lapsed Catholics, those struggling with their faith, nonbelievers, non-Christians, and agnostics. Küng hopes to offer a vision of the Christian life that is intelligible, credible, and challenging. It is also a work that is critical of the tradition. *On Being a Christian* is as much a critique of the present state of Christianity as it is an offering of that faith to the world. He warns, "The specific danger of Protestant belief is biblicism, the danger of Eastern Orthodox belief is traditionalism, the danger of Roman Catholic belief is authoritarianism. All these are defective modes of believing."[4] It is a salvage mission to recover the original "Christian program," as Küng says, "before it was covered with the dust and debris of two thousand years."[5] First, however, we need to review the principles that will guide us along the way.

In the section entitled "The Real Christ" (Section B/II), Küng engages in an effort that is known in theological circles as "the quest for the historical Jesus." Underlying this quest is the acknowledgment that the Gospels, while grounded in history, also contain embellishment and later commentary. The task of the investigator is to sift through the biblical materials and determine which teachings or events actually occurred and recover a portrait of the actual person of Jesus of Nazareth. While certainly filled with theological peril—such as excluding those elements of the Gospels that do not agree with our preconceived ideas about Jesus—it is nonetheless a logical outgrowth of the working assumption that the Gospels are not to be read at every turn as literal, biographical accounts of Jesus' life. This recovery mission, though, is not without immense theological benefit. The historical Jesus will later function as the criterion of all Christian claims. As Küng writes elsewhere, *"The source, standard and criterion of Christian faith is the living Jesus of history."*[6] Küng's conclusions regarding "the real Christ" will, therefore, impact subsequent theological and exegetical (that is, biblical interpretations) decisions.

The opening questions for a critical historical investigation of any historical person would be, "What are our sources? How reliable are they?" Küng's starting point is that the Gospels are "committed testimonies." He writes,

> They are therefore *committed testimonies of faith meant to commit their readers:* documents not by non-participants but by convinced believers wanting to appeal for faith in Jesus Christ and which therefore take the form of an interpretation or even of a profession of faith.[7]

This definition does not deny the historical accuracy of the Gospels, but neither does it seem to exclude the possibility of historical inaccuracy. Küng poses the next logical question clearly and succinctly: "But the question arises quite seriously at least for our historical consciousness: how much in these Gospels is an account of what really happened and how much is interpretation?"[8] The parameters of the investigations have now been set. Attention will be focused primarily on the Gospels. We will bring to bear on the Gospels all the tools of modern scholarship (that is, the historical-critical method). We will establish the most reliable wording of a text, employ literary analysis to determine the original form of the stories, engage in comparative studies of other texts from the same time period, and so on, to arrive at the most probable reconstruction of "what really happened." In terms of our ability to determine "what really happened," the news is either pretty good or pretty bad, depending on your perspective. Küng claims, "If we examine the state of the New Testament sources without prejudice, we shall describe the *Jesus tradition* historically as *relatively reliable.*"[9] For those who believe in the literal truth of each and every gospel story, Küng is claiming far too little. For, Küng, however, "relative reliability" is a cause for much confidence. In fact, he contends, "Because of the work of so many generations of exegetes and the results of the historical-critical method, we are able today to know better than perhaps any former generation of Christians— except the first—the true, original Jesus of history."[10]

Küng's Treatment of the Resurrection in On Being a Christian

We now examine Küng's treatment of the resurrection of Jesus (Section V of *OBC*, "The New Life"). Küng begins by identifying four difficulties, surmountable difficulties to be sure, but difficulties nonetheless:

> 1. What is true of the Gospels as a whole is particularly true of the Easter stories: they are *not unbiased reports* by disinterested observers but dispositions in favor of Jesus submitted in faith by supremely interested and committed persons.[11]

The sources from which we are working are not neutral third-party accounts. However, more positively stated, the resurrection is the most logical answer to the historical question of Christian origins. Küng poses the rhetorical questions, *"How did this condemned heretical teacher become Israel's Messiah, the Christ?" "Where did they get their strength from: these men who came forward as his apostles so soon after such a breakdown, the complete failure of his plans; who spared no efforts, feared neither adversity nor death, in order to spread this 'good' news among men, even to the outposts of the Empire?"*[12] The answer, avers Küng, is the resurrection.

> 2. We tried to understand the numerous miracle stories of the New Testament without assuming a *"supernaturalist" intervention—which cannot be proven—*in the laws of nature. It would therefore seem like a dubious retrogression to discredited ideas if we were now suddenly to postulate such a supernatural "intervention" for the miracle of the resurrection: this would contradict all scientific thinking as well as all ordinary convictions and experiences.[13]

Here Küng argues a more controversial line. Earlier in *On Being a Christian*, he tackled the question of the historicity of the miracle stories. "Miracle, 'dearest child of faith' according to Goethe, in the age of natural science and technology has become the weakest child of faith. How are we to overcome the tension which exists between the scientific understanding of the world and belief in miracles, between rational-technical world organization and the experience of miracles?"[14] Küng's final answer is probably more skeptical than many theologians or biblical scholars feel is necessary. While he admits that "miracles stories as a whole (not each individual story) belong in fact to the oldest elements of the Gospel tradition,"[15] he also believes that they are "simply unsophisticated popular narratives which are meant to call forth admiring belief."[16] Küng's central contention regarding the miracle accounts, however, is that, "people then did not think in terms of natural science and therefore did not regard miracles as a breach of the laws of nature or as a break in the otherwise uninterrupted causal sequence."[17] Küng believes that there is a historical core to the reports of Jesus curing people of various illnesses or performing exorcisms. Küng would, however, also add two points: (1) The miracle stories were embellished by the gospel writers, and (2) the miracles were not ends in themselves, but rather served as confirmations of the truth of Jesus' teachings.

3. There is *no direct evidence* of a resurrection.[18]

The New Testament does not report the resurrection as it happened. Rather, it summons us to trust that the proclamations of it having happened are true.

4. A close analysis of the Easter accounts reveals insuperable *discrepancies and inconsistencies*.[19]

The gospel stories do not agree on the precise details of who reached the tomb first, to whom Jesus first appeared, the number of angels, the places and dates of Jesus' post-resurrection appearances, and so on. Küng does not regard this as a liability; in fact, these discrepancies reflect a sense within the early church that the details of the resurrection are secondary to its significance. We will turn to Küng's own statement of the significance of the resurrection, but first he offers three clarifications.

First, he prefers the biblical language of "being raised by the Father" rather than Jesus "rising." "Throughout the New Testament," insists Küng, "resurrection is understood, not simply as Jesus' deed, but in the sense of raising as a work of the Father."[20]

Second, for Küng, the resurrection is not, strictly speaking, a historical event. He writes,

> Since according to the New Testament faith the raising is an act of God within God's dimensions, it can *not* be a *historical* event in the strict sense: it is not an event which can be verified by historical science with the aid of historical methods. For the raising of Jesus is not a miracle violating the laws of nature, verifiable within the present world, not a supernatural intervention which can be located and dated in space and time. There was nothing to photograph or to record.[21]

This claim may be in tension with Küng's earlier argument that the resurrection offers the most plausible explanation for the apostles' ardent desire to preach the gospel to all corners of the world. Küng's interest, however, seems to be focused elsewhere. Küng, it appears, wishes to remove his treatment of the resurrection from his earlier comments regarding miracles. If the resurrection is one miracle alongside other miracles, the same criticism that he voiced regarding miracles would apply to the historicity of the resurrection. Küng, therefore, speaks of the resurrection as a *real* event, but not a *historical* event. The resurrection is "beyond the bounds of history," "involves a completely new mode of existence in God's wholly different mode of existence," and as such, "is completely *intangible* and *unimaginable*."[22] Küng insists that the resurrection presents us with an offer of faith, not an object of historical knowledge.

Third, Küng argues that faith in the resurrection should not be seen as necessarily an endorsement of the belief in a bodily resurrection. Was Jesus raised bodily from the dead? Küng answers,

> Yes and no, if I may recall a personal conversation with Rudolf Bultmann. No, if "body" simply means the physiologically identical body. Yes, if "body" means in the sense of the New Testament *soma* the identical personal reality, the *same self* with its whole history.[23]

Christ's resurrection is, in other words, a transformation of Christ, a continuation of Christ himself in a new mode of existence. It is not merely that Christ's cause continues after his death: Christ himself lives.

The Significance of the Resurrection

We have now reached the critical point in Küng's discussion. What, then, is the significance of the Christ's resurrection?

> The message with all its difficulties, its time-bound concrete expressions and amplifications, situational expansions, elaborations and shifts of emphasis is basically concerned with something simple. And—despite all discrepancies and inconsistencies of the different traditions in regard to place and time, persons and the sequence of events—the different primitive Christian witnesses, Peter, Paul, and James, the letters, the Gospels and Acts, are agreed that the *Crucified lives forever with God, as obligation and hope for us.*[24]

The first half of that declaration is an acknowledgment of, and engagement with, the idea that the Gospels are "committed testimonies." Included, however, is a tacit indication that all lines of critical inquiry will arrive at one central belief. That belief, simply stated in the second half, concerns the present existence of both Christ and his followers. First, "the Crucified lives forever with God." Because this new life is new life in God, we are not to think of the resurrection as a return to an earthly existence (for example, Lazarus) nor as a miraculous event occurring within the confines of time and space. More cryptically phrased, *"Resurrection means dying into God."*[25] Second, the Christian life involves obligation and hope. Christianity is a resurrection faith. Not only do Christians believe that Christ was raised from the dead, they also believe that their lives should give testimony to that pivotal event in history. Commenting on Küng's work, Alrah Pitchers notes,

> To be a Christian today involves commitment to the resurrected Christ....Küng then underscores his point, main-

taining that to be a follower of Jesus today is to walk in the light of his resurrection. It is the resurrection that becomes one's strength through life, so persons are called by Jesus to follow him through life and death into the resurrection of God, by faithfully walking in one's Christian vocation.

Küng follows with some practical suggestions for Christians today. He says that since the resurrection was *for us* Christians live with hope as an obligation. In accepting the cause of Christ, which is one's salvation or well-being, means *"initiation into the discipleship of the One who binds me absolutely to follow my path, my own path, in accordance with his guidance."* Moreover, *"resurrection involves a daily struggle against death,"* in that the Christian is obliged to live in the power of the resurrection now.[26]

More specifically, Küng presents the resurrection as a confirmation of Jesus, a vocation for the apostles, and a motivation for believers today.

First, and most important of all, the resurrection is a statement about Jesus. "The resurrection message, that is, reveals the very thing that was not to be expected: that this crucified Jesus, despite everything *was right*. God took the side of the one who had totally committed himself to him, who gave his life for the cause of God and men....He approved of his proclamation, his behavior, his fate."[27] Küng sees in the resurrection a divine approval of the one who was said to be a heretical teacher, false prophet, and blasphemer. "His claim, his faith in God's closeness, his obedience, his freedom, his joy, his whole action and suffering were confirmed. The one forsaken by God was justified by God."[28]

Second, for the disciples, the confirmation of Jesus' message and identity was joined inextricably with the obligation to proclaim Christ and his message to the ends of the earth. Küng writes, "The 'appearances' certainly mean that the resurrection, the risen Christ are made known. But that is not all. For Paul and similarly for the apostles appearance and vocation, encounter and mission obviously go together."[29] The appearance stories are similar to Old Testament accounts of the prophetic callings. They are neither dreams nor hallucinations, but divine summonses that call for a faithful response. To this point, I believe, Küng's discussion of the effect of the resurrection on the disciples is fairly traditional. However, the question arises: On what is this faith based? What evidence, apart from the appearances, could lend support to the disciples' conviction that Christ was indeed raised from the dead? The traditional answer is, The empty tomb.

Küng regards the empty tomb story as "a legendary development"[30] rather than as an article of faith. While he acknowledges that there are "a number of influential exegetes even today who hold that the empty tomb is historically probable," Küng believes that "there should be agreement on the fact that the empty tomb alone even in the light of the stories *cannot provide any proof of the resurrection* or justify any hope of the resurrection."[31] In the earliest stratum of New Testament teachings, claims Küng, there is no mention of the empty tomb. "It is odd that the oldest testimony of the resurrection, reproduced in the first epistle to the Corinthians, says nothing about an empty tomb and does not mention the women among the witnesses, perhaps because their testimony was not accepted in law anyway."[32] Furthermore, an empty tomb does not prove the reality of the resurrection. The sight of an empty tomb could provoke any number of emotional responses (for example, fear or joy) or lead to any number of conclusions (for example, that the body was stolen). Küng concludes, therefore, that, *"Faith in the risen Christ therefore is independent of the empty tomb. The empty tomb is not a condition, but at best an illustration, of the Easter event."*[33]

Third, the resurrection should motivate Christians today, not only religiously, but politically as well. In faith, we carry on Christ's message because in faith we believe that the resurrection is God's approval of his proclamation. "The resurrection faith is not science or ideology, but an attitude of trust and hope in the light of the risen, crucified Jesus: an attitude which has to find expression in all personal and also socio-political decisions and which can be sustained throughout all doubts and despair."[34] Resurrection faith is an active faith.

The Christian concept of truth is not—like the Greek—contemplative-theoretical, but operative-practical. It is a truth which is not merely to be sought and found, but to be pursued, made true, verified and tested in truthfulness. A truth which aims at practice, which calls to the way, which bestows and makes possible a new life.[35]

This is the new life to which Christians are called. This is the new life that Christians offer the world. This is the new life that Christians believe will be revealed in its fullness at the end of time.

Critique of Küng's Treatment of Christology and the Resurrection in On Being a Christian

In a very perceptive review of *On Being a Christian*, Peter Chirico, S.S., identifies four propositions as fundamental to Küng's christology:

1. *The starting point for Christology is the real earthly Christ.*
2. *This real Christ can be partially uncovered with reasonable certitude by modern Scripture scholars. They cannot give us a chronological biography, but they can furnish us with the drives, patterns, and values which characterized the earthly Christ and which are normative for us.*
3. *A distinction must be made between the historical account of Jesus' life and subsequent interpretations. Such interpretations, whether they appear in the post-NT Church or even in the NT itself, can never have the normative value of the account of Christ's earthly existence. In fact, they have validity only insofar as they express in another context and in other thought patterns the enduring meaning of Christ's earthly life.*
4. *The Resurrection is Christ's reception into a new and glorified life by the Father. The basic function of the Resurrection is to attest that the cause of Christ, the pattern of his life, truly did manifest in its totality the work of God.*[36]

We follow Chirico's lead and examine each of these propositions and explore in part the series of arguments and counterarguments that each proposition prompts. I pair the first two propositions in a discussion of Küng's christology; the third and fourth propositions are linked in a review of Küng's treatment of the resurrection.

The first proposition in many respects is the basis for the three that follow. The "earthly Christ," as Chirico puts it, or "the historical Jesus," as others have phrased it, is the object of our inquiry. The actual Jesus of Nazareth, however, is not to be equated with the gospel portrait of Jesus, since the Gospels themselves are "committed testimonies" and contain elaboration and embellishment. Therefore, the starting point must be discovered *within* the Gospels. Various criticisms could be raised here. Those who regard the Gospels as literal, historical accounts of Jesus' life would obviously object. Even those who would concede that the Gospels contain embellishments might argue that the entire Bible is an incontestable source of revelation, that is, we cannot pick and choose which stories to believe or not believe, because all parts of the Bible are divinely inspired. For those who believe along with Küng that such an inquiry is warranted, we move to the second proposition.

If the proper starting point is the historical Jesus, then the next logical step is to offer some estimate of the probability of undercovering him. Do the sources (that is, the Gospels) contain a bedrock of history? Do we possess the necessary tools to uncover such a bedrock of historical fact?

As Chirico has highlighted in the second proposition, Küng would respond affirmatively to both questions. The Gospels do contain a core of highly probable sayings and actions of Jesus. This can be recovered, continues Küng, by a careful application of the various techniques offered by modern historical criticism. Küng reconstructs Jesus along both negative and positive lines. Jesus was not a priest, a theologian, a sympathizer with the conservative ruling class, a monk, a rigid legalist, or a violent revolutionary. Küng insists that

> we cannot make Jesus a guerrilla fighter, a rebel, a polit-
> ical agitator and revolutionary or turn his message of
> God's kingdom into a program of politico-social action,
> unless we distort and reinterpret all Gospels accounts,
> make a completely one-sided choice of the sources, irre-
> sponsibly and arbitrarily work with isolated texts—

whether Jesus' own sayings or community creations—
and largely ignore Jesus' message as a whole: in a word,
we would use the novelist's imagination instead of adopt-
ing a historical-critical method.[37]

Positively stated, *"Jesus' cause is the cause of God in the world*....He
speaks of this cause as the approaching kingdom of God *(malkut
Yahweh)"*[38] That the kingdom of God is the central concept of Jesus'
preaching is widely accepted by biblical scholars, but there is a range
of interpretation about what Jesus meant by it. For Küng,

> *It will be a kingdom where, in accordance with Jesus'
> prayer, God's name is truly hallowed, his will is done on
> earth, men will have everything in abundance, all sin will
> be forgiven and all evil overcome.*
>
> *It will be a kingdom where, in accordance with Jesus'
> promises, the poor, the hungry, those who weep and those
> who are downtrodden will finally come into their own;
> where pain, suffering and death will have an end.*
>
> *It will be a kingdom that cannot be described, but only
> made known in metaphors: as the new covenant, the seed
> springing up, the ripe harvest, the great banquet, the royal
> feast.*
>
> *It will therefore be a kingdom—wholly as the prophets
> foretold—of absolute righteousness, of unsurpassable free-
> dom, of dauntless love, of universal reconciliation, of ever-
> lasting peace. In this sense therefore it will be the time of
> salvation, of fulfillment, of consummation, of God's pres-
> ence: the absolute future.*[39]

Küng's reconstruction of the historical Jesus involves countless judgment calls, any of which, of course, could be challenged. But he implies
that while a serious, fair-minded application of the historical-critical
method to the Gospels will allow for a range of interpretations about
Jesus, it also excludes a good number of claims about him as well.

Some argue that Küng claims too much knowledge of the historical Jesus, others that he claims too little. Clark M. Williamson
argues the former. He writes,

Do Küng's claims about the historical Jesus go beyond what we can responsibly claim to know? Obviously. Küng knows full well the problem with the Gospels as sources of historical knowledge, yet on the basis of them he regularly contends that Jesus experienced God in a certain, immediate way, that he always did so, that he experienced himself as God's son and advocate, as God's final and unsurpassable prophet, that Jesus' whole life was totally dedicated to God, that he lived entirely in virtue of the One whom he called "abba," that he was always faithful to God's will, and that he "foresaw" the temple's destruction and his own death. Küng never tells us how he knows these things, because he cannot. He merely asserts them and, on that basis, attempts to "back up" his Christology.[40]

Others find Küng's treatment of Jesus overly general. Robert Krieg believes,

Küng's consideration of Jesus' actions has not resulted in an individuating account of Jesus. It has highlighted his governing objective in life: to care for other others, especially the dispossessed. But it has not revealed how Jesus' service and presence are quite distinctive. Because Küng does not recount specific things that Jesus did, Jesus' commitment remains disembodied. It is an intention that many people could have, and indeed have had.[41]

This diversity of opinion about what we can reasonably posit as true about the historical Jesus becomes a problem as we move to Chirico's third proposition: the historical Jesus is the norm by which later interpretations—both within the New Testament itself and in church tradition—are measured. Here we turn our attention specifically to the resurrection.

Küng believes that the historical Jesus should be the norm by which all christological statements are measured. The corollary to that principle, however, is that theological priority belongs to the earliest stratum of tradition. Regarding the implications of that position, Chirico writes,

This distinction between the reality grasped by the original witnesses and subsequent interpretation is crucial for Küng. The overriding importance he gives to the original witness of the reality of the earthly Christ accounts in large measure for the misgivings with which he looks upon any postresurrectional interpretation which goes beyond what was manifested to the witnesses of the earthly life....Even the shift in the later NT books from a stress on the concrete aspects of the earthly Christ to a stress on the incarnation of God's Son in John and in the deutero-Pauline writings is regarded with reserve.[42]

It is for this reason that Küng attaches no importance to the empty tomb tradition.

Küng notes, "It is odd that the oldest testimony of the resurrection, reproduced in the first epistle to the Corinthians, says nothing about an empty tomb....*Paul*, like the rest of the New Testament writers outside the four Gospels, never mentions either the witnesses of the empty tomb or the empty tomb itself."[43] But is the earliest interpretation always the truest or the most preferred interpretation? Manuel Miguens, O.F.M., writes,

Küng rejects Paul and John as sources for an understanding of Jesus because, he contends, in them we have to deal with "interpretations" of the historical Jesus. No one would deny that both Paul and John go beyond the gospel episodes and disclose the meaning/interpretation of those episodes. But a question is in order here: does not Küng offer his own interpretation of those gospel episodes that he chooses from Mark (while dismissing others) in order to present his image of Jesus? Does a critical scholar have any less right and freedom to reject Küng's interpretation than the latter has to reject Paul's and John's?[44]

In other words, is it possible that a later expression captures the fullness of truth more completely than an earlier formulation?

Chirico's fourth proposition is *"The Resurrection is Christ's reception into a new and glorified life by the Father. The basic function of the*

Resurrection is to attest that the cause of Christ, the pattern of his life, truly did manifest in its totality the work of God."[45] Küng emphasizes that the resurrection was a vindication of Jesus. Jesus' proclamation about God's cause—the kingdom of God—was right. Küng also argues that the resurrection was real, but not historical. He writes,

> Since according to the New Testament faith the raising is an act of God within God's dimensions, it can not be a historical event in the strict sense: it is not an event which can be verified by historical science with the aid of historical methods. For the raising of Jesus is not a miracle violating the laws of nature, verifiable within the present world, not a supernatural intervention which can be located and dated in space and time.[46]

Here we meet head-on a critical theological question: What is the proper relationship between historical inquiry and Christian faith? Küng argues that the resurrection was not a "supernatural intervention" within time and space. We have seen earlier his hesitation to speak of miraculous events. In fact, at certain points, Küng appears hostile to the very idea. "The time must really be gone forever when quite a few thought they could demonstrate the possibility of Christ's walking on the lake."[47] The late scripture scholar Raymond Brown noted in his review of *On Being a Christian*, "But when Küng comes to miracles and to the virginal conception and bodily Resurrection, he denies on principle all 'supernatural intervention in the laws of nature.' For many of us, even if we do not care for the 'laws of nature' approach, this is not sound exegesis, but represents the tyranny of philosophical presupposition."[48] Battista Mondin uses similar language when he asks, "What then are the fundamental principles, the supreme postulates upon which Küng builds his interpretation of the figure of Christ?"[49] Mondin believes there are three, but the first concerns us here. It is "that rationalistic postulate according to which what is true is only that which can be scientifically verified."[50] Should Christians read the Bible through the lens of what can be scientifically verified? Are the biblical stories in a different class than "ordinary events"? Should we judge the historicity of miracle stories by the standards of modern science? A related questions is, Should church doctrine control biblical interpretation or should church doctrine be revised by biblical interpretation? In Mark 9:1, Jesus says, "Amen, I say to you, there are some standing here who will not taste death until they see that the kingdom of God has come in power." Are we, from the outset, to exclude any interpretation that suggests Jesus was in error here?

Kenan B. Osborne, O.F.M., claims that "one could almost say that in our own century [the twentieth century] the major christological subject of study by theologians has been the resurrection of Jesus."[51] Why the high level of interest in the resurrection by theologians? Among other reasons, the resurrection challenges our modern scientific mindset, while at the same time, it supports all that we believe as Christians. Stanley J. Grenz and Roger E. Olson conclude their examination of Küng's theology by drawing attention to this tension in his work:

> Catherine LaCugna correctly observed that a distinction must be made between Küng's theoretical methodology (his stated intentions) and his applied methodology (what he actually does). After a rigorous investigation of the former she concluded, "Formally speaking… in Küng's theoretical theological methodology there appears to be a lively, if not difficult, tension between faith and history, in which the historical strand conditions but does not determine the strand of faith." In other words, Küng cannot make up his mind which he will choose as the ultimate norm for theological truth, should a conflict arise between critical historical reason and clear biblical teachings about Jesus Christ.[52]

Students of theology face a similar question: Should Christians unflinchingly assert the historicity of the resurrection or qualify in some way what is meant by the term "resurrection" to bring it into greater harmony with modern science?

For Christians, the resurrection is the confirmation of the truth of all that Jesus proclaimed during his ministry. This confirmation of Christ, however, soon gives way to a commission to the disciples: to carry on the ministry begun by Jesus. At Pentecost, the risen Lord commands and empowers his disciples to carry the good news to the

ends of the earth. It is to that beginning of the Christian Church that
we now turn our attention.

Notes

1. For the biographical information, I am borrowing from Leonard
    Swidler, "Hans Küng," in *A Handbook of Christian Theologians*,
    enlarged ed., ed. Martin E. Marty and Dean G. Peerman (Nashville:
    Abingdon Press, 1984); "Hans Küng" by Werner J. Jeanrond in *The
    Modern Theologians*, 2nd ed., ed. David F. Ford (Malden: Blackwell,
    1997); and Stanley J. Grenz and Roger E. Olson, *Twentieth-Century
    Theology* (Downers Grove: InterVarsity Press, 1992).
2. Swidler, "Hans Küng," pp. 720–21.
3. See Ibid., p. 725.
4. Hans Küng, *On Being a Christian* (Garden City: Doubleday, 1976), p.
    163. Hereafter *OBC*.
5. Ibid., p. 20.
6. Hans Küng and Edward Schillebeeckx, et al., *Consensus in Theology?*
    (Philadelphia: Westminster Press, 1980), p. 6.
7. *OBC*, pp. 153–54.
8. Ibid., p. 154.
9. Ibid., p. 157.
10. Ibid., pp. 160–61.
11. Ibid., p. 346.
12. Ibid., pp. 344, 344–45.
13. Ibid., p. 346.
14. Ibid., p. 226.
15. Ibid., pp. 227–28.
16. Ibid., p. 229.
17. Ibid., p. 228.
18. Ibid., p. 347.
19. Ibid.
20. Ibid., p. 349.
21. Ibid.
22. Ibid., p. 350.
23. Ibid., p. 351.
24. Ibid., p. 356.
25. Ibid., p. 359.
26. Alrah Pitchers, *The Christology of Hans Küng* (Berlin: Peter Lang,
    1997), pp. 150–51.
27. *OBC*, p. 382.

28. Ibid.
29. Ibid., p. 376.
30. Ibid., p. 365.
31. Ibid.
32. Ibid., p. 363.
33. Ibid., p. 366.
34. Ibid., p. 379.
35. Ibid., p. 410.
36. Peter Chirico, S.S., "Hans Küng's Christology: An Evaluation of Its Presuppositions," *Theological Studies* (1979), pp. 257, 258, 259, and 268.
37. *OBC*, p. 187.
38. Ibid., p. 214.
39. Ibid., p. 215.
40. Clark M. Williamson, "The Christology of Hans Küng: A Critical Analysis," *Journal of Ecumenical Studies* 30 (1993), p. 384.
41. Robert Krieg, "Is Jesus the Focus of Küng's Christology?" *Irish Theological Quarterly* 50 (1983/84), p. 255.
42. Chirico, "Hans Küng's Christology," p. 260.
43. *OBC*, p. 363.
44. Manuel Miguens, O.F.M., "Hans Küng and Catholic Teaching," in *The Teaching Church in Our Time*, ed. George A. Kelly (Boston: St. Paul Editions, 1978), p. 172.
45. Chirico, "Hans Küng's Christology," p. 268.
46. *OBC*, p. 349.
47. Ibid., p. 227.
48. Raymond E. Brown, "'On Being a Christian' and Scripture," *America* (November 20, 1976), p. 344.
49. Battista Mondin, "The Christological Experiment of Hans Küng," *Biblical Theology Bulletin* 7(2), 1977, p. 86.
50. Ibid.
51. Kenan B. Osborne, O.F.M., *The Resurrection of Jesus* (Mahwah: Paulist, 1997), p. 12.
52. Stanley J. Grenz and Roger E. Olson, *Twentieth-Century Theology* (Downers Grove: InterVarsity Press, 1992), pp. 269–70.

Discussion Questions

1. Do you agree with Küng that the Gospels are "committed testimonies"? If so, what effect does this have on their historical accuracy?
2. Do you believe that miracles occurred in biblical times? Do you believe that miracles occur today? Why? Why not?

3. What is the significance of the resurrection? Why is that meaning most important? What are some other important meanings of the resurrection?
4. Do you believe there was an empty tomb? Why? Why not?
5. What does Küng mean when he says that the resurrection is a real event, but not a historical event? Do you agree or disagree with Küng?
6. Is it reasonable to believe that the earliest statements about the historical Jesus were the most accurate and should be the standard by which all other statements should be measured?
7. Should the standards of modern science affect how we read the Bible? If so, does that diminish the sacredness of the Bible? If not, are we being asked to ignore what we accept as true in all other areas of our life?

Suggested Readings

The leading contemporary Catholic scholar on the resurrection is Gerald O'Collins, S.J. Two of his many helpful works are *The Resurrection of Jesus Christ* (Valley Forge: Judson Press, 1973), and *Jesus Risen* (Mahwah: Paulist Press, 1987). See also *Resurrection: New Testament Witness and Contemporary Reflection* (Garden City: Doubleday, 1984) by Pheme Perkins. See John P. Galvin, "The Resurrection in Contemporary Catholic Systematics," in *The Heythrop Journal* 20 (1979), pp. 123–45; and Bernard P. Prusak, "Bodily Resurrection in Catholic Perspectives," in *Theological Studies* 61(1), 2000, pp. 64–105, esp. pp. 89–92 for a discussion of Küng's views.

For overviews of Küng's theology, see Hermann Haring, *Hans Küng: Breaking Through* (New York: Continuum, 1998); *Hans Küng: New Horizons For Faith and Thought*, ed. Karl-Josef Kuschel and Hermann Haring (New York: Continuum, 1993); and *A Passion for Truth: Hans Küng and His Theology* (New York: Crossroad, 1981) by Robert Nowell.

For Küng's treatment of the resurrection, see chap. 4 of Alrah Pitchers, *The Christology of Hans Küng* (Berlin: Peter Lang, 1997). I also benefited from the dissertation of William F. Buggert, O. Carm., *The Christologies of Hans Küng and Karl Rahner: A Comparison and Evaluation of Their Mutual Compatibility* (Washington, DC: The Catholic University of America, 1978).

8

Pentecost and Yves Congar's
The Mystery of the Church

Christ's resurrection closes one chapter in the Christian narrative and opens another. In the first chapter of Acts of the Apostles, Christ ascends to heaven after telling the apostles to remain in Jerusalem to await the fulfillment of "the promise of the Father. 'This,' he said, 'is what you have heard from me; for John baptized with water, but you will be baptized with the holy Spirit not many days from now'" (1:4–5). This promise is fulfilled in dramatic fashion at Pentecost. Originally a harvest festival in Judaism, Pentecost becomes in Christian thought the occasion on which the apostles were given the gift of the Holy Spirit, empowering them to carry the gospel to the ends of the earth. A theology of Pentecost, therefore, will consider the role of the Holy Spirit, the nature and purpose of the church, and the missionary outreach to the world. These very themes were treated extensively in the writings of one of the most influential Roman Catholic theologians of the twentieth century, Yves Congar. Congar's pioneering work also impacted the deliberations at the Second Vatican Council, the most important event in the life of the Roman Catholic Church in the twentieth century.

Congar's Biography

Born in 1904 in the French city of Sedan, Yves Congar entered the novitiate of the Dominican order (the Order of Preachers, O.P.) in 1925. The French Dominican house of study, known as Le Saulchoir, was at that time located in Belgium—the French government had expelled the Dominicans at the turn of the century. At Le Saulchoir, Congar studied under Marie-Dominique Chenu, O.P., whose historical approach, ecumenical interests, and generosity of spirit were to leave a lasting impression on the young Dominican novice. Later, as colleagues at Le Saulchoir, they would develop a theological method that called for a "return to the sources" of scripture, early Christian thought, and the work of the great Dominican thinker Thomas Aquinas. Congar also shared with Chenu a deep, abiding interest in the ecumenical movement.

Ecumenism is the attempt to reunify the Christian churches. Congar's tireless commitment to that cause began early in his career and never wavered. Congar writes,

> I was a student at the Saulchoir, ordained the feast of St. James July 25, 1930. To prepare myself for ordination, I made a special study both of John's Gospel and Thomas Aquinas' commentary on it. I was completely overwhelmed, deeply moved, by chapter 17, sometimes called the priestly prayer, but which I prefer to call Jesus' apostolic prayer on Christian unity: "That they may be one as we are one." My ecumenical vocation can be directly traced to this study of 1929.[1]

Congar was a Catholic pioneer in that field. Thomas F. O'Meara, O.P., reports, "He spoke at countless meetings, large and small, on the ecumenical movement and he preached a moving series of sermons on ecumenism at Sacre-Coeur in Paris in January 1936. That week was seen as a watershed for Catholic involvement in the ecumenical movement, which until then was a Protestant movement."[2] Congar's first book, published in 1937, was a groundbreaking study in ecumenical theology entitled *Divided Christendom*. At the same time, the first signs of a form of sclerosis that would later require him to use a wheelchair began to appear.[3] At the outbreak of World War II, Congar served as a military chaplain and spent five years as a prisoner of war. During his confinement, he learned that a work by Chenu had been placed on the church's official Index of Forbidden Books. "While in prison," writes Jean-Pierre Jossua, O.P.,

> he had learned with consternation of the condemnation of Father Chenu's little book *The Saulchoir, A School of Theology*, and of its author's disgrace. Twenty-three years

later, reflecting on this episode, he was to write: "Even today, after having questioned and sought, having learned many details, I come up against so many contradictions and incomprehensible details, that I can see in this affair only an error or an unfortunate step that cannot be justified."[4]

The Chenu censure was also an ominous foreshadowing of events in Congar's own career.

At the end of the war, Congar returned to Le Saulchoir and soon produced two important works: *True and False Reform in the Church* (1950) and *Lay People in the Church* in 1953. The former work deals with the questions of reforming the church without dividing it—a "reform not *of* the church," writes Congar, "but *in* the church, since it remained within the church."[5] Jossua notes that the importance of the latter work lies in its influence on "the theology of the laity, on the relations between the Church and the world, on the Christian priesthood (especially the baptismal priesthood and the spiritual sacrifice of the baptized), on the prophetic function of the laity, and on their holiness in the world."[6] Church authorities in Rome, however, were growing increasingly suspicious of the "New Theology," as it was then called, and in 1954 Congar "was summoned to the provincial headquarters of the Dominican order in Paris for a dramatic meeting. The head of the Dominicans had driven rapidly to Paris from Rome: under threats from the Vatican that the Order in France would be dissolved. Fr. Suarez removed the French Dominicans' major superiors, the head of their publishing house, and forbade Congar, Chenu and others to teach."[7] Looking back on that period in his life, Congar writes, "As far as I was concerned in this regard, from the beginning of 1947 to the end of 1956 I was to know nothing but an uninterrupted sequence of denunciations, warnings, restrictive or discriminatory measures, suspicious interventions."[8] In an article expressing his appreciation for the life and work of Congar, Avery Dulles, S.J., discusses the church's ill treatment of the French scholar.

> Like several other precursors of Vatican II, Congar fell under suspicion during the 1950's. He was suspended from teaching and at one point exiled from his native France. Some of his books were forced out of print and prevented

from being reprinted or translated. Convinced that "the cross is the condition for every holy work," Congar took these setbacks without complaint. He was a deeply spiritual man, content to wait for the time to be ripe. Those who labor for the reform and renewal of the church, he said, must cultivate the virtue of "active patience."[9]

Congar's "active patience" and ardent desire for church renewal were to be realized during the papacy of Pope John XXIII.

When reading Congar's work *True and False Reform in the Church,* Angelo Roncalli was reported to have asked, "A reform of the Church—is it possible?"[10] It was the very same Roncalli who was elected pope in 1958 and took the name John XXIII. Within six months Pope John XXIII stunned the church by calling an ecumenical council—a meeting of all the bishops of the world. In 1960 John XXIII appointed Congar to the Theological Commission charged with preparing documents for the consideration of the bishops. Congar also served as a *peritus,* or expert, during the council. Congar's tireless efforts resulted in the incorporation of many of his ideas in the official documents of Vatican II. Soon after the close of Vatican II, Congar's health declined. "In 1967," notes Victor Dunne,

> he suffered a rather severe relapse into a form of sclerosis which had afflicted him, on and off, from 1936. From then on he was largely confined to a wheelchair and his travelling and lecturing were increasingly restricted. In spite of this disease and even when he was confined to bed, a steady stream of writings issued from his pen until his condition deteriorated so much that he was unable to continue the work of theological research and writing.[11]

He produced a three-volume work entitled *I Believe in the Holy Spirit* in 1979–1980. He continued to publish throughout the 1980s. As a final tribute to the man and his work, Pope John Paul II named Congar a cardinal in 1994. He died June 22, 1995, at the age of ninety-one.

The Mystery of the Church

In the opening essay in *The Mystery of the Church,* Congar offers an extended reflection on the meaning of Pentecost. As A. V. Littledale notes, it "purports to be a discourse delivered to a group of pilgrims as they made their dusty way towards Chartres, where they were due to arrive for the feast of Pentecost."[12] Congar himself tells us that the subject of the meditation is "the *fact* of Pentecost and all that it means for ever and for the faith and life of the Church."[13] The essay falls into three sections: the first discusses the place of Pentecost in God's plan for the world; the second identifies the gifts bestowed on the church by God at Pentecost; and the third locates the missionary work of the church in the Pentecost event. This essay, entitled simply "The Church and Pentecost," serves as the foundational piece in our investigation of Congar's ecclesiology—the branch of theology concerned with the church (literally, "the study of the church").

In the first section of his essay, Congar situates Pentecost in the overall plan of God. This plan of God is revealed in the narrative of the Bible, beginning with creation, centered in Christ, and consummated at the end of time. This pattern reflects the trinitarian nature of God. Congar writes,

> God's plan in our regard, as made known by Revelation—what, following our Fathers, we might call the "Economy" (of salvation) follows, so to speak, the structure of God himself. It is fundamentally the plan of the Creed, which is Trinitarian, and which follows at one and the same time of the "procession" of the divine Persons and the order of God's work, for the three great decisive moments of this are appropriated to these Persons. The three of which we speak are the creation, the redemption, and the work of sanctification or the communication of the divine life.[14]

In the unfolding of this divine plan, Pentecost is a pivotal moment. "All that we find in the Gospels and the writings of the apostles cries out that God's purposes and his gifts do not stop short at the incarnation....In short, *there is a dynamism coming from God for men through Christ.*"[15] This dynamic power of God at work in the world is the Holy Spirit received at Pentecost. "The moving force, the animating principle, of everything Christian, everything holy, since Christ, is the Holy Spirit…who leads us back to the God of holiness, and unites us to him."[16]

In the second section of his essay, Congar elaborates on the Spirit's role in the creation of the church by insisting that "at Pentecost, the Church received, with the Holy Spirit, both its law and its soul."[17] By "law," Congar means more than simply the rules and regulations that govern church life. He notes,

> What is the law? It is the order authoritatively decreed by the head of the community, and giving it its form of life, its rule of collective living; and so it harmonises and adjusts the conduct of individuals to make of them a social unity. It is at once clear that when, as is the case with the Church, we are dealing with a community whose aim is salvation, whose life is that of the spirit, the law is much more than something imposed by external force.[18]

Rather than "something imposed by external force," the law of the church is the internal organization that helps the community achieve its desired spiritual goals. If the church is, as Paul insists, the body of Christ (1 Cor 12), then the law of the church is the coordination of the various organs that creates a state of well-being for the entire body. The law of the church, therefore, is "communion." As Michael Fahey explains,

> The Christian word "communion" is a translation from the Greek term *koinonia* used by Paul to indicate sharing, fellowship, or close association. Paul frequently combines the word communion with the modifier, "by the Holy Spirit." His conviction is that Christians, through the Holy Spirit, enjoy communion with the triune God and are also "in communion" with other baptized Christians. Communion therefore has a vertical dimension (contact with God) and a horizontal dimension (bonding with other Christians).[19]

Just as a human being requires both body and soul to function, the church requires both law and soul. Referring to Augustine, Congar writes, "What the soul is for man's body, he says, the Holy Spirit is for the Body of Christ, which is the Church; and as the Holy Spirit over-shadowed the Virgin Mary to form in her the temporal individual body of Christ, so he was given to the Church at Pentecost to make it into the spiritual, 'communional' Body of the Lord."[20]

Congar's discussion of the law and soul of the body of Christ has two important implications for his understanding of the church. First, the hierarchy and the laity play distinct, yet vital roles in the life of the church. Congar writes,

> The idea of the Church as an organism explains two things so necessary to grasp clearly and to bear in mind together whenever we speak of the Church, particularly when we try to estimate the respective roles of the ordinary faithful and of the Hierarchy. On the one hand, it is the whole Body which is indwelled, animated and in action. On the other, there exist, within the Body, hierarchical functions, which themselves are functions of service (Eph. iv. 16); and those who exercise them are animated and moved by the Spirit for this purpose. All members are living and ani-mated, but each according to what he is and to perform what he is called to do within the body.[21]

Second, Congar recognizes the limits of the depiction of the church as the body of Christ. "In Scripture, the description of the Church as the Body of Christ is completed and, in a sense, corrected by its being also spoken of as the Bride of Christ. The two form one flesh, not by physical fusion—for then the Church would be strictly identical with Christ, impeccable even in its individual members and, like him, wor-thy of adoration—but by a spiritual union."[22] The church, in other words, is comprised of both human and divine elements. As such, the concept of reform in the church is not antithetical to the Catholic understanding of the church as divine in origin. Congar writes, "The bride and the bridegroom are faithful to one another; but, though the latter is divine, the former is yet human. Along with her essential fidelity, divinely guaranteed by that of God himself, she still has the possibility, in each and all of the smaller details of her life, of falling short of the absolute of holiness and truth which is God."[23]

In the third section of the essay, Congar discusses one more consequence of Pentecost: "At Pentecost, the Church set out on its missionary work."[24] Congar emphasizes the point that this mission is universal in scope.

> At the breath of the Spirit, there then occurred, through the dispersion of the apostolic preaching throughout the world, a kind of bursting asunder of Jerusalem. From then on the temple of God would be wherever there were worshippers in spirit and truth, in other words men who, receiving in faith the apostolic message, had become members of the Body of Christ. That is the law of Christian universality.[25]

The significance of Pentecost, therefore, is not merely the interior transformation of the individual brought about by the Spirit. Important as that may be, it is also true that "Pentecost is for the sake of the whole world, to renew the face of the earth."[26] The apostolic mission of the church that began at Pentecost continues to the end of time.

> "The seed is the word of God" (Mt. xiii; Mark iv; Luke 8), and the field is the whole world; not only the small land of Palestine, not only the Roman Empire, traversed in part by St. Paul, but the entire world, the world of all times, the world of today with its problems, its complexities, its immense ramifications in the matter of classes and races and all those new spheres constantly being opened up to the mind with bewildering rapidity.[27]

The dynamism unleashed at Pentecost generates conversion within the heart of the Christian, reform throughout the universal church, and transformation of the wider society.

A Brief Summary of Congar's Views

Congar's essay, "The Church and Pentecost," deals with the nature of the church, the relationship between the hierarchy and the laity, and

the role of the church in the world. Before moving to the impact of
Congar's theology on the bishops at Vatican II, we need to pause to
summarize Congar's views on these important areas in church life and
point to their appearance in some of the other essays in *The Mystery
of the Church*.

Congar's understanding of the nature of the church illustrates
his theological commitment to a "return to the sources." Congar saw
in the ecclesiology of the early twentieth century a continuation of a
trend begun in the aftermath of the Protestant Reformation. In reaction to the challenges of Luther, Calvin, and the other leaders of the
Protestant Reformation, the Roman Catholic Church increasingly
defined itself in legal terms, emphasizing the hierarchical structure of
the church, the authority of the pope and other bishops to define doctrine, and the external conditions to be met for inclusion into the one
true church. While such an understanding of the church provided
great clarity as to the structure, belief, and membership of the
church, it failed to capture the spiritual dimension of church life. In a
1972 piece, Congar reflects on his forty years of ecclesiological
thought. He states that

> the Church was presented around 1930 (the date of my
> own presbyteral ordination) as an organized society consti-
> tuted by the exercise of powers with which pope, bishops
> and priests were invested. Ecclesiology consisted almost
> entirely of a treatise of public law. I coined for this the
> word "hierarchology," which has been taken up often
> enough since. But that kind of thing is impotent in drawing
> men, while Catholic Tradition—in Scripture, the Fathers,
> and the Liturgy—gave us a different notion of Church:
> generous, vital, religious. My aim from that point,
> expressed in the founding of the *Unam Sanctam* collection
> (announced in September, 1935) was to recover for eccle-
> siology the inspiration and resources of an older and
> deeper Tradition....[28]

Congar's essay, "The Idea of the Church in St. Thomas Aquinas,"
which appears as chapter 3 in *The Mystery of the Church*, represents
his effort to retrieve a pre-Reformation Catholic ecclesiology. Congar

finds in Aquinas an ecclesiology permeated with a sense of the presence of Christ active in the church, in which the Holy Spirit produces the faith, hope, and love that lead humans back to their Creator.

Aidan Nichols rightly observes, "There is no one Congarian ecclesiology."[29] Throughout his career, Congar considered numerous images for the church, drawing from them the insights that captured the nature and purpose of the Christian community: body of Christ, communion, society, sacrament, and people of God. One of the most important images in both the church's own official pronouncements and Congar's early work is the concept of the church as the mystical body of Christ. In 1943, Pope Pius XII issued an encyclical (that is, "a formal pastoral letter from the pope [lit., a circular letter] written by, or under the authority of, the pope concerning moral, doctrinal, or disciplinary issues addressed to the universal Church"),[30] entitled *Mystici Corporis Christi*. This image of the church that appears in the letters to the Ephesians and Colossians sees Christ as head of the body that is the church. The image conveys the sense of each Christian's unity with Christ through the church, especially through the sacramental life of the church. It also, however, suggests that the life of Christ continues in the world through the church. In his essay devoted to the mystical body of Christ in *The Mystery of the Church*, Congar writes, "The conformity of our life to that of Christ, which is the substance of the Mystical Body, is not brought about, as we have said, so much by our own effort to reproduce Christ as by the gift of Christ continuing and prolonging himself in mankind."[31] Despite his initial attraction to this understanding of the church, Congar eventually became aware of the limitations of this approach to ecclesiology, especially how it was put to use in *Mystici Corporis Christi*. As Wendell Sanford Dietrich reports,

> In a retrospective remark in 1961, Congar commented further on this encyclical and its ramifications. He candidly acknowledged that theologians of his persuasion came slowly, in the fifties, to abandon the notion of the body of Christ as the exclusive focus for their definition of the church. They made this move precisely because, despite its excellences, the notion of the body of Christ could be exploited as it was in the first sections of *Mystici Corporis*.

It could be used to promote a monarchical notion of the church in which authority descends from the papal "head" to the various members.[32]

Congar's reservations about *Mystici Corporis* reflect his long-standing desire to develop an ecclesiology that respected the distinct yet related roles of both the hierarchy and the laity.

Congar's ongoing reflections on the relationship between the laity and the hierarchy have yielded some of his most enduring and influential theological insights. Timothy I. MacDonald, S.A., believes,

> One of the most significant contributions that Yves Congar had made to Roman Catholic ecclesiology was his theological development of the role of the laity in the church. The importance of this development for ecclesiology is based on Congar's conviction that this theology of the laity is an essential ingredient within a whole ecclesiological system in which the mystery of the church is described in all its dimensions. As Congar states: "At bottom there can only be one sound and sufficient theology of the laity and that is a 'total ecclesiology.'"[33]

A "total ecclesiology" could not reduce the definition of the laity to merely "those not ordained." Rather, the entire body of Christ is animated by the Holy Spirit. As Richard McBrien concludes,

> Thus, the notion of the church as the body of Christ contributed to the widening of active participation in the eucharist and in the church's sacramental life generally. And this active participation, in turn, disclosed the church to itself as an assembly convoked by God without regard for hierarchical status. The whole community worships God, in and through Christ. The whole community is a priestly people. The whole community is a creation of the Holy Spirit.[34]

Congar himself observes, "I have always insisted on the part that laymen may rightfully take in the internal life of the Church insofar as it is a positive, divine institution....Laymen share in the priestly, royal, and prophetic dignity and life which comes to the Church from Christ. One must add: and in its apostolic life too, which turns into a finished work all that precedes."[35] This "lay apostolate" in particular, and the social mission of the church in the world in general, is the final topic that we summarize before we turn our attention to the implementation of Congar's ideas at Vatican II.

Congar's early enthusiasm for the "Catholic Action" movement reflects his eager desire to have the laity play a vital role in the apostolic mission of the church, though Catholic Action itself viewed the laity's involvement as a participation in the apostolic mission *of the hierarchy*. Congar will later argue that all baptized members of the church have a share in the apostolic mission of the church, but certainly his early endorsement of the role of the laity in the church must be regarded as prophetic in terms of Vatican II. In his 1937 essay ,"The Church and Its Unity," which appears as chapter 2 of *The Mystery of the Church*, Congar identifies movements within the church that he believes hold great promise for the future. He notes that Pope Pius XI gave "the communal apostolic movement the form of Catholic Action, that is to say of an apostolate of the laity in their own special surroundings," and praises Catholic Action, claiming that "it has already yielded, particularly in the Young Christian Workers, a splendid harvest of fields won for Christ" and created "a pure, deep and generous interior life."[36] Congar sees a vital role for the laity in the church's apostolic mission to the world, while at the same time preserving a difference in how the hierarchy and the laity carry out that mission.

The Second Vatican Council

Ecumenical councils are momentous occasions in the history of the church. Vatican II was the twenty-first such gathering in the history of the Roman Catholic Church, and only the third since the Protestant Reformation. The two previous ecumenical councils were the Council of Trent (1545–1563), which responded to the theological challenges of the Protestant Reformers, and Vatican I (1869–1870), at which the doctrine of papal infallibility was promulgated. John XXIII felt that the time was ripe for another council, one that would be pastoral in nature. The church needed to address the concerns of the modern world in a way that engaged the thoughts and energies of modern Catholics.

There was a need for an *aggiornamento,* an Italian word meaning an "updating" of the church. It was, in the estimation of Congar, an event in keeping with the spirit of Pentecost. "A Council is also a Pentecostal type of event. John XXIII was not wrong to speak of Vatican II in terms of…'When…they were all together in one place' (Acts 2:1)—and a visit of the Holy Spirit or a kind of new Pentecost."[37]

John XXIII announced his intention to call a council on July 25, 1959. Preparation began immediately. As Richard P. McBrien informs us,

> The preparation for this council was the most extensive in the history of the Church. Ideas for the conciliar agenda were solicited from every bishop, from the head of clerical religious orders (but not orders of religious women), from Catholic universities and theological faculties, as well as from members of the Roman Curia. Over 9,300 proposals were submitted. The material was indexed and distributed to eleven preparatory commissions appointed by Pope John XXIII in June 1960 to prepare draft documents for discussion. These commissions met between November 1960 and June 1962 and produced over seventy documents, or schemata.[38]

"In July 1960," Joseph Komonchak writes, "Congar learned that he had been appointed to the Theological Commission established to prepare texts for consideration by the Second Vatican Council. Rumors that his appointment, and that of Henri de Lubac, had been ordered by Pope John XXIII were not enough to convince him that their presence would be able to affect the largely conservative orientation of the commission."[39] Initially Congar's fears were realized; his criticisms of the schemata had little effect. However, in the first session of Vatican II, the bishops rejected the documents produced by the Theological Commission and called for the creation of new groups that would redraft the texts. The council had taken the direction Congar had hoped, and many of the documents that were finally produced either reflected his influence or came directly from his pen. The beloved John XXIII died on June 3, 1963, and was succeeded by

Cardinal Montini, who took the name Paul VI. He reconvened Vatican II and presided over it until its completion in 1965.

The deliberations that had taken place during four sessions from 1962 to 1965 produced sixteen documents. Of these sixteen, four were constitutions—the most important statements coming out of an ecumenical council. These constitutions have English titles, but they are more commonly known by their Latin titles, which are drawn from the first few words of the work's opening sentence. The four are the "Dogmatic Constitution on the Church" *(Lumen Gentium)*, the "Pastoral Constitution on the Church in the Modern World" *(Gaudium et spes)*, the "Dogmatic Constitution on Divine Revelation" *(Dei verbum)*, and the "Constitution on the Sacred Liturgy" *(Sacrosanctum concilium)*. We focus in our discussion on the nature of the church, the relationship between the hierarchy and the laity in the church, and the role of the church in the world, as expressed in *Lumen Gentium* and *Gaudium et spes*.

Yves Congar's influence can be detected most clearly in *Lumen Gentium (LG)*. First, the very structure of the document reflects Congar's approach: the first four chapters are "The Mystery of the Church" (chapter 1), "The People of God" (chapter 2), "The Church Is Hierarchical" (chapter 3), and "The Laity" (chapter 4). The church is first understood as a mystery, not as an institution or a perfect society. Second, the leading expression for the church is "the People of God." Congar argues that the idea of the people of God,

> in the first place, enables us to express the continuity of the Church with Israel. It at once invites us to consider the Church inserted in a history dominated and defined by God's Plan for man....
>
> The People of God is rediscovering once again that it possesses a messianic character and that it bears the hope of fulfillment of the world in Jesus Christ.
>
> The idea of the People of God, therefore, introduces something dynamic into the concept of the Church. This People possesses life and is advancing toward an end established for it by God. Chosen, established, consecrated by God to be his servant and his witness, the People of God is,

in the world, the sacrament of salvation offered to the world.[40]

Congar has admitted that significant portions of chapter 2, "The People of God," come directly from his hand. "At the Council...I worked on Chapter II of *Lumen gentium* (numbers 9, 13, 16 and 17 are mine, and also parts of number 28 and of chapter I)."[41] Third, by not directly identifying the people of God with the Catholic Church (as, for example, when Pius XII equated the mystical body with the Catholic Church in *Mystici Corporis*), the bishops opened the door for dialogue with other Christian churches (especially the Orthodox). Vatican II endorsed the ecumenical outreach initiated by Congar decades earlier. While the fullness of the sacramental life and doctrinal truth resides in the Catholic Church, argued the bishops, the church of Christ extends beyond the boundaries of the Catholic Church.

The relationship of the laity and the hierarchy takes on a different shape when viewed from the perspective of the church as the people of God. First, there is an emphasis on the unity of all the baptized members of the church. In the words of *Lumen Gentium,* all members of the church share in the priestly, prophetic, and kingly offices of Christ (see *LG* #31). Second, the church is a "structured community." He writes, "Let us briefly say that Jesus has instituted a structured community which is...entirely holy, priestly, prophetic, missionary, apostolic; it has ministries at the heart of its life, some freely raised up by the Spirit, others linked by the imposition of hands to the institution and mission of the Twelve."[42] In other words, there are different gifts, but the same Spirit (1 Cor 12:4) at work throughout the church. Some ministries arise from the prompting of the Spirit, but this does not eliminate the need for structure in the church. Third, since all share in the Spirit, and are united into the one people of God, a spirit of collegiality should pervade all levels of decision making in the church—the pope with his fellow bishops from around the world, bishops with priests in the diocese, and pastors with their parishioners.

Finally, *Gaudium et spes* addressed the question of the relationship of the church and the modern world. Congar's sense of history is again relevant. He writes,

Catholics had a defensive, siege mentality. They thought
that the world was conspiring against them and were therefore closed to everything that came from outside. From the
time of Leo XII onwards (1823–29), the number of specifically Catholic societies and activities increased enormously.
The clergy protected themselves by apologetics that were
always triumphant. I was very familiar with all that!

Paul VI's attitude and that of the Council were very different. The Council knew and said publicly that the
Church was not the same as the world and that Christian
life made certain distinctive claims, but it formulated a
programme for the Church within the world no longer
restricting it to the Christian world.[43]

The church must, in the words of *Gaudium et spes,* read "the signs of
time" and interpret them in light of the gospel (LG #4). The bishops
insisted that the church must enter into genuine dialogue with the
wider currents of thought in the world, and they called upon all
Catholics to join with others of good will to create a more just and
peaceful world.

Controversies have abounded in the Catholic Church since
Vatican II. Some feel its changes were too sweeping; some feel the
changes were insufficient. There have been countless debates
between liberals and conservatives as to the "intention" of Vatican II,
or whose positions are most in keeping with the teachings of Vatican
II. In an interview conducted late in his life, Congar offered spiritual
advice to those caught in the turmoil swirling around the church:
"Now the fate of the Church seems to me increasingly to be bound up
with a spiritual and even supernatural life, that of the Christian life. I
think that in present conditions the only Christians who can stand the
pressures are those who have an inner life."[44] As *Lumen Gentium*
(chapter VII) reminds us, the church is a pilgrim church, a people on
a journey in time in the hope that the yearnings of the inner life will
not go unfulfilled. It is to that very hope that we now turn.

Notes

1.   Yves Congar, O.P., "Letter from Father Yves Congar, O.P.," *Theology
Digest* 32(3), 1985, p. 213.

2.   Thomas F. O'Meara, O.P., "Congar, Yves," *HarperCollins Encyclopedia of Catholicism*, ed. Richard P. McBrien (San Francisco: Harper San Francisco, 1995), pp. 351–52.

3.   See William Henn, "Yves Congar, O.P. (1904–95)," *America* 173(4), 1995, p. 23.

4.   Jean-Pierre Jossua, O.P., *Yves Congar: Theology in the Service of God's People* (Chicago: Priory Press, 1968), p. 29.

5.   "Letter from Father Yves Congar," p. 214.

6.   Jossua, *Yves Congar,* p. 31.

7.   Thomas F. O'Meara, O.P., "Ecumenist of Our Times: Yves Congar," *Mid-Stream* 27 (1988), p. 73.

8.   Quoted in Jossua, *Yves Congar*, p. 32

9.   Avery Dulles, S.J., "Yves Congar: In Appreciation," *America* 173(2), 1995, p. 6.

10.   See Henn, "Yves Congar," p. 24.

11.   Victor Dunne, *Prophecy in the Church* (Frankfurt am Main: Peter Lang, 2000), p. 17.

12.   A. V. Littledale, "Translator's Note," *The Mystery of the Church* (Baltimore: Helicon Press, 1960), p. vi.

13.   Yves Congar, "The Church and Pentecost," in *The Mystery of the Church* (Baltimore: Helicon Press, 1960), p. 4.

14.   Ibid., pp. 11–12.

15.   Ibid., pp. 5–6.

16.   Ibid., p. 7.

17.   Ibid., p. 21.

18.   Ibid., p. 22.

19.   Michael A. Fahey, "Communion, Church as," *HarperCollins Encyclopedia of Catholicism*, p. 337.

20.   Congar, *Mystery of the Church*, p. 34.

21.   Ibid., pp. 36–37.

22.   Ibid., pp. 35–36.

23.   Ibid., p. 40.

24.   Ibid., p. 43.

25.   Ibid., p. 48.

26.   Ibid., pp. 49–50.

27.   Ibid., p. 51.

28.   Yves Congar, "My Path-Findings in the Theology of Laity and Ministries," *Jurist* XXXII (1972), p. 170.

29.   Aidan Nichols, *Yves Congar* (Wilton, CT: Morehouse-Barlow, 1989), p. 52.

30. Michael O'Keefe, "Encyclical," *HarperCollins Encyclopedia of Catholicism*, p. 465.
31. Yves Congar, "The Mystical Body of Christ," in *The Mystery of the Church*, p. 123.
32. Wendell Sanford Dietrich, "Yves Congar," in *The New Day*, ed. Wm. Jerry Boney and Lawrence E. Molumby (Richmond: John Knox Press, 1968), p. 25.
33. Timothy I. MacDonald, *The Ecclesiology of Yves Congar* (Lanham: University Press of America, 1984), p. 88.
34. Richard McBrien, "Church and Ministry: The Achievement of Yves Congar," *Theology Digest* 32(3), 1985, p. 205.
35. Congar, "Path-Findings," pp. 173–74.
36. Yves Congar, "The Church and Its Unity," in *The Mystery of the Church*, p. 94.
37. Yves Congar, O.P., "A Last Look at the Council," in *Vatican II Revisited by Those Who Were There*, ed. Alberic Stacpoole (Minneapolis: Winston Press, 1986), p. 350.
38. Richard P. McBrien, "Vatican Council II," *HarperCollins Encyclopedia of Catholicism*, pp. 1301–2.
39. Joseph A. Komonchak, "A Hero of Vatican II: Yves Congar," *Commonweal* 122(21), December 1, 1995, p. 15.
40. Yves Congar, O.P., "The Church: The People of God," in *The Church and Mankind*, Concilium: Dogma vol. 1, ed. Edward Schillebeeckx (Glen Rock: Paulist Press, 1965), pp. 19–20.
41. Quoted in Noelle Hausman, "Le Pere Yves Congar au Concile Vatican II," in *Nouvelle revue theologique* 120 (1998), p. 268. Christopher M. Bellitto directed me to this article.
42. Congar, "Path-Findings," p. 178.
43. Yves Congar, O.P., "Moving Towards a Pilgrim Church," in *Vatican II Revisited*, pp. 138–39.
44. Yves Congar, O.P., *Fifty Years of Catholic Theology: Conversations with Yves Congar*, ed. Bernard Lauret (Philadelphia: Fortress Press, 1988), p. 5.

Discussion Questions

1. What importance does Pentecost play in the life of the church?
2. What is the Holy Spirit? In what ways does the Holy Spirit act in the church and in the world today?
3. What is a helpful image or expression for describing the church (body of Christ, people of God, and so on)? What are the strengths and weaknesses of that concept?

4. Interview someone who was raised in the pre–Vatican II church. Does he or she think the changes introduced at Vatican II were positive or negative?
5. How are important decisions made in your parish? What roles do laypeople play in the life of your parish?
6. Speaking of the ill treatment suffered by Congar and others at the hands of church authorities, Father Laurentin once commented, "Probably we shall never know what price has been paid for Vatican II" (Quoted in Jossua, p. 33). Does a comment such as this discourage or encourage you?
7. What, in your opinion, are the most difficult challenges the church will confront in the next five or ten years?

Suggested Readings

Two very helpful book-length discussions of Congar's theology are Aidan Nichols, *Yves Congar* (Wilton, CT: Morehouse-Barlow, 1989), and Jean-Pierre Jossua, O.P., *Yves Congar: Theology in the Service of God's People* (Chicago: Priory Press, 1968).

For a book-length introduction to Congar's ecclesiology, see Timothy I. MacDonald, *The Ecclesiology of Yves Congar* (Lanham: University Press of America, 1984). For a helpful shorter piece, see Wendell Sanford Dietrich, "Yves Congar," in *The New Day*, ed. Wm. Jerry Boney and Lawrence E. Molumby (Richmond: John Knox Press, 1968).

For Congar's views on ministry, see "Church and Ministry: The Achievement of Yves Congar," in *Theology Digest* 32(3), 1985. See also Congar's own piece, "My Path-Findings in the Theology of Laity and Ministries," *Jurist* XXXII (1972).

For Congar's theology of the Holy Spirit, see Elizabeth T. Groppe, "The Contribution of Yves Congar's Theology of the Holy Spirit," in *Theological Studies* 62(3), 2001.

For background on Vatican II, see "The Basic Teaching of Vatican II," which appears as chap. 2 in Avery Dulles, S.J., *The Reshaping of Catholicism* (San Francisco: Harper and Row, 1988), and the Introduction by Alberic Stacpoole to *Vatican II Revisited by Those Who Were There*, ed. Alberic Stacpoole (Minneapolis: Winston Press, 1986). Chaps. 8 and 23 are by Congar.

9

The End of Time and Wolfhart Pannenberg's Ingersoll Lecture on Immortality

Wolfhart Pannenberg's theology can be seen as a counterproposal to much of what had become the norm in twentieth-century German theology. Pannenberg brings to his theology a confidence in human reason's ability to recognize God's revelation, in history's ability to display that revelation, and in scripture's ability to preserve that revelation. Pannenberg resists the tendency on the part of many theologians to insist that faith is a necessary component to recognize the revelation of God. By contrast, as Stanley J. Grenz and Roger E. Olson explain, Pannenberg

> sees theology as a public discipline related to the quest for universal truth. For him the truth question is to be answered in the process of theological reflection and reconstruction. He criticizes any attempt to divide truth into autonomous spheres or to shield the truth content of the Christian tradition from rational inquiry. Theological affirmations must be subjected to the rigor of critical inquiry concerning the historical reality on which they are based. Theology, in other words, must be evaluated on the basis of critical canons, just as other sciences, for it also deals with truth.[1]

Pannenberg also repeatedly insists that God's revelation does not exist in a realm of eternity separate and distinct from the flow of history or in the recesses of the human heart apart from public view. Instead,

174

God's revelation is historical. Pannenberg speaks of the "indirect self-revelation of God through the history in which God is active."[2] Pannenberg also rejects the claims of those who argue that the scriptures are hopelessly compromised as historical sources. Though he certainly employs the tools of modern biblical scholarship, he does not believe that this necessitates a wholesale discounting of the historical reliability of the scriptural stories. Pannenberg argues for the historicity of the resurrection stories of the empty tomb (which, he argues, could easily have been disproven if they were false), and of the tradition of the appearances of the resurrected Lord.

The significance of the resurrection, contends Pannenberg, is twofold: first, it sheds light on the pre-Easter career of Jesus; second, it anticipates the future. In terms of its meaning for the pre-Easter career of Jesus, James C. Livingston and Francis Schüssler Fiorenza explain, "Pannenberg also asserts the retroactivity of the resurrection in a creative attempt to take into account the full humanity of Jesus and those New Testament verses that speak of Jesus's inauguration as Son of God at his resurrection. Pannenberg asserts that although Jesus is appointed the Son of God at his resurrection, he is retroactively the Son of God from the beginning of his life."[3] Pannenberg, in other words, argues from the resurrection to the incarnation. Our present investigation, however, requires that we follow his second line of reasoning that is anticipatory or "proleptic" in nature. Livingston and Fiorenza continue, "What Pannenberg means by the proleptic and anticipatory nature of the resurrection is that the end of history is already anticipated and realized in the event of Jesus's resurrection."[4] It is this second meaning, this anticipatory or proleptic meaning, that occupies our attention in this chapter.

Our investigation divides into three parts. First, we situate Pannenberg's discussion of anticipatory or proleptic meaning of resurrection in the theological category called "eschatology." Second, we examine the critical and constructive role eschatology plays in Pannenberg's theology. We conclude by examining Pannenberg's eschatology as presented in his 1983 Ingersoll Lecture on Immortality.

Eschatology in the Bible

Zachary Hayes, O.F.M., offers a useful summary of the issues involved in a discussion of eschatology, literally, a study of, or view about, the end of history.

> Christians are people of hope. But they are not alone in this, for hope is a common element in human experience. What distinguishes Christians is not the mere fact that they hope, but the peculiar way in which they hope and the distinctive reasons for which they hope. In the Scriptures, the object of Christian hope is called the Kingdom of God. The ground for Christian hope is that which God has done in Jesus of Nazareth for the salvation of the world. Here, in seminal form, is the heart of the Christian faith. It is from this center that theology attempts to explicate the vision which Christian hope has for the future of the world.[5]

Christians pin their hopes for the future on what God has done in Jesus of Nazareth, but the content of that hope varies from one Christian group to the next. What does the future hold? What significance does that future have for the present moment? What is the kingdom of God?

The roots of biblical eschatology are to be found in the ancient concept of a covenant, a binding pledge between God and Israel, expressed simply as "I will take you as my people, and I will be your God" (Exod 6:7). This divine promise was inextricably linked with the promise of the land of Canaan. But, as Richard H. Hiers notes,

> then came a series of oppressors and conquerors. In 721 B.C., the Assyrians totally defeated Israel, and in 586 B.C., the Babylonians overcame the surviving kingdom of Judah, destroying Jerusalem and the Temple, and carrying most of the Jews into exile. Pre-exilic prophets interpreted these disasters as God's judgment against his people for worshiping other gods and failing to do justice and mercy (e.g., Amos 4–8; Hos. 4–10; Jer. 2–8). Generally these prophets also expected God to punish foreign nations for their false

religion, pride, and wickedness (e.g., Isa. 38; Jer. 46; Ezek. 30). Most of them promised that God would restore the fortunes of Israel and Judah afterwards. Oracles of future redemption envisioned not only the restoration of national strength and status but also the establishment of an era of everlasting peace and blessing (e.g., Hos 2:14–23; Isa. 2:2–4; 11; 35; Jer. 31:1–37; Ezek. 16:53–63).[6]

These passages predicting an era of everlasting peace and blessing profoundly shape early Christian proclamation (especially the Immanuel passages in Isaiah).

A second development in the Old Testament that exerts a significant influence on Christian thought is the rise of apocalyptic thinking. The word *apocalyptic* itself refers to the revelations granted, usually in symbolic form, to an individual, regarding the unalterable course of human history. The message of apocalyptic is that God, for reasons unknown to us, has allowed evil nations to oppress the righteous ones of the Lord, but that their dominion will soon be overturned in spectacular fashion by God. The righteous ones who are being persecuted need to persevere in their struggles in the hope that God will soon intervene in human history and bring all people to judgment. That judgment could be carried out by God, or God could delegate authority to another figure (for example, "the Son of Man"). Before that judgment, however, there will be a time of great tribulation. This time of tribulation was commonly compared to the pangs of labor experienced by expectant mothers before they give birth (for example, Mark 13:8). This apocalyptic outlook, evident in Daniel 7, also appears in various passages in the Gospels and letters, and most dramatically in the Book of Revelation.

One of the most significant features of the apocalyptic tradition is the belief in the future resurrection of the dead. Daniel 12:7 is often cited as the first instance of this belief in the Old Testament. "Many of those who sleep in the dust of the earth shall awake; Some shall live forever, others shall be an everlasting horror and disgrace." In the New Testament, Paul speaks of Christ's resurrection as the "first fruits" (1 Cor 15:20) of those who have died. This agricultural metaphor compares the initial harvest of a crop and its relation to an assured, imminent, and abundant harvest of that crop to the resurrection of Christ and the hope of future resurrection of "those who belong to Christ" (1 Cor 15:23) that will follow the *parousia* or return of Christ.

Jesus' preaching centered on the coming of the kingdom of God (or its equivalent expressions "reign of God" or "kingdom of heaven"). In Mark's Gospel, Jesus' opening proclamation is, "The time is fulfilled, and the kingdom of God has come near; repent, and believe in the good news" (1:15).What did Jesus preach by this proclamation? Did Christ expect the imminent end of the world as we know it? Was Jesus speaking in spiritual terms or political terms or both? To what extent did Jesus think and act apocalyptically? These questions have been at the center of New Testament studies for decades, and there is no indication that they will be supplanted anytime soon. To add greater confusion, the Gospels themselves seem to give clues leading in different directions. Jesus at times speaks of the kingdom as a present reality in rather unapocalyptic terms.

> Once Jesus was asked by the Pharisees when the kingdom of God was coming, and he answered, "The kingdom of God is not coming with things that can be observed; nor will they say, 'Look, here it is!' or 'There it is!' For, in fact, the kingdom of God is among you. (Luke 17:20–21)

On other occasions, Jesus speaks in starkly apocalyptic tones: "Truly I tell you, there are some standing here who will not taste death until they see that the kingdom of God has come in power" (Mark 9:1, see also Mark 13).

Eschatology in Modern Theology

A brief history of the twists and turns of the modern biblical scholarship on the question of Jesus' eschatological outlook will lead us directly to Pannenberg's place in that tradition. In the theological tradition called Protestant liberalism, the eschatological dimension of Jesus' teachings was either minimized or eliminated. Norman Perrin offers the following assessment of the work of one of the leading voices of that tradition, Albrecht Ritschl (1822–1889):

> In all of this the Kingdom of God is conceived by Ritschl
> in purely ethical terms. Jesus saw in the Kingdom of God
> the moral task to be carried out by the human race, and…it
> is the organization of humanity through action inspired by
> love. Christianity itself is completely spiritual and thor-
> oughly ethical. It is completely spiritual in freedom given
> to the children of God through redemption, which involves
> the impulse to conduct through the motive of love—and it
> is thoroughly ethical in that this conduct is directed
> towards the moral organization of mankind, the establish-
> ment of the Kingdom of God.[7]

The challenge to Ritschl came from one of his students who was also
his son-in-law, Johannes Weiss. Weiss insisted that his former teacher
had not given sufficient attention to the eschatological and apocalyptic elements in Jesus' preaching and had overemphasized the human
involvement in the bringing about of the kingdom of God. Modern
biblical scholarship has generally attempted to do justice to both the
present and the future dimensions in Jesus' preaching about the kingdom of God (compare Luke 11:20 and Luke 13:29). For example,
Norman Perrin writes in a later work, "In the teaching of Jesus the
emphasis is not upon a future for which men must prepare, even with
the help of God; the emphasis is upon a present which carries with it
the guarantee of the future. The present that has become God's present guarantees that all futures will be God's future."[8]

One twentieth-century biblical scholar who was a "notable
exception to the developing tendency among scholars to recognize
the Kingdom as both present and future in the teaching of Jesus"[9] was
Rudolf Bultmann, whose work we discussed briefly in chapter 4, on
Dietrich Bonhoeffer. Jesus' preaching centered for Bultmann on the
future coming of the kingdom. This may seem to be a liability, since
it leaves open the possibility that Jesus mistakenly expected the imminent end of the world. Bultmann, however, sees this future aspect of
Jesus' preaching as the perfect complement to modern existentialist
thought. Bultmann writes, "Rather, the Kingdom of God is a power
which, although it is entirely future, wholly determines the present. It
determines the present because it now compels man to decision; he
is determined thereby either in this direction or in that, as chosen or

as rejected, in his present existence."[10] Bultmann's strategy was to uncover the existential message embedded in the mythological language of the New Testament writings. Given the nature of the Gospels as faith documents, he did not feel the historical accuracy of individual sayings or incidents could be definitively determined. More important, Bultmann believed that Christian faith does not rest upon the Jesus of history, but rather on the Christ of faith. It is the risen Christ who confronts us in Christian preaching, and it is the risen Christ who challenges us with the existential decision to place our trust in a power beyond ourselves in order that we might live authentic human lives.

The Place of Eschatology in Pannenberg's Theology

Pannenberg places eschatology at the center of his theology. More particularly, he highlights the importance of apocalyptic thinking for Christian faith. In an early programmatic essay, Pannenberg insists, "It is only within this tradition of prophetic and apocalyptic expectation that it is possible to understand the resurrection of Jesus and his pre-Easter life as a reflection of the eschatological self-vindication of Jahweh."[11] In another influential early essay, "Theology and the Kingdom of God," Pannenberg situates his work in the modern history of biblical scholarship. He writes,

> From Kant to Ritschl and the religious socialists, the Kingdom of God and its propagation were goals to be achieved though man's labor. Today such thinking is dismissed as being simplistic or even dangerously naive. But theologians of the past correctly asserted that where men comply with the will of God, there is the Kingdom of God. Taking this a step farther, they asserted that to extend the sphere of obedience to God's will means the extension and establishment of his Kingdom.
>
> This assumption was upset by Johannes Weiss toward the end of the nineteenth century. He discovered that, according to the New Testament and Jesus' message, the Kingdom of God will be established not by men but by God alone. The coming of the Kingdom will involve cosmic revolutions and

change far beyond anything conceivable as a consequence of man's progressive labor. God will establish his Kingdom unilaterally. Therefore Jesus, and John the Baptizer before him, only announced the Kingdom of God, exposing every present condition under the light of the imminent future. This future is expected to come in a marvelous way from God himself; it is not simply the development of human history or achievement of God-fearing men.[12]

Pannenberg then concludes, "This resounding motif of Jesus' message—the imminent Kingdom of God—must be recovered as a key to the whole of Christian theology."[13] We focus on three features of Pannenberg's theology that take seriously "this resounding motif of Jesus' message."

First, Pannenberg gives theological priority to the future. As he states in his *Systematic Theology*,

The truth of the revelation of God in Jesus Christ is dependent, then, on the actual in-breaking of the future of God's kingdom, and we maintain and declare it today on the premise of that coming. The coming of the kingdom is the basis of the message of Jesus, and without the arrival of this future it loses its basis....As the work and history of Jesus were essentially an anticipation of this reign, and as they depend on the future of the ultimate coming for their meaning and truth, so do the liturgical life of the church, the presence of Jesus Christ at celebrations of his Supper, and the saving efficacy of baptism, along with the Christian sense of election and faith's assurance of justification. As regards its content and truth all Christian doctrine depends on the future of God's own coming to consummate his rule over his creation.[14]

Pannenberg declares that Christianity is based on a divine promise. If the promise is not kept, then the framework of Christian belief and practice crumbles. The future is, of course, not unrelated to the present. In fact, much like a mariner charts a course based on the final destination, the Christian sees every day against the backdrop of

God's kingdom that is yet to come. Christians' eschatological hope is that "what turns out to be true in the future will then be evident as having been true all along."[15]

Second, the Christian life is characterized by anticipation. Simply stated, "in the fate of Jesus, the end of history is experienced in advance as an anticipation."[16] The concept of anticipation is so important to Pannenberg's theology that Philip Clayton labels it "the central systematic principle of his theology." Clayton writes,

> It was thinking through the logic of Jesus' resurrection, along with the resultant authority of his message and divinity of his person, that led Pannenberg to the central systematic principle of his theology, the concept of anticipation. As the apocalyptic horizon criterion suggests, *the anticipatory structure that characterizes most of what Pannenberg has written is generalized directly from the conclusions of his Christology.*[17]

The resurrection is a foretaste, a glimpse, or a down payment (2 Cor 1:22; Eph 1:14). Christians walk by faith (2 Cor 5:7) that the end of history has been previewed in Christ.

The third feature of Pannenberg's theology that follows from his eschatological focus is the provisional view of human endeavors. As Richard John Neuhaus explains,

> Provisionality in Pannenberg's thought is not a condition that excuses a lack of commitment. This is as true of the intellectual life as it is of commitment to social change. That is, we must have the maturity to recognize the tentative character of existence on the one hand and the urgency of embracing it as the only existence we have on the other. For many, not only for Christians, there is an unbreakable connection between commitment and certitude; we can only be thoroughly committed to what we are absolutely sure about. Christians frequently appeal to some authority, revelation perhaps, to establish the certitude of the premises on which they act. To Pannenberg's radically provisional view of existence it is objected that if

we cannot know for sure, we cannot act with religious seri-
ousness. Pannenberg counters that religious faith is con-
nected not so much to certitude as it is to venturing risk on
the basis of reasonable probabilities.[18]

Pannenberg explains, "A commitment to the provisional is essential to
Christian faith in the Kingdom of God. To withhold such a commitment because the absolute remains out of reach of human endeavors
would mean betraying the Kingdom. And yet it is the special contribution of the eschatological understanding of the Kingdom that it
does not allow any particular social program to be mistaken for the
Kingdom."[19] The eschatological orientation, therefore, translates into
neither social indifference nor theocratic politics.

"Constructive and Critical Functions of Christian Eschatology"

We now delve into Pannenberg's Ingersoll Lecture on Immortality,
delivered at the Harvard Divinity School on October 13, 1983. The
lecture consists of a brief introduction and four sections. In the space
of twenty pages, the lecture summarizes nicely the themes we have
been discussing so far in Pannenberg's theology.

Pannenberg begins by providing a brief history of the past century's theological engagement with eschatology. The starting point—
as we discussed earlier—is the work of Johannes Weiss.

But a recovery of the eschatological concern in systematic
theology has been due for some time, since Johannes
Weiss' successful thesis of 1892 that Jesus' proclamation of
the kingdom of God was not primarily a program for moral
or social action, but had its roots in Jewish apocalypticism
and envisages a cosmic catastrophe that would occur when
God in the imminent future would replace this present
world by the new creation of his own kingdom without any
human ado.[20]

"Three decades later," continues Pannenberg, "in 1922, Karl Barth
wrote in the second edition of his commentary on Romans: 'A

Christianity that does not thoroughly and without remainder consist of eschatology, would be thoroughly and totally devoid of Christ.'"[21] Pannenberg argues that Barth's insight was not adequately appropriated by theologians because of the evolutionary outlook of the modern mind. In the apocalyptic tradition, the present world is ended in dramatic fashion by the unilateral action of God; in the evolutionary outlook, this present world is set on a gradual course of transformation. For this reason, contends Pannenberg, "it was no accident that Barth and Bultmann recovered the apocalyptic urgency of Jesus' message at the price of stripping it of its temporal prospect of a final future of this world."[22] Pannenberg sees in Moltmann's work a proper refocusing on an actual end-time, but believes Moltmann has incorrectly defined that in terms of certain political consequences rather than "the transcendent content of the biblical hope itself."[23] We are then left with the natural question: What then is the proper place of apocalyptic eschatology in Christian theology? With that question in mind, let us turn to the first of four parts in Pannenberg's lecture.

In the first part of the lecture, Pannenberg comments on the traditional grouping of biblical images about the end-times into individual and social eschatology. He notes, "Individual eschatology focuses on a future life of the individual in terms of bodily resurrection, immortality of the soul, and communion with God and with Christ. In the center of social eschatology there is the hope for the kingdom of God that will bring about true justice and peace among all creatures."[24] Rahner, for example, connects his views on human nature as created by God with the fulfillment of that nature in God's kingdom. What is now known indistinctly will be made clear in the final consummation. Protestant theologians have shied away from this approach and have largely argued in terms of a promise-fulfillment scheme based on divine promises contained in scripture. Pannenberg sees both approaches as preserving an important ingredient in any Christian eschatology. The future will bring about human fulfillment so that the fulfillment will bear a resemblance to the present state of humans and that fulfillment will, of course, take place at the time and in the manner determined by God.

In the second part of the lecture, Pannenberg addresses the common criticism that eschatology introduces an "otherworldly" element to Christian faith that Karl Marx rightly criticized. This otherworldly dimension encourages those suffering political, social, or economic injustice to quietly endure their hardship in the hope that they will be rewarded in heaven. Pannenberg counters this charge with the assertion that

> the otherworldliness of religious eschatology questions the alleged self-sufficiency of the secular world. In declaring the consummation of human existence to be a matter of hope beyond death, religious eschatology denounces the illusions of secular belief in the attainability of a perfect and unambiguous happiness in this world. In proclaiming the eschatological kingdom of God to be the place of the achievement of true peace and justice among human beings, Christian eschatology denounces at the same time the pretensions of the politicians who claim that by taking the measures they advocate, ultimate justice and perfect peace could be achieved in our secular societies.[25]

In other words, this otherworldliness does not reduce Christian faith to escapism or social indifference, but rather it serves as the standard by which to judge the present state of the world. This is the vital, *critical function* of Christian eschatology. Rather than denying the world, "it clears the stage for a realistic involvement in its struggles, without admitting illusions of obtaining ultimate solutions to its problems and without the psychological need for considering the opponent as a foe of the ultimate truth itself."[26]

With the struggle for social justice comes the inevitable frustration, despair, or sense of being overwhelmed. Here Christian eschatology plays a *constructive function*.

> The constructive functions of eschatology are closely related to its critical functions, because it is precisely the insufficiency of the secular world—the endemic and recurrent injustice (though different in degree) in all the different systems of social order, the sufferings and fragmented existence of human individuals—that legitimates the conception of a consummation of human destiny in another world and beyond the death of the individual.

> Eschatological hope empowers the individual to carry the burden of its finite existence with all its irremovable limitations and disgraceful frustrations. It encourages the human person to face the evils of this world as they are, without illusion. Hope in a transcendent completion of human existence in communion with God illumines the present existence in spite of its shortcomings.[27]

The eschatological backdrop of Christian faith provides the standard by which the conditions of the world are measured (the critical function) and is the source of hope for those struggling to bring about that better world (the constructive function). It shatters the illusion that any government or human cause represents the unambiguous fulfillment of divine promises (the critical function), yet calls upon all humans to organize their efforts to address the urgent needs of their fellow human beings (the constructive function).

Pannenberg further argues that the destiny of the individual and the destiny of society are linked in the biblical eschatological tradition, but that in the modern age Christian thinkers have unfortunately separated what God has joined together.

> But it was only in the eighteenth-century thought that the question of the future of the individual beyond death was thoroughly separated from the concern for the destiny of society and for the complete achievement of peace and justice in social life....The dissolution of social eschatology rendered the expectation of a general resurrection at the end of history meaningless, a mythological remnant. Individual eschatology was rephrased in terms of immortality of the soul, and each individual soul was understood to enter the realm of eternity immediately after death.[28]

How, then, should we view the future end-time? What is the content of the Christian hope? Pannenberg addresses these questions in the third part of the lecture, when he turns his attention to the "problem of how a life beyond death can be conceived."[29]

The Christian tradition has preserved two ways of conceiving the future life of an individual beyond death: a future resurrection of the body and an immortal soul. Both provide a means for speaking about a real continuity between a person's identity in this life and the next. The former belief—a hope in a future resurrected body—is found in Paul's letters (for example, 1 Cor 15; 1 Thess 4). The latter belief of the immortal soul figured prominently in Greek philosophy and was incorporated into Christian thought, according to Pannenberg, to handle the vexing problem: "If resurrection does not occur within a short time after the person's death, if, on the contrary, the body decays or is devoured by wild animals or burnt to ashes and the ashes are dispersed: how, then, can a bodily existence at some later time, in the day of the resurrection, be continuous with the unique life of the individual person who died long ago?"[30] The immortal soul provided the mechanism for preserving personal identity over the long expanse of time between a person's death and the general resurrection at the end of time. Pannenberg sees human identity as derived from both body and soul, so the resurrected state must include both. Between now and the end-time, we remain present to the Lord: "What happens in the moment of death, then, is that we are no longer present to ourselves, nor to other creatures, although we remain present to God. It is this inextinguishable presence to God's eternity that provides the condition of the possibility that the same life of ours can come alive again."[31] What exactly would such an event entail? Pannenberg now advances his own position regarding this future event.

He develops his position in response to the criticisms of John Hick.[32] Since Pannenberg has ruled out the mind's disembodied survival of death, Hick argues, then the resuscitation of a corpse in this world would be no less impossible. Pannenberg responds:

> If our life remains present to God, is it not conceivable that God could restore its ability of relating to itself, a form of self-awareness, though different from self-consciousness in the present world, because it would not occur in a succession of perishing instants of time, but in the eternal present and therefore could relate to the simultaneous whole of one's life? Such a possibility would be different from the continuance of a disembodied consciousness, because it is rather the totality of our bodily life, as preserved in the

presence of God, that would recover self-awareness. Nor would it be a "resuscitation of corpses in this world," because self-awareness would be restored to the simultaneous whole of our life as it is present to the eternal God. Still, the realization of such a possibility would come close to an act of creation.[33]

Second, Hick wonders whether Pannenberg's view of eternal life would be nothing more than an eternal reminder of all the evils and tragedies that have befallen a person in his or her earthly life. Pannenberg believes Hick "underestimates the implications of the *transformation* that occurs to the finite life in light of eternity."[34] This involves both judgment and glorification. "Eternal judgment does not mean a violent reaction of a punishing God against his creatures. It rather means that the sinner is left to the consequences of his or her own behavior."[35] Eternal bliss arises when a person sees his or her own life as a participation in the life of God. "The presence of God means glorification as well as judgment, and whether it will be one or the other depends on the relation of the creature to God and to his kingdom."[36]

Hick's third objection is prompted by his interest in world religions. Hick sees in Pannenberg's theology a link between salvation and the gospel message. Hick argues, "Such a doctrine can only apply to those who have lived to responsible maturity during the centuries since Jesus lived and in the lands in which his gospel has been known. It cannot apply…to those who have lived before Jesus or outside the influence of historic Christianity; and yet these of course constitute the large majority of the human race."[37] Pannenberg believes such a problem disappears if "Jesus and his message are considered to stand as a *criterion* of God's eternal judgment, but not as the indispensable *means*, the explicit acceptance of which would be a precondition of participation in the kingdom of God."[38]

The fourth and final part of Pannenberg's lecture deals with the notion of an "end of history." Pannenberg insists that "the end of time does not border on some other time, but the notion of an end of time expresses the finite character of time as such."[39] Pannenberg instead sees "God himself is the end of time, and as the end of time he is the final future of his creation. This does not entail the annihilation of time, but the lifting up of temporal histories into the form of an eternal presence."[40] In the meantime, "We travel through the history of our lives in the light of some continuing presence that travels with us."[41]

Conclusion

The end of time is the final moment in the tapestry of the biblical narrative. Like any important art of work, the Bible continues to influence generations of believers who see in the story of Creation, Exodus, Conquest, Exile, Incarnation, Crucifixion, Resurrection, Pentecost, and the End of Time the framework for understanding their own lives. In that way—to echo a theme in the Ingersoll Lecture—the biblical tapestry serves a critical and constructive role in the tapestry of our own lives.

Notes

1. Stanley J. Grenz and Roger Olson, *Twentieth-Century Theology* (Downers Grove: InterVarsity Press, 1992), p. 189.
2. Wolfhart Pannenberg, "Introduction," *Revelation as History*, ed. Wolfhart Pannenberg (London: Collier-Macmillan, 1968), p. 19.
3. James C. Livingston and Francis Schüssler Fiorenza, *Modern Christian Thought,* 2nd ed., vol. 2 (Upper Saddle River: Prentice Hall, 2000), p. 344.
4. Ibid., p. 345.
5. Zachary Hayes, O.F.M., *Visions of a Future: A Study of Christian Eschatology* (Collegeville: Liturgical Press, 1990), p. 15.
6. Richard H. Hiers, "Eschatology," *Harper's Bible Dictionary,* ed. Paul J. Achtemeier (San Francisco: Harper and Row, 1985), pp. 275–76.
7. Norman Perrin, *The Kingdom of God in the Teaching of Jesus* (Philadelphia: Westminster Press, 1963), p. 16.
8. Norman Perrin, *Rediscovering the Teaching of Jesus* (New York: Harper & Row, 1976), p. 205.
9. Perrin, *Kingdom of God,* p. 112.
10. Rudolf Bultmann, *Jesus and the Word* (New York: Charles Scribner's, 1958), p. 51.
11. Wolfhart Pannenberg, "Dogmatic Theses on the Doctrine of Revelation," in *Revelation as History,* p. 127.

12. Wolfhart Pannenberg, "Theology and the Kingdom of God," in *Theology and the Kingdom of God*, ed. Richard John Neuhaus (Philadelphia: Westminster, 1969), pp. 51–52.
13. Ibid., p. 53.
14. Wolfhart Pannenberg, *Systematic Theology*, vol. 3 (Grand Rapids: William B. Eerdmans, 1998), p. 531.
15. Pannenberg, "Theology and the Kingdom of God," p. 63. Critics have rightly pointed out the tension in Pannenberg's theology on this point. At times, he speaks of history as open-ended, with God being affected by the course of history; at other times, he speaks of God as unaffected by history. See Philip Clayton, "Anticipation and Theological Method," in *The Theology of Wolfhart Pannenberg*, ed. Carl E. Braaten and Philip Clayton (Minneapolis: Augsburg, 1988), pp. 139–40.
16. Pannenberg, "Dogmatic Theses," p. 134.
17. Clayton, "Anticipation and Theological Method," p. 131. Emphasis his.
18. Richard John Neuhaus, "Wolfhart Pannenberg: Profile of a Theologian," in *Theology and the Kingdom of God*, pp. 19–20.
19. Wolfhart Pannenberg, "The Kingdom of God and the Foundation of Ethics," in *Theology and the Kingdom of God*, pp. 114–15.
20. Wolfhart Pannenberg, "Constructive and Critical Functions of Christian Eschatology," *Harvard Theological Review* 77(2), 1984, p. 119.
21. Ibid.
22. Ibid.
23. Ibid., p. 120.
24. Ibid.
25. Ibid., p. 124.
26. Ibid.
27. Ibid.
28. Ibid., p. 126.
29. Ibid., p. 128.
30. Ibid., p. 129.
31. Ibid., p. 131.
32. Hick's criticisms can be found in his work *Death and Eternal Life* (San Francisco: Harper and Row, 1976), pp. 221–26. See also Pannenberg's response to Hick's lecture in his "A Note on Pannenberg's Eschatology" in *Harvard Theological Review* 77 (1984), pp. 421–23.
33. Pannenberg, "Note on Eschatology," p. 133.
34. Ibid., p. 134.
35. Ibid.
36. Ibid., p. 135.

37.   Hick, *Death and Eternal Life*, p. 225.
38.   Pannenberg, "Note on Eschatology," p. 136.
39.   Ibid., p. 137.
40.   Ibid., p. 138.
41.   Ibid.

Discussion Questions

1.   How do you believe the world will end? Are there events that will sig-
     nal that the end is near? Do you interpret biblical language about Jesus
     returning on the clouds of heaven literally or figuratively?
2.   In what concrete ways do beliefs about the end-time influence how we
     live in the present?
3.   In what ways does Christian eschatology help free the Christian to
     involve him- or herself in the affairs of this world? What are, in your
     opinion, the critical and constructive uses of Christian eschatology?
4.   On what is Christian hope for the future based? Is it a promise in scrip-
     ture, the general direction of human history, or some element of
     human nature?
5.   Do you believe that the human personality survives death in some
     form? If so, in what form? If not, why not?

Suggested Readings

For a brief introduction to the theme of eschatology, see "Eschatology:
Conceptions of" by Josef Finkenzeller, and "Eschatology: Contemporary
Issues" by Roger Haight, both in *Handbook of Catholic Theology*, ed.
Wolfgang Beinert and Francis Schüssler Fiorenza (New York: Crossroad,
1995). See also "The Kingdom of God and the Life Everlasting," by Carl E.
Braaten in *Christian Theology*, ed. Peter C. Hodgson and Robert H. King
(Philadelphia: Fortress Press, 1982); and "Eschatology" by David Fergusson
in *The Cambridge Companion to Christian Doctrine* (Cambridge:
Cambridge University Press, 1997), ed. Colin E. Gunton. For two book-
length treatments by Zachary Hayes, O.F.M., see *Visions of a Future*
(Collegeville: Liturgical Press, 1989), and *What Are They Saying About the
End of the World?* (New York: Paulist, 1983).

     For an introduction to Pannenberg's theology, see Carl E. Braaten,
"Wolfhart Pannenberg," in *A Handbook of Christian Theologians*, enlarged
ed., ed. Martin Marty and Dean G. Peerman (Nashville: Abingdon Press,
1984); and Richard John Neuhaus, "Wolfhart Pannenberg: Profile of a
Theologian," in Wolfhart Pannenberg, *Theology and the Kingdom of God*
(Philadelphia: Westminster, 1969). I also found the master's thesis of Brian

John Walsh, *Futurity and Creation* (Toronto: Institute for Christian Studies, 1979), to be very helpful.

Students in upper-level courses looking for treatments of Pannenberg's eschatology should see Philip Clayton, "Anticipation and Theological Method," and Ted Peters, "Pannenberg's Eschatological Ethics," in *The Theology of Wolfhart Pannenberg* (Minneapolis: Augsburg, 1988), ed. Carl E. Braaten and Philip Clayton. Also helpful in that volume is Stanley Grenz, "The Appraisal of Pannenberg: A Survey of the Literature." See also chap. 6 of Stanley Grenz's work *Reason for Hope* (New York: Oxford University Press, 1990). Also helpful, but difficult, is *The Theology of Wolfhart Pannenberg* by E. Frank Tupper (Philadelphia: Westminster Press, 1973), chaps. 8 and 9.

Related to Pannenberg's discussion of eschatology is his treatment of the Eucharist in chap. 2 of his *Christian Spirituality* (Philadelphia: Westminster Press, 1983). There he writes, "The worship of the Christian community anticipates and symbolically celebrates the praise of God's glory that will be consummated in the eschatological renewal of all creation in the new Jerusalem" (p. 36).

Conclusion

After this rather close examination of several individual strands of the biblical narrative, we conclude by stepping back and seeing how they fit together to form one piece. If we return to the idea that theology is the horizontal line representing the flow of the Christian tradition, and spirituality is the vertical line connecting heaven and earth, we can better appreciate the mutual dependence and creative tension between the two as they are woven into one work, which is the Christian life.

Theology

The chief similarity between theology and tapestry-making that I have emphasized throughout this study is that both are crafts.[1] Like any craft, theology can be done very poorly or very well, but when it is done right, it creates an object that is beautiful to behold. Like tapestry-making, theology is a creative endeavor in which the thinker draws elements from scripture and tradition, assembles them in a unique way, and submits the finished product for consideration by the wider Christian community. Ruether's feminist theology, Gutiérrez's call for liberation, and Moltmann's thesis of the cross as an intra-trinitarian affair are just a few of the many bold theological proposals that were constructed and submitted for scrutiny by the wider theological community.

If theology is a craft, there is certainly a diversity of opinion about how it should be practiced. The twentieth century saw great changes in both Catholic and Protestant theology. The Second Vatican Council stands as the watershed of the liturgical and theological *aggiornamento* or updating of the Roman Catholic Church. In Protestant circles, the optimism of nineteenth-century theology was tempered by the horrors of the First and Second World Wars. It was also a time when traditional lines of demarcation became blurred and, in some cases, were erased. For example, the typical division between

Protestant and Catholic theology does not always seem the most useful categorization, since liberal Protestants and liberal Catholics often seem more closely aligned in terms of methodology than do conservative Catholics and liberal Catholics. It is for this reason that the work of the Lutheran theologian and ecumenist George Lindbeck rightly captured so much attention in the closing decades of the twentieth century.

Lindbeck identifies three understandings of religion and doctrine. First, traditional orthodoxy has held that religious doctrines are true propositions. Religion in this school of thought is primarily a matter of holding factually true beliefs. Second, in liberalism (or in Lindbeck's words, an "experiential-expressive" view of religion), experience replaces belief as the essence of religion. Doctrines are the conceptualization of the experience. In this way, discrepancies between the various religions' belief systems are seen as different cultural formulations of the one universal experience of transcendence at work in the universe. Lindbeck proposes a third model, which he labels "cultural-linguistic." Here attention shifts away from experience to the language of the particular religious community. The language shapes the person's experience of the world.

There is a different conception of the task of theology in each of the three theories of religion. The chief theological task in orthodoxy is the formulation of correct beliefs. Liberal theologians seek to draw out the dimension of transcendence from human experience and demonstrate the experiential truth of religious language. In the cultural-linguistic model, the task of the theologian is to articulate the self-understanding of the Christian community and describe the proper beliefs and actions for Christians.

The image of the tapestry presented here suggests that all three approaches outlined by Lindbeck could be seen as mutually corrective endeavors being carried on simultaneously by the Christian community. Clark Pinnock puts the matter in the following way:

> Perhaps it would be wise for Lindbeck to come right out and admit that doctrines do all three things. They make truth claims, they express inner experience, *and* they serve as rules for God's people. What he is actually doing here is emphasizing and exploring the third function as something

that has been neglected. In this respect he surely has a point.[2]

Each of the approaches standing alone strikes most believers as deficient—not wrong, merely incomplete. Beliefs are obviously important, and Christians have suffered hardship or even died for their faithful conviction that central Christian beliefs were true, that is, that they correspond to the actual nature of God, or that Christ's message was true. This approach, however, seems to overlook the spiritual dimension that the liberal tradition captures so well. The liberals see all human endeavors as imbued with the presence of God—that is a religiously compelling vision. The liberal willingness to abandon traditional religious language or compromise traditional beliefs, however, makes many Christians uneasy. The cultural-linguistic model that Lindbeck advocates gives priority to the language of the church. The primary role of the Christian community, in an increasingly secular world, is the formation and support of Christians. The danger lurking here, however, is a sectarian disengagement from the causes of justice and peace in the world.[3] It also overlooks the fact that currents of thought outside the church have corrected the Christian tradition, prompting various Christian denominations to alter their beliefs about slavery, women's rights, and evolution.[4]

If this assessment is accurate, then theology needs to be multidimensional.[5] It needs to articulate proper beliefs for Christians (orthodoxy). It should connect believers with the presence of God in their lives and reach out to those outside the bounds of the church (liberalism). It ought to form and sustain personal and communal lives of Christian character and virtue (cultural-linguistic model). In short, theology is a multidimensional exploration that draws from a number of sources (Clark Pinnock identifies four: scripture, tradition, experience, and reason);[6] assumes a number of tasks (Schubert Ogden speaks of theology being differentiated into historical, systematic, and historical theology);[7] and addresses a number of audiences (David Tracy lists three: society, the academy, and the church).[8]

In order to achieve these lofty goals, Christian theology needs, I believe, to possess three characteristics.

First, since it is unreasonable to ask any one theologian to meet all of these demands, theology needs to be communal, that is, the work of the entire body of Christ. Theological positions bear the personal mark of the thinker, but the most enduring positions have withstood the scrutiny of the wider Christian community.

Second, theology needs to be pluralistic. Just as thousands of strands make a tapestry, the fullness of truth is not found in any one theology. This is not to suggest that any theology is just as good as the next. Nor does it address the very difficult questions each Christian body faces on how to distinguish true from false belief, how to determine when change is a good thing or a bad thing, or how to maintain church unity without imposing stifling uniformity. Despite these difficulties, the exchange of ideas and the confrontation of contrasting theological styles is the lifeblood of theology. Psychology has also taught us that different personality types respond differently to the same stimuli. What is clear and orderly for one reader is rigid and lifeless to another. A plurality of theological arguments, therefore, seems to benefit both church and academy.

Third, theology needs to be historical. One of the greatest resources for doing theology is the historical memory of the Christian community. With that memory, overlooked ideas can be retrieved, acknowledgment of sin can take place, and cherished ideas can be transmitted. Theologians who bring a historical perspective to bear on their work can help correct overemphases or highlight neglected elements in the prevailing theological opinions of the day. For example, commenting on the negative view of "the world" in John's Gospel (especially, "I do not pray for the world," John 17:9), Raymond Brown wrote,

> This attitude toward the world strikes many modern Christians as strange and even as a distortion of the true Christian apostolate. In an age of involvement where men are considering the role of the Church in the modern world, the refusal of the Johannine Jesus to pray for the world is a scandal....Distrust for a world that is looked on as evil is, of course, not the whole NT message, and there are many passages that inculcate involvement in the world. But, if Christians believe that Scripture has a certain power to judge and correct, then the latter passages are more meaningful in eras when the Church tends to be

sequestered from the world, while passages such as those we have found in John have a message for an era that becomes naively optimistic about changing the world or even about affirming its values without change.[9]

Brown's intellectual honesty allowed him to see a place in theology for a theme in John's Gospel that was unpopular in many circles at the time of his writing (1970).

A similar type of mutual correction exists among the theologians in this study. For example, Moltmann believes that Pannenberg's attention to the future in Jesus' preaching results in a diminished role for the cross. Moltmann writes, "In his emphasis on the anticipatory character of the message and the resurrection of Jesus from the dead, however, Pannenberg has neglected the contradictory character of this message and of the cross of Jesus."[10] The supporters of Niebuhr's approach often lock horns with those who advocate liberation theology over many issues: the proper role of the church, the relevance of Christian faith to power politics, and the best strategy for effecting social and political change.[11]

Types of Theological Arguments

Drawing on the work of the theologians presented in this study, we can identify five types of arguments Christian theologians often make when engaged in the craft of theology. These five are in addition to the usual arguments that the opponent's position is factually incorrect or internally inconsistent, or that the author is overlooking an important piece of data or is failing to advance a compelling theological argument.

1. One of the most common Christian theological arguments is the cry, "Back to Jesus." This appeal calls for a return to the words and actions (and perhaps intentions) of Jesus of Nazareth and measures all subsequent developments against the founder's spiritual vision. Küng's argument was perhaps the clearest example of this approach. Typically such an argument is a call to return to an original pristine state of Christianity before later non-essential and even harmful elements were added by religious leaders and others. This argument sometimes sees an early spirit-filled Christian movement with few

rules and charismatic leaders, which eventually became less sponta-
neous and more preoccupied with rules and church structure (a state
some scholars call "early catholicism").[12]

2. The second type of argument is related to the first. Here an
appeal is made to the "essence of Christianity." That essence may be
a crystallization of Jesus' message and hence may be a form of the
"Back to Jesus" argument, but it need not be. For example, in his survey of contemporary theology, Clark H. Pinnock writes, "In my judge-
ment, the central message of Christianity and therefore its essence is
the epic story of redemption, enshrined in its sacred texts and litur-
gies, that announces the salvation and God's liberation of the human
race."[13] As we read Bonhoeffer's letters, we get the sense that he was
sifting through Christian beliefs in hopes of preserving those elements of Christianity that are still relevant for a godless world. The
prominence of grace in Rahner's theology argues for its place in any
Rahnerian description of the essence of Christianity. The same goes
for Moltmann's argument for the centrality of the cross to Christian
faith.

3. A third type of argument is known as "a hermeneutic of suspicion." *Hermeneutics* is the technical name given to the process of
interpretation. The element of suspicion arises from the conviction
that people often conceal their true motives. Therefore, an evaluation
of any position entails an analysis of the vested interests of the person
making the argument. Powerful people, whether in the church, the
halls of government, or business, it is argued, espouse positions that
best ensure their continued possession and exercise of power. As a
theological argument, it appears in authors influenced by Marx's critique of religion. The Niebuhr of *Moral Man and Immoral Society*,
Gutiérrez's *A Theology of Liberation,* and Moltmann's *The Crucified
God* all bring a healthy dose of suspicion to arguments advanced by
the powerful.

4. A fourth set of arguments revolves around the concept of
authority. Why should I accept something as true? What assurance
can I have that a religious belief is true? As Jaroslav Pelikan explains,

> Lurking behind every theological issue is the problem of
> authority. As it is possible to stop any argument in its tracks
> by raising the epistemological question, "How do you know

that, and how is that related to the way you know other things?" so the appeal to authority carries the specious appearance of promising to resolve all other matters of theological inquiry by making them its corollaries. Then the correlative of authority, which is obedience to Bible or Church, assumes the position of the principal virtue from which all others can be derived.[14]

Congar and Rahner explicitly relate their own theological positions to the official teachings of the Roman Catholic Church. Even when advocating a new line of thinking or practice in the church, both thinkers did so on the basis of orthodox Catholic belief as expressed in the church's doctrine and dogma.

5. Questions of authority are linked with the last category of arguments—those dealing with starting points or fundamental assumptions. Here theological problems are diagnosed as manifestations of a mistake made earlier in the reasoning process. Gutiérrez argues along these lines when he traces the modern separation of politics from religion to certain assumptions about the temporal and the spiritual.[15] Niebuhr seems to operate with the assumption that Jesus is largely irrelevant to the shaping of international policy. Lindbeck's cultural-linguistic model summons us to see language, not experience, as the proper starting point for Christian theology.

One of the key assumptions that is frequently challenged is the claim that some universal aspect of the human personality or human experience exists. Is there a universal human nature that is affected by culture but not obliterated by it? Are there certain fixed structures of the human mind? Are there certain universal or cross-cultural human experiences (for example, an innate drive to find meaning in life)? If so, what function should they play in Christian theology? This question is most evident in Rahner's theology, since he explicitly grounds his theology in certain assumptions about human nature. As Robert Kress notes, "Rahner's transcendental theological method 'mediates' between the 'changeless a priori structure of the human mind, which, as Lonergan has shown, is the unrevisable revisor of all conceptual frameworks,' and the historically contingent revelation of Christ, whom Christianity proclaims as the answer to that infinite questioning which transcendental philosophical reflection has shown the human being to be."[16] On the other end of the theological spectrum, Hans Frei's theological dictum was, "Respect the local, mistrust the universal."[17] I suspect that most theologians smuggle (knowingly or unknowingly) a few universal claims into most arguments, and most critics approach a theological argument with a few (acknowledged or unacknowledged) beliefs that are universal in scope.

Spirituality

We now turn our attention to the vertical dimension of this investigation—spirituality. In the Introduction to this book I proposed the following thesis: *The Christian life may be understood as the gradual interiorization of the biblical narrative so that it eventually becomes the overarching interpretive framework through which believers understand the events of their lives.* If this proposal has merit, then in order to obtain that goal, we need to root the spiritual vision in scripture and tradition, expand our reading of scripture, and locate our lives in a larger context that is divine in origin.

The central idea I have emphasized is that the structure of Christian faith is temporal. In other words, there is a certain sequence of events (scripture and tradition) that forms and informs Christian belief and action. As the bishops at Vatican II put the matter:

> Sacred Tradition and sacred Scripture, then are bound closely together, and communicate one with the other. For both of them, flowing out from the same divine wellspring, come together in some fashion to form one thing, and move towards the same goal. Sacred Scripture is the speech of God as it is put down in writing under the breath of the Holy Spirit. And Tradition transmits in its entirety the Word of God which has been entrusted to the apostles by Christ the Lord and the Holy Spirit.[18]

Within this temporal framework, however, special emphasis could be placed on the past, present, or future. This is evident, for example, in eucharistic piety. For some, the Eucharist is a remembrance of a past event, namely Christ's Last Supper. The words, "Do this in remembrance of me" (1 Cor 11:24), are central in this view of the Eucharist.

For other Christians, the Eucharist is a participation in the present, eternal, heavenly liturgy. As Joseph Martos explains,

> Especially in their instructions to new Christians the fathers often explained every detail of the liturgy, giving the sacred meaning of every word and action in the sacred space and time of the ritual. The eucharistic liturgy, for example, represented Christ offering himself to the Father, the bread and wine symbolized his body and blood, the candles stood for the light of faith, the attending deacons symbolized ministering angels, and so on. According to John Chrysostom, when the "Holy, holy, holy" is chanted, "one is as it were transported into heaven itself, for this is actually the hymn of the seraphim; and at the moment of consecration, one should stand in the presence of God with fear and trembling" *(On the Incomprehensible)*. For the fathers, then, there was a close parallel between the details of the sacramental rituals and the mysterious realities that they symbolized; and by understanding the symbolism it was possible to enter into those realities experientially.[19]

In the present moment, Jesus' promise that "where two or three are gathered together in my name, there I am in the midst of them" (Matt 18:20) is central. For still other Christians, the Eucharist is an anticipation of eternal life with God. "In the earthly liturgy we share in a foretaste of that heavenly liturgy which is celebrated in the Holy City of Jerusalem toward which we journey as pilgrims, where Christ is sitting at the right hand of God."[20] Central to this understanding is the verse, "Whoever eats my flesh and drinks my blood has eternal life, and I will raise him on the last day" (John 6:54).

A second feature that is essential to a contemporary spirituality is a willingness to explore the spiritual meaning of biblical texts. For example, the story of Jacob's vision at Bethel (Gen 28) of a stairway or ladder on which angels move back and forth between heaven and earth presents a number of interesting historical questions: Where is Bethel? What type of worship took place there before the construction of the Temple? What were other prominent shrines in the ancient world? These questions, however, do not represent the sum

total of important questions to ask of the story. This story has functioned as a spiritual lesson for countless readers down through the
centuries. Saint Francis de Sales offers the following commentary:

> Consider Jacob's ladder, for it is a true picture of the
> devout life. The two sides between which we climb upward
> and to which the rungs are fastened represent prayer,
> which calls down God's love, and the sacraments, which
> confer it. The rungs are the various degrees of charity by
> which we advance from virtue to virtue, either descending
> by deeds of help and support for our neighbor or by con-
> templation ascending to a loving union with God.[21]

This is not to suggest that the historical questions are unimportant,
for obviously they are essential to any critical study of the text. The
question is whether those are the only questions believers should
bring to the biblical text.

Most Christians would, I believe, insist that the historical questions do not exhaust their own inquiries into the Bible. As Luke
Timothy Johnson has argued, "If Scripture is ever again to be a living
source for theology, those who practice theology must become less
preoccupied with the world that produced Scripture and learn again
how to live in the world Scripture produces."[22] Johnson contends that
the historical reconstructions are important, but so too are the spiritual questions raised by Christians struggling to live lives of faithful
discipleship. In "The Interpretation of the Bible in the Church," the
Pontifical Biblical Commission speaks of the literal sense, the spiritual sense, and the fuller sense of scripture. In describing the "fuller
sense," the document states,

> It has its foundation in the fact that the Holy Spirit, princi-
> pal author of the Bible, can guide human authors in the
> choice of expressions in such a way that the latter will
> express a truth the fullest depths of which the authors
> themselves do not perceive. This deeper truth will be more
> fully revealed in the course of time—on the one hand,
> through further divine interventions that clarify the mean-
> ing of texts and, on the other, through the insertion of texts

into the canon of Scripture. In these ways there is created a new context, which brings out fresh possibilities of meaning that had lain hidden in the original context.[23]

This deeper sense of meaning is often more explicitly surfaced in treatments of the Bible by literary critics. Their attentiveness to and appreciation of metaphor, puns, and symbolism often help them see the spiritual dimension of the text better than their theological counterparts.[24]

Christians have traditionally remembered certain verses that speak to them at particular moments in their spiritual journeys. These would include, among other things, proverbs, psalms, or particular sayings of a biblical personality that seem to transcend time and apply to the lives of all Christians. All of us at one time or another have had a spiritual kinship with the prodigal son who returns to his merciful father or the father of the boy possessed by a demon who cries out, "I believe; help my unbelief!" (Mark 9:24). Peter seems especially interesting as a role model. He cries, "Go away from me, Lord, for I am a sinful man!" (Luke 5:8); he proclaims, "Lord, to whom can we go? You have the words of eternal life" (John 6:68); yet he also denies Christ and gets called on the carpet by Paul (Gal 2:11–14). The letters in the New Testament contain a number of gems:

> I have fought the good fight, I have finished the race, I have kept the faith. (2 Tim 4:7)

> Above all, maintain constant love for one another, for love covers a multitude of sins. (1 Pet 4:8)

> Be angry but do not sin; do not let the sun go down on your anger, and do not make room for the devil. (Eph 4:26–27)

It is also amazing how single verses or ideas penetrate so deeply into a given theologian's thought process. James Walsh, S.J., once wrote of the great spiritual writer, Saint Bernard of Clairvaux, "The central core of Bernard's message is contained in the words 'God is love' and 'He has first loved us.'"[25] "Seek first the kingdom of God" exercises a determinative role in Pannenberg's theology. Gutiérrez's work is filled with references to the prophets, and Bonhoeffer refers often to the forty-fifth chapter of Jeremiah.

William James once wrote, "Were one asked to characterize the life of religion in the broadest and most general terms possible, one might say that it consists of the belief that there is an unseen order, and that our supreme good lies in harmoniously adjusting ourselves thereto."[26] James's observation captures the third aspect I believe needs to be included in a contemporary Christian spirituality. There needs to be a connection between the "unseen order" established by God and the heights and depths of our lives—the struggles we confront, the victories we enjoy, and the sufferings we endure. Bultmann's strategy was to translate all christological statements into existential statements, thereby driving a wedge between faith and history. A powerful existential message cut off from history will soon wither or drift into flights of fantasy. A historical reconstruction of the life of Jesus with no connection to the actual real-life experiences of Christians is religiously lifeless.[27] The bridge connecting believers and God that I have proposed here is the process of interiorization of the moments of the biblical narrative as the "interpretive framework" for Christian existence. Paul expresses this connection when he exclaims, "I have been crucified with Christ; and it is no longer I who live, but it is Christ who lives in me. And the life I now live in the flesh I live by faith in the Son of God, who loved me and gave himself for me" (Gal 2:19–20).

The ancients made more deliberate efforts to connect the structure of the person and the structure of the universe. They often spoke of the human as a *microcosm*, literally, a "little universe," which means that the human personality in some significant way parallels the nature of the cosmos or universe. Plato, for example, spoke of the human personality as being a conflict among reason, spirit, and appetite. For the individual to have well-being, reason must control the person's spirited enthusiasm and fleshly desires. The ideal state mirrored this structure. There would be three classes of individuals: the wise philosopher-king, the courageous soldiers, and industrious producers of goods. Theologians likewise reasoned that since humans are created in the image and likeness of God, it is reasonable to see vestiges of the Trinity in the human personality. Saint Augustine (354–430) saw the divine triune imprint at work in the dynamic relation of human memory, understanding, and will. What is essential in both Plato's and Augustine's theory is the grounding of the dynamics of human life in something beyond itself that is unseen, yet real. Time, I would argue, has not diminished the necessity of that correspondence for the spiritual lives of Christians. The proposed model of spirituality in this study sees the dynamics of the internal life of a Christian as a microcosm of the dynamics occurring in the larger biblical narrative.[28]

The Christian Life

When spirituality and theology are interwoven, the tapestry of the Christian life takes shape. Mark McIntosh has summarized nicely the necessity of both spirituality and theology in the Christian life. He writes, "Put as bluntly as possible, theology without spirituality becomes ever more methodologically refined but unable to know or speak of the very mysteries at the heart of Christianity, and spirituality without theology becomes rootless, easily hijacked by individualistic consumerism."[29] The horizontal and vertical lines need to be joined securely to prevent the unraveling of the entire work. Just as two tapestry-makers can construct radically different pieces from the same materials, so, too, Christians have crafted a variety of expressions of faithful Christian discipleship. We conclude, however, with some general observations about the creative process that is the Christian life.

First, the Christian life involves the conformity of our entire selves to Christ. In an influential essay, Paul Tillich speaks of religion as "the aspect of depth in the totality of the human spirit."[30] As Gabriel Fackre notes, "The three dimensions of human experience— rational, moral and affective—appear in the Tillichian terms of metaphysical, ethical and mystical and their equivalents."[31] While thought, action, and feeling are three distinct aspects of our personalities, they are interrelated. We can, therefore, speak of all three as essential elements in the single process of conforming ourselves to Christ.

The idea of conformity with Christ has its roots in Paul's admonition:

> I urge you, therefore, brothers by the mercies of God, to offer your bodies as a living sacrifice, holy and pleasing to God, your spiritual worship. Do not conform yourself to this age but be transformed by the renewal of your

mind, that you may discern what is the will of God, what is
good and pleasing and perfect. (Rom 12:1–2)

This union with Christ is described in various ways throughout the
New Testament, for example, as having the mind of Christ (1 Cor
2:16), being baptized into Christ (Rom 6:3), having Christ living
within us (Gal 2:20), or having a life hidden with Christ in God (Col
3:3).[32]

In the Roman Catholic tradition, conforming one's self to Christ
takes place in the context of the sacraments. The *Catechism*, for
example, states,

> The Church affirms that for believers the sacraments of
> the New Covenant are *necessary for salvation*, "Sacra-
> mental grace" is the grace of the Holy Spirit, given by
> Christ and proper to each sacrament. The Spirit heals and
> transforms those who receive him by conforming them to
> the Son of God. The fruit of the sacramental life is that the
> Spirit of adoption makes the faithful partakers in the divine
> nature by uniting them in a living union with the only Son,
> the Savior.[33]

In the Roman Catholic tradition, therefore, conforming oneself to
Christ is inextricably joined with participation in the liturgical life of
the church.

Second, conforming ourselves to Christ is an ongoing activity.
The Christian life, in other words, is always a work in progress. For
some, such as Paul after his experience on the road to Damascus,
great shifts in the pattern are evident; for others it is a work marked
by one continuous, ever-widening band of holiness. For some it is a
life filled with heartache and tragedy; for others it is a life barely
touched by the senselessness of evil, the burden of poverty, or the
pain of neglect. It could be a work in which threads that once domi-
nated the piece are slowly eliminated or a work in which threads long
forgotten resurface at the most opportune time.

Third, conformity to Christ does not annihilate our individuality.
Each Christian brings the particularities of his or her life to the loom
and, drawing on the vast resources supplied by the biblical narrative,

fashions a unique expression of that shared desire to conform our wills to God's will. The nine moments in the biblical narrative we have explored are, as one would expect, applicable in varying degrees to each person's life. For someone who has experienced little geographical or psychological displacement, the concept of exile may play a negligible role in his or her spirituality. From the hymns sung by slaves in North America, we know that many understood their entire time on Earth to be an exile that would end only when they passed on to eternal life.[34] In this way, the biblical narrative is not a cookie cutter that produces the same design without deviation. Its raw materials can be combined in various ways, depending on a variety of factors. The goal, however, is to preserve both the contours of the biblical narrative and the person's individuality in the finished product.

Fourth, conformity to Christ necessarily involves a concern for the poor and oppressed of this world, but the proper use of the biblical narrative in a public forum is a complex issue. Michael E. Allsopp and Edward R. Sunshine identify "two basic questions of social spirituality: what is the best way for believers to foster the faith life in their communities and what is the best way for them to address non-believers?"[35] This involves a host of questions about the proper relationship of the church and the wider culture, church catechesis, and so on. One interesting example drawn from American history is the "I've Been to the Mountaintop" speech delivered by Dr. Martin Luther King, Jr., on April 3, 1968, at the Memphis Masonic Temple. In this address, King masterfully blends biblical imagery, U.S. history, and social commentary as he brings his speech to its dramatic conclusion:

> Well, I don't know what will happen now: we've got some difficult days ahead. But it really doesn't matter with me now, because I've been to the mountaintop. And I don't mind. Like anybody, I would like to live a long life— longevity has its place. But I'm not concerned about that now. I just want to do God's will. And He's allowed me to go up to the mountain. And I've looked over, and I've seen the Promised Land. I may not get there with you. But I want you to know tonight, that we, as a people, will get to the Promised Land. And so I'm happy tonight; I'm not

worried about anything; I'm not fearing any man. Mine eyes have seen the glory of the coming of the Lord.[36]

What, then, are the threads that make up the Christian life? In the biblical narrative they are the stories of Creation, the Exodus, the Conquest, the Exile, the Incarnation, the Crucifixion, the Resurrection, Pentecost, and the End of Time. In the group of theologians presented here, they are Ruether's relentless critique of the status quo, Gutiérrez's uncompromising commitment to the poor, Niebuhr's hard-nosed pragmatism, Bonhoeffer's penetrating analysis of modern secular culture, Rahner's grand vision of the presence of God's grace, Moltmann's lifting up of the cross into the inner life of God, Küng's apologetic concerns, Congar's balance of spirit and structure, and Pannenberg's reminder that we have not here a lasting city, but we seek the one that is to come (Heb 13:14). In the Christian life, they are the creativity of the human spirit, the exhilaration of liberation from bondage, the responsibility to use power justly, the pain of displacement, the sacramental sense of creation, the disruption of suffering and death, the hope for new life, the trust in the abiding presence of God, and the anticipation of God's final restoration. The blending of these strands is an individual effort undertaken by each Christian, and a communal endeavor carried on by the church over time. It is our hope and our responsibility that we create a tapestry worthy of the One who commissioned us to do the work.

Notes

1. The metaphor of craft appears in Avery Dulles, *The Craft of Theology* (New York: Crossroad, 1992).
2. Clark H. Pinnock, *Tracking the Maze* (San Francisco: Harper and Row, 1990), p. 59. I first discovered this quotation in Ed. L. Miller and Stanley J. Grenz, *Fortress Introduction to Contemporary Theologies* (Minneapolis: Fortress Press, 1998), p. 216.
3. For a very balanced assessment of the strengths and weaknesses of postliberal theology, see James J. Buckley, "Postliberal Theology: A Catholic Reading," in *Introduction to Christian Theology*, ed. Roger A. Badham (Louisville: Westminster John Knox Press, 1998).
4. See John Noonan, "Development in Moral Doctrine," *Theological Studies* 54 (1993), pp. 662–77, and Jim Hill and Rand Cheadle, *The*

Bible Tells Me So: Uses and Abuses of Holy Scripture (New York: Anchor Books, 1996).

5. A concept I am borrowing from Kenan B. Osborne, O.F.M., *The Resurrection of Jesus* (Mahwah: Paulist Press, 1997), p. 16.

6. Pinnock, *Tracking the Maze*, chap. 11.

7. See Schubert M. Ogden "What is Theology?" in *Readings in Christian Theology*, ed. Peter C. Hodgson and Robert H. King (Philadelphia: Fortress Press, 1985), p. 21.

8. See chap. 1 of David Tracy, *The Analogical Imagination* (New York: Crossroad, 1981).

9. Raymond E. Brown, S.S., *The Gospel According to John* (The Anchor Bible), vol. 29A (Garden City: Doubleday, 1970), p. 764.

10. Jürgen Moltmann, *On Human Dignity* (Philadelphia: Fortress, 1984), p. 112, n. 6.

11. See Dennis P. McCann, *Christian Realism and Liberation Theology: Practical Theologies in Creative Conflict* (Maryknoll: Orbis Books, 1981).

12. See chap. 12, "Paul and Early Catholicism," in Ernst Kasemann, *New Testament Questions of Today* (Philadelphia: Fortress, 1969).

13. Pinnock, *Tracking the Maze*, p. 153.

14. Jaroslav Pelikan, *The Melody of Theology* (Cambridge: Harvard University Press, 1988), p. 18.

15. See Leslie Griffin, "The Integration of Spiritual and Temporal: Contemporary Roman Catholic Church-State Theory," *Theological Studies* 48 (1987), pp. 225–57.

16. Robert Kress, *A Rahner Handbook* (Atlanta: John Knox Press, 1982), p. 32.

17. Hans Frei, *Theology and Narrative: Selected Essays* (New York: Oxford University Press, 1993), ed. George Hunsinger and William C. Placher. The quote is attributed to Frei on p. 16 of the Introduction by William Placher.

18. *Dei Verbum*, §9. I am using *Documents of Vatican II*, ed. Austin P. Flannery (Grand Rapids: Eerdmans, 1975), p. 755.

19. Joseph Martos, *Doors to the Sacred* (Garden City: Doubleday, 1981), p. 44.

20. Quoted in the *Catechism of the Catholic Church* §1090 (New York: Sadlier, 1994), p. 283.

21. St. Francis de Sales, *Introduction to the Devout Life*, trans. John K. Ryan (Garden City: Image Books, 1966), p. 42.

22. Luke Timothy Johnson, "Imagining the World Scripture Imagines," in

Theology and Scriptural Imagination, ed. L. Gregory Jones and James J. Buckley (Oxford: Blackwell Publishers, 1998), p. 3.

23.   "The Interpretation of the Bible in the Church" (II,B,3). (Washington, DC: United States Catholic Conference, 1998), p. 24.

24.   For an excellent example, see Northrup Frye, *The Great Code* (New York: Harcourt Brace Jovanovich, 1982).

25.   James Walsh, *Spirituality Through the Centuries* (New York: P. J. Kenedy and Sons, 1964), p. 113.

26.   William James, *The Varieties of Religious Experience* (New York: The Modern Library, 1902), p. 53.

27.   Scripture scholars who share a common concern to connect the gospel accounts (or the Bible in general) and history will not, of course, necessarily arrive at similar conclusions about the historicity of specific events in the Bible.

28.   This position does not depend on whether one holds that it is the biblical narrative that creates those experiences or whether those experiences fit perfectly into the narrative. Neither does it require a direct correspondence between the sequence of events of the biblical narrative and the person's life.

29.   Mark A. McIntosh, *Mystical Theology* (Malden: Blackwell Publishers, 1998), p. 10.

30.   Paul Tillich, "Religion as a Dimension in Man's Spiritual Life," in *Theology of Culture* (New York: Oxford University Press, 1959), p. 7.

31.   Gabriel Fackre, *The Doctrine of Revelation* (Grand Rapids: Eerdmans, 1997), p. 67.

32.   For a discussion of the biblical passages that speak of Christians being "in Christ," see Bernard McGinn, *The Foundations of Mysticism* (New York: Crossroad, 1991), chap. 3, esp. pp. 73–74.

33.   *Catechism of the Catholic Church* ¶1129 (New York: Sadlier, 1994), p. 292.

34.   See Paul Nathanson, *Over the Rainbow* (Albany: State University of New York Press, 1991), pp. 203–8.

35.   Michael E. Allsopp and Edward R. Sunshine, "Speaking Morally: The Thirty Year Debate Between Richard A. McCormick and Stanley Hauerwas," *Irish Theological Quarterly* 63(1), 1998, p. 64.

36.   I am using the text available on the Stanford University Web site, "The Martin Luther King, Jr. Papers Project" at www.stanford.edu/group/King/speeches/I've_been_to_the_mountaintop.html.

Index